INTRODUCTION

George Whitefield (1714-1770) was, by far, the most popular transatlantic preacher of the eighteenth century, an early American icon, even surpassing Jonathan Edwards, his co-revivalist in the Great Awakening, in the number of people who came to hear him. As a huge eighteenth-century success, Whitefield was able to utilize not only open-air preaching in the fields but also the power of the popular press, which was instrumental in spreading the infectious news of the revivals that so characterized his life. Newspaper reports of the immense crowds to which he preached in England in 1739 (rumored to be over twenty-five thousand) spread to the New World; so much so, that by the time Whitefield arrived in Philadelphia later that year, after a short stay in Ireland, he had already attained celebrity status, attracting crowds upwards of six to ten thousand, a rather remarkable feat given that Philadelphia's population at the time was estimated at thirteen thousand. And yet, unlike celebrities in our own day, Whitefield hated press notices, even when favorable, and was annoyed by them; in the words of D. M. Lloyd-Jones, "he was … an extraordinarily humble and saintly man" (*The Puritans: Their Origins and Successors*, p. 119). Thus, Whitefield was a man for his times; his preaching was loved and revered by the common sort but was often ridiculed or criticized by the established church; reasons for this criticism varied greatly; some suspected charlatanry; others feared his power to persuade the masses – "enthusiasm" was, perhaps, their most common label. But whatever critiques the established church had against itinerant preachers like Whitefield it could not dismiss the massive social change that occurred in the colonies because of revivalist preaching.

One of Whitefield's most influential friends in America, and the publisher of eight editions of his *Journals*, Benjamin Franklin, wrote of this social change: "It was wonderful to see the change soon made in the manners of our inhabitants, from being thoughtless or indifferent about religion, it seemed as if all the world were growing religious, so that one could not walk through the streets in an evening without hearing psalms sung in different families of every street ..." Franklin afterward attended one of Whitefield's meetings and suspecting that a collection might be taken, resolved, silently, to refrain from giving: "I had in my pocket a handful of copper money, three or four silver dollars, and five pistols in gold." By the end of the sermon, however, Franklin had emptied all his money into the collection; such was Whitefield's persuasion; and yet, in spite of Whitefield's critics, he never misused the funds raised but rather spent them for the establishment of orphanages and other social causes. Franklin later concluded, "Some of Mr. Whitefield's enemies affected to suppose that he would apply these collections to his own private emolument, but I who was intimately acquainted with him (being employed in printing his sermons and journals, etc.) never had the least suspicion of his integrity, but am to this day decidedly of the opinion that he was in all his conduct a perfectly honest man" (Richard Middleton, *Colonial America: A History, 1565-1776*, Wiley-Blackwell, 3rd ed. pp. 266-67).

While Whitefield's relation to Franklin was only one of business (they were near opposites in their views about orthodox Christian doctrine), he would often pray for Franklin's conversion; such prayers, however, seemed unfruitful, and Whitefield, according to Franklin, "never had the satisfaction of believing his prayers were heard." Their friendship lasted until Whitefield's death in 1770. Franklin had lost a valuable ally in social reform.

It may seem strange why Franklin, a Deist, liked Whitefield so much. Ever since they first met in Philadelphia, they kept up a warm exchange of letters. There were several reasons that fostered this friendly disposition: First, as hinted at, Whitefield often supported specific social causes that Franklin could not help but admire – the founding of an orphanage in Georgia is just one example. Second, Whitefield was profoundly influential in affecting social change – something Franklin greatly admired in a newly settled and often immoral society; in fact, Franklin praised the awakenings for their positive effect in his *Pennsylvania Gazette*: "The alteration in the fact of religion here is altogether surprising" – thus echoing the former "surprising" work of God in Northampton in 1735. "Religion is become the subject of most conversations. No books are in request but those of piety and devotion; and instead of idle songs and ballads, the people are everywhere entertaining themselves with psalms, hymns, and spiritual songs." One of the great things about the Great Awakening was its international and ecumenical character, its ability to cross social barriers, political and private sectors, and its innovative use of communication and its use of the press to affirm social change.

Whitefield, of course, was not the only one who preached in the fields of Philadelphia. Other, lesser-known evangelists, such as William Tennent, Sr., and his two sons, William Jr. and Gilbert, were all influential in promoting an awakening culture. Other than his well-famed relationships and fall-outs with the Wesley brothers, Whitefield corresponded with such prominent preachers as Ralph and Ebenezer Erskine in Scotland (though he too had a falling out with them because he refused to join their "Associate Presbytery"). This actually raises an important aspect of Whitefield's ministry: he refused to associate himself with any one church or denomination. As he wrote to Ebenezer Erskine in 1741, "I come only as an occasional preacher, to preach the simple gospel, to all who are willing to hear me, of whatever denomination. It will be wrong in me to join in a reformation, as to church government, any further than I have light given me from above … My business seems to be to evangelize." Whitefield was only twenty-six years old and the most popular preacher in England; he did not want to use his fame to advance a cause other than the gospel and he stuck to this sense of urgency throughout his life. The evangelicalism that he promoted crossed denominational and churchly lines; at the height of the Great Awakening, spiritual awakenings were reported throughout the colonies, affecting Presbyterians and Methodists alike.

Whitefield has received a lot of attention since his first rise in eighteenth-century evangelical circles. Contemporaneous accounts varied in their portrayals. The first published biography issued from the press in 1772 by John Gillies. Called *Memoirs of the Life of the Reverend George Whitefield, M.A.*, this biography was dedicated to the Countess of Huntingdon, arguably one of most influential women in England and an endorser of evangelicalism. Whitefield had served, for a time, as Huntingdon's chaplain. The most expansive biography published in the nineteenth century was Methodist-scholar Luke Tyerman's two-volume *The Life of the Rev. George Whitefield, B.A. of Pembroke College, Oxford* (Anson D.F. Randolph, London, 1876).

Twentieth-century historians have both praised and criticized Whitefield for the evangelical Calvinism that he endorsed and the methods he used to do so. He has been called a "saint," a "divine dramatist," a "pedlar in divinity," "prince of pulpit orators," the "Grand Itinerant," among many other names. The reasons for these diverse portrayals have as much to do with the historians' assumptions as anything else. Those historians who deny the existence of God and thus rule out his operative work in the world are most likely to depict Whitefield as a charlatan or pedlar – this is in essence the argument of Frank Lambert's *"Pedlar in Divinity": George Whitefield and the Transatlantic Revivals* (Princeton, 1994). Harry S. Stout's *The Divine Dramatist: George Whitefield and the Rise of Modern Evangelicalism* (Grand Rapids, 1991) provides a more balanced account, though still too critical for most readers. The best and most sympathetic narrative is Arnold A. Dallimore's two-volume *George Whitefield: The Life and Times of the Great Evangelist of the Eighteenth Century* (Edinburgh, 1970-1980) and its much-abridged version, *George Whitefield: God's Anointed Servant in the Great Revival of the Eighteenth Century* (Wheaton, 1990). Those wishing to read more of Whitefield's life should begin with Dallimore's abridged biography or John Pollock's *George Whitefield: The Evangelist* (Ross-shire, 2009), and then move on to Dallimore's two-volume *magnum opus*.

Though numerous reprints of Whitefield's sermons and journals continue to be printed, amazingly, no one has ever compiled a devotional. This absence is surprising given the fact that Whitefield employed language borrowed from Puritan sermons, diaries, and devotional works – in fact, Whitefield was an avid reader of the Puritans and recommended them wherever possible. Whitefield's own life was riddled with doubts, torments, anguish, and an abiding frustration over his own sin – a common *motif* found in Puritan diaries. He found guidance in Juan de Castaniza's *Spiritual Combat* (1644), a well-known Catholic devotional manual favored by the Puritans and printed numerous times throughout the seventeenth century. Castaniza, like his Protestant counterpart, John Downame, had compared the sinner's struggle with immense warfare, likening the mortification of the flesh to the converting of Indians – something Whitefield knew well, having little success with their conversions. The most immediate reason for the absence of a devotional is, perhaps, that Whitefield was a far better orator than an author. His chief power lay as a preacher of the spoken word; men and women would flock in great numbers to hear him preach, some out of novelty, and others out of a more sincere concern for their souls. That his voice would reach to the outermost crowds shows how permeating his voice was. Still, the popularity of Whitefield's *Journals* should not be underestimated. Whitefield was among the first Methodist journalists and his early notoriety can no doubt be traced to its success.

It is never easy to edit another person's work, let alone someone who has been dead for 240 years. Whitefield's language and expressions are at times antiquated, reflecting the eighteenth century in which he lived and hoped. Thus, while editing, I have strived to be true to Whitefield's sense and message. At times repetitive and wordy, I have had to condense and occasionally paraphrase his work. Further, I have standardized biblical citations to the English Standard Version (ESV), though a few times I have retained the KJV. All selections have been taken from the standard six-volume set of Whitefield's works, *The Works of the Reverend George Whitefield, M.A.,* published posthumously in 1771, one year after his death. While most excerpts are taken from sermons, I have also included a few selections from his letters, tracts, hymns, and miscellaneous writings. All changes, overall minor, will enable modern readers more immediate access to the "Grand Itinerant" and his usefulness for our time. As you read, you will see Whitefield for who he was – an evangelist concerned for the salvation of souls.

As with my earlier *Matthew Henry: Daily Readings*, this small devotional is meant to provide rather brief and easy access to the treasures of the past. Its entries can be read in less than five minutes, and the book itself can be kept in one's pocket or purse. It is printed to be mobile – whether on the train, on the bus, or in a plane; *George Whitefield: Daily Readings* will inspire, convict, and encourage you in your daily walk.

I am dedicating this book to my son, Tyler, who someday, the Lord willing, will be able to read it for himself. He has been and continues to be a constant source of joy and delight. I love you, Tyler; let us continue to rejoice in God's great gift for us.

Thanks, as always, to good friends from Kuyper days, including Terreth Klaver, Brett Schut, Durell Flood, and Steve Carr.

I also wish to thank Willie MacKenzie, Director of Publishing at Christian Focus, for his vision and patience as I finished the manuscript amid the flurry of academic life; Anthony and Lorraine Gosling, for their winsome visits; Jonathon and Allyson

Beeke, for their kindness; James and Courtney Dolezal, for their godly life and witness; Micah and Eileen Bickford, for their friendship; Joel and Mary Beeke, for their love of books; Donald and Sally Pederson, Tom and Hannah Beeke, Ron and Leah Chi, for their love; Gary and Rosa Pederson, my parents, for their encouragement through many winters; Richard and Emma DeRuiter, my other parents, for their prayers; and, lastly, Sarah, my wife, and Tyler, my son, for putting up with all my projects over the years, the books I continue to acquire, and the necessary mess that ensues.

With Jonathan Edwards, Whitefield remains among the most popular preachers of the modern era. It is hoped that this small devotional will contribute to a further spread of Whitefield's fame as a preacher for our time. Like so many other luminaries in church history, though dead, Whitefield yet speaks to us who are living. Throughout the pages that follow you will hear Whitefield calling, pleading, urging you to close with Christ, to love Christ, and to love one another. My hope is that the same Spirit who revived Britain and America in the colonial period would do so in our day.

Randall J. Pederson
Cheltenham, Pennsylvania
March 2010

JANUARY 1

The Natural Man

For the mind that is set on the flesh is hostile to God, for it does not submit to God's law; indeed, it cannot.

ROMANS 8:7

Walking with God implies that the prevailing power of the enmity of a person's heart be taken away by the blessed Spirit of God. Perhaps it may seem a hard saying to some, but our own experience daily proves, what the Scriptures in many places assert, that the carnal mind, the mind of the unconverted natural man, and even the mind of the regenerate, so far as any part of him remains unrenewed, is enmity, not only an enemy, but "enmity [itself] against God: for it is not subject to the law of God, neither indeed can be" (Rom. 8:7, KJV). Indeed, one may well wonder that any creature, especially that lovely creature man, made after his Maker's own image, should ever have any enmity, much less a prevailing enmity, against that very God in whom he lives, moves, and has his being. But, alas! So it is. Our first parents contracted it when they fell from God by eating the forbidden fruit … and this same enmity rules and prevails in every man that is naturally engendered of the offspring of Adam … He that cannot set his seal to this knows nothing yet, in a saving manner, of the Holy Scriptures, or of the power of God. And all that do know this, will readily acknowledge, that before a person can be said to walk with God, the prevailing power of this heart-enmity must be destroyed: for persons do not walk and keep company together, who entertain an irreconcilable enmity and hatred against one another … It is destroyed in every soul that is truly born of God, and gradually more and more weakened as the believer grows in grace, and the Spirit of God gains a greater and greater ascendancy in the heart.

JANUARY 2

Pray for Us

Finally, brothers, pray for us, that the word of the LORD may speed ahead and be honored, as happened among you …

2 THESSALONIANS 3:1

You ought to pray for those whom the Holy Spirit has made overseers over you. This is what Saint Paul begs again and again of the churches to whom be writes … surely, if the great Saint Paul, that chosen vessel, that favorite of heaven, needed the most importunate prayers of his Christian converts, much more do the ordinary ministers of the gospel stand in need of the intercession of their respective flocks … Much good is frequently withheld from many by reason of their neglecting to pray for their ministers, and which they would have received, had they prayed for them as they ought. Not to mention, that people often complain of the want of diligent and faithful pastors. But how do they deserve good pastors, who will not earnestly pray to God for such? If we will not pray to the Lord of the harvest, can it be expected he will send forth laborers into his harvest? Besides, what ingratitude is it, not to pray for your ministers! For shall they watch and labor in the word and doctrine for you and your salvation, and shall not you pray for them in return? … Add to this, that praying for your ministers will be a manifest proof of your believing, that though Paul plant, and Apollos water, yet it is God alone who gives increase. And you will also find it the best means you can use, to promote your own welfare; for God, in answer to your prayers, may impart a double portion of his Holy Spirit to them, whereby they will be qualified to deal out to you larger measures of knowledge in spiritual things, and be enabled more skillfully to divide the word of truth.

JANUARY 3

Psalm 46

God is our refuge and strength, a very present help in trouble.
PSALM 46:1

There was a tradition among the ancient Jews that the manna which came down from heaven, though it is was a little grain like coriander-seed, yet it suited every taste, as milk unto babes, and strong meat to grown persons. Whether this supposition be founded on fact or not, the observation will hold good in a great measure respecting the sayings of David, for if we have eyes to see, and ears to hear, if God has been pleased to take away the veil from our hearts, we shall find, by happy experience, that let our circumstances be what they will, the book of Psalms may serve as a spiritual magazine, out of which we may draw spiritual weapons in the time of the hottest fight, especially those that are under trouble, when the hand of the Lord is gone seemingly forth against them. When unbelief is apt to make them say, "All these things are against me!" If we can have the presence of mind to turn to the book of Psalms, we may find something there suitable to our case, a word to refresh us in pursuing our spiritual enemy. This is true of the 46th Psalm in particular … It is uncertain at what time, or upon what occasion, David wrote it; probably under some sharp affliction, which made him eloquent; or when the affliction was over, when his heart was swimming with gratitude and love, and when out of the fullness of it his pen was made the pen of a ready writer. It was a favorite Psalm with Luther. And whenever Philip Melanchthon or any other of his friends told him some sad news, he used to say, "Come, come, let us sing the 46th Psalm;" and when he had sung that, his heart was quiet.

JANUARY 4

Due Thanks

The one who offers thanksgiving as his sacrifice glories me; to one who orders his way rightly I will show the salvation of God!

PSALM 50:23

When God placed the first man in Paradise, his soul no doubt was so filled with a sense of the riches of divine love, that he was continually employing that breath of life, which the Almighty had not long before breathed into him, in blessing and magnifying that all-bountiful, all-gracious God, in whom he lived, moved, and had his being. And the brightest idea we can form of the angelical hierarchy above, and the spirits of just men made perfect, is that they are continually standing around the throne of God, and cease not day and night, saying, "Worthy is the Lamb who was slain, to receive power and wealth and wisdom and might and honor and glory and blessing!" (Rev. 5:12). That which was man's perfection when time first began, and will be his employment when death is swallowed up in victory, and time shall be no more, without controversy is part of our perfection, and ought to be our frequent exercise on earth. I doubt not that those blessed spirits, who are sent forth to minister to them who shall be heirs of salvation, often stand astonished, when they encamp around us, to find our hearts so rarely enlarged, and our mouths so seldom opened, to show forth the loving-kindness of the Lord, or to speak of all his praise.

JANUARY 5

Our Birthright

... that the God of our Lord Jesus Christ, the Father of glory, may give you a spirit of wisdom and of revelation in the knowledge of him ...

EPHESIANS 1:17

God is love. Could our own wills, or the world, have made us happy, he never would have sent his own dear Son, Jesus Christ, to die and rise again, to deliver us from the power of them. But because they only torment, and cannot satisfy, therefore God bids us to renounce them. Had anyone persuaded profane Esau not to lose so glorious a privilege, merely for the sake of gratifying a present corrupt inclination, when he saw him about to sell his birth-right for a little red pottage, would not one think that man to have been Esau's friend? And just thus stands the case between God and us. By the death and resurrection of Jesus Christ, we are new-born to an heavenly inheritance amongst all them which are sanctified; but our own corrupt wills, would tempt us to sell this glorious birth-right for the vanities of the world, which, like Esau's red pottage, may please us for a while, but will soon be taken away from us. God knows this; he bids us to renounce them for a season, than for the short enjoyment of them lose the privilege of that glorious birthright, to which, by knowing the power of the resurrection of Jesus Christ, we are entitled. O the depth of the riches and excellence of Christianity! Well might the great Saint Paul count all things but garbage and dross for the excellence of the knowledge of it. Well might he desire so ardently to know Jesus and the power of his resurrection! For even on this side of eternity it raises us above the world, and makes us to sit in heavenly places in Christ Jesus.

JANUARY 6

The Dead shall Rise

In their case the god of this world has blinded the minds of the unbelievers, to keep them from seeing the light of the gospel of the glory of Christ, who is the image of God.

2 CORINTHIANS 4:4

There are more unbelievers within the pale than without the pale of the church. Let me repeat it again, you may think of it when I am tossing upon the mighty waters, there are more unbelievers within the pale of the church than without. All are not possessors that are professors, all have not got the thing promised, all are not partakers of the promise, that talk and bless God they have got the promised Savior. I may have him in my mouth and upon my tongue, without having the thing promised, or the blessed promise in my heart. A moral man that can walk touching the law blameless, a person that thinks he is righteous, because he does not know why a person who has got no other religion but to go to a particular place of worship, values himself upon being a churchman or dissenter … These, however they may think themselves safe, will before long go to one place, whether they think so, or no. They will be soon summoned to one bar, and the voice of the archangel sounding, "Arise, you dead, and come to judgment." The dead shall arise, and appear before the Son of God, as Judge of all mankind. These, as well as the infidels, would gladly be excused; and as they once said, "I wish to have me excused from coming to Christ," so too they will fain be excused from appearing before and being condemned by him – but they must all go to one place – and as they know not God and are unacquainted with the divine life they must hear and suffer this dreadful sentence, "Depart from me, you cursed, into the eternal fire prepared for the devil and his angels" (Matt. 25:41).

JANUARY 7

Thorough Change

Let the evildoer still do evil, and the filthy still be filthy, and the self-righteous still do right, and the holy still be holy.
REVELATION 22:11

Our Lord denounced dreadful woes against the self-righteous Pharisees. So, too, must ministers cut at them, and warn them, saying, "woe, woe, woe" to all those who will not submit to the righteousness of Jesus Christ. I could almost say that this is the last stroke that Jesus gave Paul, in turning him to real Christianity; for having given him a blow as a persecutor of true religion, he then brought him out of himself by revealing his person and office as a Savior. "I am Jesus," said our Lord. Hence the apostle writes, "I count everything as loss because of the surpassing worth of knowing Christ Jesus my Lord. For his sake I have suffered the loss of all things and count them as rubbish, in order that I may gain Christ" (Phil. 3:8). You do not hear him speak only as a blasphemer, but also as a Pharisee; and in vain we may talk of being converted until we are brought out of ourselves and come as poor, lost, and undone sinners, to the Lord Jesus Christ, there to be washed in his blood and to be clothed in his glorious imputed righteousness. The consequence of this imputation, or application of our Mediator's righteousness to our souls, will be a conversion from sin to holiness … They that are truly converted to Jesus and who are justified by faith in the Son of God will take care to evidence their conversion, not only by the having grace implanted in their hearts, but by that grace diffusing itself through every faculty of the soul, and making a universal change in the whole man.

JANUARY 8

Gasping after God

Indeed, I count everything as loss because of the surpassing worth of knowing Christ Jesus my Lord. For his sake I have suffered the loss of all things and count them as rubbish, in order that I may gain Christ and be found in him.

PHILIPPIANS 3:8-9

O the depth of the riches and excellence of Christianity! Well might the great Saint Paul count all things but dung and dross for the excellence of the knowledge of it; well might he desire so ardently to know Jesus, and the power of his resurrection. For even on this side of eternity it raises us above the world, and makes us to sit in heavenly places. Well might that glorious company of worthies, recorded in the Bible, supported with a deep sense of their heavenly calling, despise the pleasures and profits of this life, and wander about in sheepskins, and goatskins, in dens and caves of the earth, being destitute, afflicted, tormented. O that we were all like-minded and that we felt the power of Christ's resurrection as they did! How should we, then, count all things as but loss for the sake of knowing Jesus … How should we then recover our primitive dignity, trample the earth under our feet, and with our souls be continually gasping after God! What hinders us that we may be thus minded? Has Jesus Christ, our great High Priest, altered from what he was? No, he is the same yesterday, today, and forever … though the world may cast us out, and separate from our company, yet Jesus will walk with and abide in us.

JANUARY 9

Spirit of Love

Having purified your souls by your obedience to the truth for a sincere brotherly love, love one another earnestly from a pure heart.

1 PETER 1:22

Praying for others will fill your hearts with love one to another. He that every day heartily intercedes at the throne of grace for all mankind cannot but be filled with love and charity towards all. The frequent exercise of love in this manner, will insensibly enlarge your heart, and make you a partaker of that exceeding abundance, which is in Christ Jesus our Lord! Envy, malice, revenge, and such-like hellish tempers, can never long harbor in a gracious intercessor's breast; but he will be filled with joy, peace, meekness, long-suffering, and all other graces of the Holy Spirit. By frequently laying his neighbor's wants before God, he will be touched with a fellow-feeling of them; he will rejoice with those that do rejoice, and weep with those that weep. Every blessing bestowed on others, instead of exciting envy in him, will be looked on as an answer to his particular intercession, and fill his soul with joy unspeakable and full of glory. Abound, therefore, in acts of general and particular intercession; and when you hear of your neighbor's faults, instead of relating them to, and exposing them before others, lay them in secret before God, and beg of him to correct and amend them. When you hear of a notorious sinner, instead of thinking you do well to be angry, beg of Jesus Christ to convert and make him a monument of free grace. You cannot imagine what a blessed alteration this practice will make in your heart, and how much you will increase day by day in the spirit of love and meekness towards all!

JANUARY 10

Real Conversion

Therefore I despise myself, and repent in dust and ashes.

JOB 42:6

The author of conversion is the Holy Ghost; it is not our own free will; nothing short of the influence of the Spirit of the living God can effect change in our hearts; therefore, we are said to "be born again, born of the Spirit;" and though there is and will be a contest between these two opposites, flesh and spirit, yet if we are truly converted, the spirit will get the ascendancy; and though for a while nature and grace may struggle in the womb of a converted soul, like Jacob and Esau, yet the elder shall serve the younger, Jacob shall supplant and turn out Esau, or at least keep him under. God grant we may all thus prove that we are converted. This conversion, however it begins at home, will soon walk abroad; as the virgin Mary was soon found out to be with child, so it will be soon found out whether Christ is formed in the heart … At first it begins with terror and legal sorrow, afterwards it leads to joyfulness. First we work for spiritual life, afterwards from it. First we are in bondage, afterwards we receive the Spirit of adoption to long and thirst for God because he has been pleased to let us know that he will take us to heaven. Conversion means being turned from hell to heaven, from the world to God … I think it is said of a sunflower, though I question whether it will always hold true, that it turns to the sun; I am sure it is true of the Redeemer's flowers that grow in his garden, they not only look to the sun, but they find fresh life, warmth, and transforming influence, from him who is their all in all.

JANUARY 11

Too much Sunshine

But God chose what is foolish in the world to shame the wise; God chose what is weak in the world to shame the strong.

1 CORINTHIANS 1:27

Sheep, you know, generally love to be together; we say a flock of sheep, we do not say a herd of sheep; sheep are little creatures, and Christ's people may be called sheep because they are little in the eyes of the world, and they are yet less in their own eyes. Oh, some people think, if the great men were on our side, if we had king, lords, and commons on our side, I mean if they were all true believers, Oh, if we had all the kings upon the earth on our side! Suppose you had this … Do you think the church would go on the better? Why, if it were fashionable to be a Methodist at court, if it were fashionable to be a Methodist abroad, they would go with a Bible or a hymnbook instead of a novel. But religion never thrives under too much sunshine. "But God chose what is foolish in the world to shame the wise; God chose what is weak in the world to shame the strong" – Not many mighty, not many noble, are called, but God has chosen the foolish things to confound the wise and mighty. Dr. Isaac Watts says, "Here and there I see a king, and here and there a great man in heaven, but their number is but small." Sheep are looked upon to be the most harmless, quiet creatures that God has made: Oh, may God, of his infinite mercy, give us to know that we are his sheep!

JANUARY 12

The Burning Fire

Praise him, sun and moon, praise him, all you shining stars!
PSALM 148:3

I believe the minutest philosophers, and those who have the greatest skill in astronomy, cannot perceive there has been any abatement in the heat of the sun since God first commanded it to rule the day. Then surely, if my God can make a sun that for so many thousands of years shall irradiate, enlighten, and warm the world, without losing any of its light and heat, so does the Sun of righteousness, the Son of God, arise upon the children of God with healing under his wings; he raises, warms, nourishes, and comforts his people, and we have the gospel on the ends of the earth, as well as those who had the honor of conversing with him in the days of his flesh. I mention this in answer to all those who have wrote against the Methodists, and represented them as fanatics. There is no other way of talking against the divine influence, but by allowing it was so formerly, but that it is not so now – they say the primitive Christians had it but it is not to be so with us now as it was formerly. O, my brethren, what fools these great men are when they talk about things they know nothing of. Give them a polyglot [i.e. a Bible with many translations], give them a lexicon, give them a geographical text, or the chronological part of the Scripture, and they have something to say – but when they come to talk of the Spirit of God they see the word "Spirit," and they read the "word" grace but while they read it their hearts cry because their knowledge puffs them up.

JANUARY 13

Solomon's Wisdom

Vanity of vanities, says the Preacher, vanity of vanities! All is vanity.

ECCLESIASTES 1:2

I remember an ingenious writer who had been very copious in his publications, observed that the best and most profitable were written after he was fifty years of age. It is supposed, then the judgment is ripened, and the genius is as it were advanced to maturity and knowledge; and experience gathered when young, will be more useful in the decline of life, when grey hairs are seen here and there upon them. It is said, indeed, that old men are twice children; but there are some whose geniuses are so very low that they cannot be twice children because they are no better than children from their cradle to their grave; but this is not the case with God's children, for upon a reflection of the wrong steps they have taken, if it proceed from the sanctified sense of afflictions, they serve to make them more instructive in their latter day. This was the case of Solomon, though highly favored when young, for the Lord appeared to him twice, yet he fell most awfully, and had we not read of his recovery again, the doctrine of the final perseverance of the saints must seem to fall to the ground. But we have reason to think that he was restored and gave evidence of his recovery by writing in such a manner that none could but one that knew much of God and himself. Witness the Book of Ecclesiastes, which in all ages of the church has been received with a peculiar respect. Ecclesiastes writes of a Preacher; such Solomon was from his own experience and exceeded by none but him who spoke as no man ever did.

JANUARY 14

Dying Grace

So then, whether we live or whether we die, we are the LORD's.
ROMANS 14:8

The grace of the Lord Jesus Christ is with his people when sick and when dying. O, my dear souls, what shall we do when death comes? What a mercy it is that we have a good Master to carry us through that time! As a poor converted servant that saw a believer who was dying in comfort, said, "Master, do not fear, Jesus Christ will carry you safe through the dark valley of the shadow of death." But the time would fail, if I were to show you in how many respects the grace of the Lord Jesus Christ helps us; but what I have said will show that we need all join in a hearty "Amen; Amen, I pray God it may be so, so it is, so may it be!" May be what? Why, that the grace of the Lord Jesus Christ, convicting, restraining, converting, establishing, and comforting grace, may be with us in his ordinances, in his providences, in sickness, and when dying: then, blessed be God, we shall carry it with us after time. Now, my dear hearers, by the help of my God, in whose strength I desire once more to go upon the waters, I shall pray, wherever I am, that this grace of the Lord Jesus Christ may be with you all … May God grant that this grace may be with you all, particularly those young men that have given up their souls to Christ! It delights my soul when I go round the communion table, to see how many young souls have given themselves to Christ. May the Lord grant that you return not again to folly – that you may study the beauties of the mind, shine in the beauties of holiness, and be wise to everlasting salvation.

JANUARY 15

Friend of God

The friendship of the LORD is with those who fear him.
PSALM 25:14

Walking with God is a very honorable thing. O that it may have its due weight and influence with you! I suppose you would all think it a very high honor to be admitted into an earthly prince's private council, to be trusted with his secrets, and to have his ear at all times. It seems Haman thought it so, when he boasted in Esther 5:11 of being "advanced above the officials and servants of the king." And when afterwards a question was put to this same Haman in chapter 6:6, "What shall be done to the man whom the king delights to honor?" he answered in verse 8, "Let royal robes be brought, which the king has worn, and the horse that the king has ridden, and on whose head a royal crown is set. And let the robes and the horse be handed over to one of the king's most noble officials. Let them dress the man…and let them lead him on the horse through the square of the city, proclaiming before him: 'Thus shall it be done to the man whom the king delights to honor.'" This was all then, it seems, that an ambitious Haman could ask, and the most valuable thing that he thought Ahasuerus could give. But, alas, what is this honor in comparison to that which the lowliest of those that walk with God enjoy! Psalm 25:14 says, "The friendship of the LORD is with those who fear him." Jesus says in John 15:15, "No longer do I call you servants … but I have called you friends." David was so sensible of the honor attending a walk with God that he declares, "I would rather be a doorkeeper in the house of my God than dwell in the tents of wickedness." O that all were like-minded with him!

JANUARY 16

Doctrines of Peace

And, as shoes for your feet, having put on the readiness given by the gospel of peace.

EPHESIANS 6:15

The doctrines of the gospel are doctrines of peace, and they bring comfort to all who believe them; they are not like the law given by Moses, which consisted of troublesome and painful ceremonies; neither do they carry with them that terror which the law did; as, "For all who rely on works of the law are under a curse; for it is written, 'Cursed by everyone who does not abide by all things written in the Book of the Law, and do them'" (Gal. 3:10). If you were to keep the whole law and break it but in one point, you are guilty of the breach of all. The law denounces threatenings against all who do not conform to her strict commands; but the gospel is a declaration of grace, peace, and mercy; here you have an account of the blood of Christ, blood which speaks better things than Abel; for Abel's blood cried aloud for vengeance; but Jesus Christ cries mercy, mercy, mercy upon the guilty sinner. If he comes to Christ, confesses and forsakes his sin, then Jesus will have mercy upon him; and if, my brethren, you are but sensible of your sins, convinced of your iniquities, and feel yourselves lost, undone sinners, and come and tell Christ of your lost condition, you will soon find how ready he is to help you; he will give you his Spirit; and if you have his Spirit, you cannot be reprobates: you will find his Spirit to be quickening and refreshing; not like the spirit of the world, a spirit of reproach, envy, and all uncharitableness.

JANUARY 17

A Better Righteousness

He leads the humble in what is right, and teaches the humble his way.

PSALM 25:9

I will venture to affirm that if your souls prosper you will grow downwards. What is that? Why, you will grow in the knowledge of yourselves … the knowledge of ourselves is the first thing God implants: "Lord, let me know myself," was a prayer that one of the fathers put up for sixteen years together. If you have high thoughts of yourselves, you may know you are light-headed, you forget what poor silly creatures you are. As our souls prosper, we shall be more and more sensible, not only of the outside, but of the inside; we first battle with the outward man, but as we advance in the divine life, we have nearer views of the chambers of imagery that are in our hearts; and one day after another we shall find more and more abominations there, and consequently we shall see more of the glory of Jesus Christ, the wonders of that Immanuel, who daily delivers us from this body of sin and death; and I mention this because there is nothing more common, especially with young Christians … Some trees I fancy grow downward; and the deeper you grow in the knowledge of yourself, the deeper you grow in the knowledge of God and his grace, that discovers the corruptions of your hearts … I never knew a person in my life that diligently used the word, and other means, but as they improved in grace, saw more and more the necessity of depending upon a better righteousness than their own.

JANUARY 18

A King's Pardon

For if you forgive others their trespasses, your heavenly father will also forgive you.

MATTHEW 6:14

If persons can give credence to an earthly king who offers a pardon, why cannot believers have a sense of the pardon of his or her sins from God? … Some think we may not be pardoned until we come to judgment, but away with it – O blessed creatures, this modern divinity our reformers knew nothing of. We are to be declared, if you please, *justified* in the day of Jesus Christ, who will pronounce it before all mankind, yes, but, my brothers, and I will insist upon it, that assurance is necessary in the present day for the well-being of a Christian. The comfortable thing is that a soul was never brought to Christ but had some ground of assurance of pardon; though, for want of knowing better, he put it by, and did not know the gift of God when it came. But, my brothers, we shall all be saved from our sins. Here are glad tidings of great joy. Let Satan hear that; I am glad to see poor creatures come, so that I may tell them, "God is love." Believers, you shall be saved from all your sins, every one of them; they shall all be blotted out. Generally, when persons are convinced, the devil preaches despair; some great sin lies upon them; and, says the poor sinner, I shall be saved from all but that; had I not been guilty of such a crime, I might have hope, but I am guilty of such a sin, which is so awful, with such dreadful aggravations, I am afraid I shall never be pardoned. But, my dear souls, Christ is love; and when he loves to forgive, *he forgives like a God*: "though your sins are like scarlet, they shall be as white as snow" (Isa. 1:18b).

JANUARY 19

Mercy and Benevolence

Beloved, I pray that all may go well with you and that you may be in good health, as it goes well with your soul.

3 JOHN 2

John, the writer of this epistle, had the honor of leaning on Christ's bosom, and of being called, by way of emphasis, "the disciple whom Jesus loved," and that very disciple, which is very remarkable concerning him, though he was one of those whom the Lord himself named sons of thunder, Mark 3:17, and was so suddenly, as Bishop Hall observes, turned into a son of lightning, that he would have called down fire from heaven to consume his Master's enemies. Consequently, though he was of a naturally fiery temper, yet the change in his heart was so remarkable, that if a judgment may be formed by his writings, he seems as full of love, if not fuller, than any of his fellow apostles. He learned pity and benevolence of the Father of mercies: and to show how Christian friendship is to be cultivated, he not only wrote letters to churches in general, even to those he never saw in the flesh, but private letters to particular saints, friends to whom he was attached, and wealthy rich friends, whom God had, by his Spirit, raised up to be helpers of the distressed. Happy would it be for us, if we could all learn that simplicity of heart, which is displayed in these particular words. Happy if we could learn this one rule, never to write a letter without something of Jesus Christ in it; for, as Matthew Henry observes, if we are to answer for idle words, much more for idle letters; and if God has given us our pens, especially if he has given us "the pen of a ready writer," it will be happy if we can improve our literary correspondence for his glory and one another's good.

JANUARY 20

Adore His Gracious Hand

All the ends of the earth shall remember and turn to the L*ORD*, *and all the families of the nations shall worship before you.*

PSALM 22:27

Come, let us adore
The Lord's gracious Hand,
Who gave a Command
And Charge to his Angels
To watch round our Bed,
To guard us from Evils,
From Dangers and Dread.

Our Shepherd alone
The Lord let us bless,
Who reigns on the Throne
The Prince of our Peace;
Who ever more saves us
By shedding his Blood;
All hail, holy Jesus,
Our Lord and our God!

We daily will sing
Your Merits, your Praise,
You, merciful Spring
Of Pity and Grace:
Your Kindness for ever
To Men we will tell;
And say, our dear Savior
Redeems us from Hell.

Preserve us in Love,
While here we abide;
Nor ever remove,
Nor cover, nor hide,
Your glorious Salvation;
'Till joyful we see
The beautiful Vision
Completed in you.

JANUARY 21

The Holy Spirit

By this we know that we abide in him and he in us, because he has given us of his Spirit.

1 JOHN 4:13

The Holy Spirit is the Third Person of the ever-blessed Trinity … He is emphatically called "holy," because he is infinitely holy in himself, and the author and finisher of all holiness in us. This blessed Spirit, who once moved on the face of the great deep; who overshadowed the blessed Virgin before that holy child was born of her; who descended in a bodily shape, like a dove, on our blessed Lord, when he came up out of the water at his baptism; and afterwards came down in fiery tongues on the heads of all his apostles at the day of Pentecost; this is the Holy Spirit who must move on the faces of our souls; this power of the Most High must come upon us, and we must be baptized with this baptism and refining fire, before we can be styled true members of Christ's mystical body. Thus says the Apostle Paul, "Examine yourselves, to see whether you are in the faith. Test yourselves. Or do you not realize this about yourselves, that Jesus Christ is in you? – unless indeed you fail to meet the test!" (2 Cor. 13:5); and, "Anyone who does not have the Spirit of Christ does not belong to him" (Rom. 8:9); and again, says Saint John, "By this we know that he abides in us, by the Spirit whom he has given us" (1 John 3:24). It is not necessary that we should have the Spirit now given in that miraculous manner in which he was at first given to our Lord's apostles, by signs and wonders; but it is absolutely necessary that we should receive the Holy Spirit in his sanctifying graces, as really as they did. So it will continue to be till the end of the world.

JANUARY 22

Nothing but Sin

If we say we have not sinned, we make him a liar, and his word is not in us.

1 John 1:10

I do not know what you may think, but I can say that I cannot pray but I sin – I cannot preach to you or any others but I sin – I can do nothing without sin; and, as one expresses it, my repentance wants to be repented of, and my tears to be washed in the precious blood of my dear Redeemer. Our best duties are as so many splendid sins. Before you can speak peace to your heart, you must not only be sick of your original and actual sin, but you must be made sick of your righteousness, of all your duties and performances. There must be a deep conviction before you can be brought out of your self-righteousness, it is the last idol taken out of your heart. The pride of our heart will not let us submit to the righteousness of Jesus Christ. But if you never felt that you had no righteousness of your own, if you never felt the deficiency of your own righteousness, you cannot come to Jesus Christ. There are a great many now who may say that they well believe all this, but there is a great difference between talking and feeling. Did you ever feel the want of a dear Redeemer? Did you ever feel the want of Jesus Christ upon the account of the deficiency of your own righteousness? And can you now say from your heart, "Lord, you may justly damn me for the best duties that ever I did perform?" If you are not thus brought out of self, you may speak peace to yourselves, but yet there is no peace.

JANUARY 23

Preaching Jesus

Also, preaching the Lord Jesus.

ACTS 11:20B

There is no idle word in God's book. It is said, "the Lord Jesus opened his mouth;" but what for? Why, to get in breath that he might speak loud to the people, when the heavens were his sounding board. Then did he open his mouth, and taught them in earnest, powerfully; and therefore the people made this observation when he had done speaking, "that he spoke as one having authority, and not as the scribes." There is no dispensation from preaching, but sickness or want of abilities, to those that are ordained to preach; and therefore it was a proverb in the primitive church, "that is becomes a bishop to die preaching." Bishop Jewell, that blessed minister of the Church of England, gave that answer to a person that met his Lordship walking on foot in the dirt, going to preach to a few people. "Why does your Lordship, weak as you are, expose yourself thus?" Says he, "It becomes a bishop to die preaching." May the entire world have such bishops such jewels as he was! What are they to preach? Not themselves. What are they to preach? – they are to preach not morality: Not morality! I say, not morality; that is, morality is not to be the grand point of their preaching; they are not to preach as a heathen philosopher would. A late bishop of Lincoln, who has not been dead a long while, said to his chaplain, "You are not a minister of Cicero, or any of the heathen philosophers; you are not to entertain your people with dry morality, but remember you are a minister of Christ … Go into all the world, and preach the gospel."

JANUARY 24

Tender Souls

Woe is me! For the LORD has added sorrow to my pain. I am weary with my groaning, and I find no rest.

JEREMIAH 45:3

We go on quietly and in great peace. The Lord keeps you and me, my dear brother, from a hot, rash, positive, overbearing temper. This, I think, is the predominant failing in my dear brother Harris. I think you do not deal gently enough, nor lead those gently that are with young … My dear brother, it is a meet thing to give reproof in a proper manner. If a brother or sister were overtaken with a fault I would not say "The devil is in you," but endeavor to restore him or her with the utmost gentleness and love. Ministers must not be wolves to worry the sheep, but shepherds to lead and feed them. Tender souls are not to be used like obstinate, and unawakened sinners. To one we are to be sons of thunder, and to the other the sons of consolation. If we deal roughly with Christ's lambs it will prejudice them against us and make them afraid to come near us. What is most to be regarded is that it will displease our Great Shepherd himself. Let us, therefore, my dear brother, pray for more of the mind of Christ. And the more we drink into his Spirit, the more tenderly and lovingly shall we deal with those under our care. I doubt but your roughness has been overruled for good. But that does not justify your conduct. Everything is not good that God brings good out of. I know the dear man to whom I am writing will not be offended.

[From a Letter to Howell Harris, October 28, 1741]

JANUARY 25

Eternal Rest

So then, there remains a Sabbath rest for the people of God … Let us therefore strive to enter that rest …

HEBREWS 4:9, 11

When we consider the persecutions those who live righteously and godly in the present world are exposed to, it is amazing to consider that the people of this generation should be so fond of a name to live while, in effect, they are dead. The people of God are to expect little else but troubles and trials while they are in this world; common experience is a contradiction to my text, that there is a rest to the people of God; but the author of the Hebrews, when speaking of this rest, did not mean that they should have a rest here, in this world. No; he too well knew that the people of God, all who would seek and serve the Lord Jesus, must be despised, hated, scoffed, slandered, and evil entreated; but the time was hastening when they should have a perfect rest: there is a rest laid up for them, and this is an encouragement for you, my brethren, to hold on, and hold out your way rejoicing. After death there will be a rest forever; at judgment, you shall be taken up to dwell with the Lord Jesus Christ. There, you shall be forever exempted from sin; you shall rest from all manner of sorrow and be no more troubled with the temptations of Satan. Here, you can set about nothing for the glory of God, or for your own soul's welfare, but the devil dissuades you from it, or distracts you in it, or discourages you after it. Here we are scoffed and derided; as the world hated the Lord Jesus Christ…but in that rest which is prepared for us, we shall then be gazed at for our glory.

JANUARY 26

Tasting Christ's Love

Greater love has no one than this, that someone lay down his life for his friends.

JOHN 15:13

If you are zealous for the Lord and seek Jesus, if your zeal is according to godliness, and you pray to him for his Spirit, you shall certainly have an answer of peace; you shall find it is good to seek the Lord, you will be adopted into his family, and by his Spirit be enabled to cry, "Abba, Father." O then, do not leave, but be continually waiting at wisdom's gate, and you shall find all her ways to be ways of pleasantness, and all her paths are peace; then, you shall find that it is worth waiting on the Lord Jesus; and, when you have got his Spirit within you, all the power of men or devils cannot make you forsake the ways of the Lord Jesus Christ. If you do but once taste his pardoning love, it will be so delightful unto you that you will cry for more and more; you will be as full as you can hold, and still not be satisfied; you will desire more and more of this love of Jesus; you will hunger and thirst, and hunger and thirst again, and never be satisfied till you come to that rest which is prepared for the people of God … As many of you as design to partake of the emblems of the body and blood of our dying Lord, examine well yourselves, lest by eating and drinking unworthily, you eat and drink damnation unto yourselves: remember the dying love of your dying Lord, and eat and drink in commemoration; do not let the world keep you from partaking; and when you have eaten and drunk, do not go away and run into the world – let the world see that you have been with Jesus.

JANUARY 27

Walking with God

But grow in the grace and knowledge of our Lord and Savior Jesus Christ. To him be the glory both now and to the day of eternity. Amen.

2 PETER 3:18

Walking, in the very idea of the word, seems to suppose a progressive motion. A person that walks, though he moves slowly, still goes forward, and does not continue in one place. So it is with those that walk with God. They go on, as the Psalmist says, "from strength to strength," or, in the language of the apostle Paul, they "are being transformed into the same image from one degree of glory to another" (2 Cor. 3:18). Indeed, in one sense, the divine life admits neither increase nor decrease. When a soul is born of God, he is a child of God, and though he should live to the age of Methuselah, yet he would then be only a child of God after all. But in another sense, the divine life admits of decays and additions. Hence it is, that we find the people of God charged with backslidings and losing their first love. And hence it is that we hear of babes, young men, and fathers in Christ. Upon this account it is that the apostle exhorts Timothy, "Practice these things … so that all may see your progress" (1 Tim. 4:15). Peter says to Christians in general, "But grow in the grace and knowledge of our Lord and Savior Jesus Christ" (2 Pet. 3:18). For the new creature increases in spiritual stature; and though a person can but be a new creature, yet there are some that are more conformed to the divine image than others, and will after death be admitted to a greater degree of blessedness.

JANUARY 28

Crosses Enough

Do you not know that all of us who have been baptized into Christ Jesus were baptized into his death?

ROMANS 6:3

We are baptized into Christ when we study to glorify Christ. That is the reason that God Almighty sends you so many trials, so that you may be baptized into his death; and generally you will find, when you have had most communications from God that some cross trials soon follow. Have you been praying for resignation? Perhaps God takes away a beloved child; you have been praying for great patience; perhaps a cross wife, a Nabal of a husband, bad servants, undutiful children, or something or other, and the devil at the head of them, making you uneasy, so that you find you have not so much patience as you thought you had. You never were upon the mount in your lives, but when you came down you were tempted to break the tables. Was it not so with Moses, after forty days communion with God? Down he came, and seeing the people dancing round the calf, down he throws the tables, and breaks them all to pieces; and if God were not to keep us, after all our communion with him, we should break the tables to pieces, and be damned. After all, that person then is dying every day, who looks upon himself every morning as one that is to be crucified afresh, that looks for crosses, and at the same time walks so inoffensively as to bring no cross upon himself. I spoke to a person yesterday about the cross. Pray, sir, says he, would you have me bring a cross upon myself? No, said I, only be honest, and you will find crosses enough.

JANUARY 29

Joys and Comforts

But we do not want you to be uninformed, brothers, about those who are asleep, that you may not grieve as others do who have no hope.

1 THESSALONIANS 4:13

It is in the midst of the tortures of a burning fever, a raptured soul can cry, "O the joys! O the comforts! Lord, I am coming! I am coming!" – what must that be when enclosed in a Redeemer's arms? In order to which, the glorious angels stand at the top of the ladder, to take a poor wearied pilgrim home. May the Lord give us not only such a frame when we are dying, but while we are living. For, if it is comfortable to die in such a frame, why should we not to live in it? Why should we not live in heaven while on earth? O, say you, "I thank God I walk by faith; I have got the promise." Well, thank God you have the promise, but, with the promise, learn to walk by that faith which is the evidence of things unseen – that faith which brings God down and brings heaven near, and gives the soul a heart-felt experience, which says, "God is love." Here is a salvation worthy of a God! Here is a salvation worthy of the Mediator's blood! – For this he groaned, for this he bled, for this he died, for this he arose, for this he ascended, for this he sent the Holy Spirit and for this purpose he now sends him into the hearts of his people. My brethren, what say you to this?

JANUARY 30

At Christ's Feet

For out of the heart come evil thoughts, murder, adultery, sexual immorality, theft, false witness, slander.

MATTHEW 15:19

If I am beloved of the Lord, how is it that I am harassed with blasphemous thoughts and suffer the trials that bring down the outward man? If I am beloved of the Lord, how is it that instead of living in plenty, I now want bread to eat, and should be glad to have it from those who I once scorned? Remember, he whom the Lord loves, he chastens and scourges every son whom he receives. Our dear Jesus was never more beloved of his Father than when he cried out, "My God, my God, why have you forsaken me?" (Mark 15:34) – never more beloved of his Father than when he was sweating great drops of blood, when he cried, "Father, if it be possible, let this cup pass from me." I remember a dear minister of Christ who told me that when he was in Scotland and went to the sacrament of the Lord's Supper, he was so dry and dark, and benumbed and tempted, that he thought he would go away without partaking and feasting with Jesus; as he was leaving, this thought came to his mind: "When was Jesus most acceptable to his Father? When did he give the greatest trial of his love? – When he cried out, 'My God, my God, why have you forsaken me?'" Upon this, then, he would venture; and if he perish, he perishes at Christ's feet; and he came away filled with comfort from his blessed God and Father in Christ.

JANUARY 31

Practice your Profession

You are the light of the world. A city set on a hill cannot be hidden.

Matthew 5:14

Permit me to exhort you, "if there is any encouragement in Christ … any participation in the Spirit" (Phil. 2:1), again and again to consider, that all Christians are as houses built upon a hill. Therefore it highly concerns you to walk circumspectly towards those that are without, and to take heed to yourselves, that your conversation in common life be as becomes such an open profession of the gospel of Christ, knowing that the eyes of all men are upon you. Labor therefore, my beloved brethren, to let your practice correspond to your profession. Think not that it will be sufficient for you to plead at the last day, "Lord, have we not assembled ourselves together in Thy name, and livened each other by singing psalms, hymns, and spiritual songs?" For verily I say unto you, in spite of this, our blessed Lord will bid you depart from him. You shall receive a greater judgment if, in the midst of these great pretensions, you are found to be workers of iniquity. Oh, may you be found at the last day, holy, sincere disciples of a crucified Redeemer! And may you adorn the gospel of our Lord Jesus Christ in all things! Thus will you anticipate the happiness of a future state, and by attending, and improving, the communion of saints on earth, be made fit to join the communion and fellowship of the spirits of the just made perfect, of the holy angels, and of the ever-blessed and eternal God in heaven.

FEBRUARY 1

Be Thankful

And let the peace of Christ rule in your hearts, to which indeed you were called in one body. And be thankful.

COLOSSIANS 3:15

Out of the many thousands that receive blessings from the Lord, how few give thanks in remembrance of his holiness! The account given us of the ungrateful lepers, is a lively representation of the ingratitude of mankind in general, who, when under any humbling providence, can cry, "Jesus, Master, have mercy on us," (Luke 17:13), but when delivered from their distress, only one in ten can be found returning to give thanks to God. Yet as common as this sin of ingratitude is, there is nothing we ought more earnestly to pray against. For what is more absolutely condemned in Scripture? The Apostle Paul wrote, "Rejoice always … give thanks in all circumstances;" (1 Thess. 5:16, 18). As for our sins, God puts them behind his back, but his mercies he will have acknowledged. We generally find that when God sent any remarkable punishment upon a particular person, he reminded him of the favors he had received, as aggravations of his ingratitude…O that you would declare by your lives that you are truly thankful for the wonders he has shown to us, who are less than the least of the sons of men. For to give him thanks with your lips, while your hearts are far from him, is a mock sacrifice and an abomination unto the Lord. O then let me beseech you, give to God your hearts, your whole hearts, and suffer yourselves to be drawn by the cords of infinite love, to honor and obey him.

FEBRUARY 2

Christ's Resurrection

That I may know him and the power of his resurrection, and may share his sufferings, becoming like him in his death.

PHILIPPIANS 3:10

Jesus, who dy'd a World to save,
Revives and rises from the Grave,
By his Almighty Pow'r;
From Sin, and Death, and Hell set free,
He Captive leads Captivity,
And lives to die no more.

Children of God, look up and see,
Your Savior cloth'd with Majesty,
Triumphant o'er the Tomb:
Give o'er your griefs, cast off your Fears,
In heav'n your Mansions he prepares,
And soon will take you Home.

His Church is still his Joy and Crown,
He looks with Love and Pity down,
On her he did Redeem;
He tastes her Joys, he feels her Woes,
And prays that she may spoil her Foes,
And ever reign with him.

FEBRUARY 3

Beauties of Age

Give ear, O heavens, and I will speak, and let the earth hear the words of my mouth. May my teaching drop as the rain, my speech distill as the dew, like gentle rain upon the tender grass, and like showers upon the herb.

DEUTERONOMY 32:1-2

Oh, what a dismal sight it is to see an old man with his hoary head grown grey in sin and hardened in iniquity. On the other hand, I believe, to all that consider rightly, there is no grander sight almost under the sun than to see an old grey-headed man keeping up a consistent character; and proving, by his conduct, that his path, like that of the just, is as the shining light that shines more and more to the perfect day … It is on this account that I admire old Jacob; how grand he looked when leaning on his staff, with all the composure in the world, under a divine influence, blessing his children standing round him! But, I think, there is one who was called to act a more public part, namely, Moses, who was honored of God to be a great legislator, king in Jeshurun, a lawgiver between Judah's feet, as pupils used to be at the feet of their teachers, to receive their instruction. If you have a mind to see how bright he shines, you must read Deuteronomy 32; indeed, you must read all of Deuteronomy, which is nothing but a sermon that Moses, at various times, preached to the children of Israel; and having done preaching, he sang a hymn of his own composing, and that too at a time when he knew, at the very finishing of the song, he should immediately have his soul kissed away, and be called to sing a better song in the kingdom of heaven.

FEBRUARY 4

Soul Prosperity

His is like a tree planted by streams of water that yields its fruit in its season, and its leaf does not whither. In all that he does, he prospers.

PSALM 1:3

If your souls prosper, the more you will fall in love with the glorious Redeemer and with his righteousness. I never knew a person in my life that diligently used the word and other means but as they improved in grace saw more and more the necessity of depending upon a better righteousness than their own. Generally, when we first set out, we have got better hearts than heads; but if we grow in the divine life, our heads will grow as well as our hearts; and the Spirit of God leads us out of abominable self, and causes us to flee more and more to that glorious and complete righteousness that Jesus Christ wrought for us. The more your souls prosper, the more you will see of the freeness and distinguishing nature of God's grace, that all is of grace. We are all naturally free-willers, and generally young ones say, "O we have found the Messiah, of whom Moses and the prophets spoke." Which is right, except that phrase "we have found"; for the believer a little after learns that the Messiah had found him. I mention this, because we ought not to make persons offenders for a word. We should bear with young Christians and not confuse them because they do not yet understand the doctrines of grace. Let it not be forgotten also, that the more your souls prosper, the more you will get above the world. Do not think that you should be negligent in life … in paradise Adam and Eve were to dress the garden, and not to be idle. After the fall, they were to till the ground.

FEBRUARY 5

Glory in Fire

For the LORD is good; his steadfast love endures forever, and his faithfulness to all generations.

PSALM 100:5

We glorify God in the fire when we bear it patiently. It is a dreadful thing when we are saying, with Cain, "My punishment is greater than I can bear" (Gen. 4:13)! But the language of the soul that glorifies God in the fire is this: "Shall I, Lord; shall I, a sinful man, complain for the punishment of my sins?" It is a glorious thing when we can say with a good man…that when he was racked with pain, and groaning all night with trouble, he would often say, "Lord, I groan; but, Lord Jesus, I appeal to you, you know I do not grumble." Then we glorify God in the fire, when, though we feel pain and anguish, we at the same time can tell the Lord that we deserve this and ten thousand times worse … We glorify God in the fire also when we are really and fully persuaded that God will not put us in the fire but for our good and his own glory. I am afraid some people think God does as some cheating apothecaries, that bring five things when they need not bring but one, especially when they have some silly patients that love to be taking physic; they send one after another, when, perhaps, the best thing would be to throw them all away; so we think of God – but this is a mistake. God never sends but what is necessary, when there is something that needs be purged away; we glorify God in the fire when we say, "Lord, do not let the fire go out until it has done its work." Then we glorify God when we wish for the good of the fire and can say from our hearts, "Lord, do with me as seems good in your sight."

FEBRUARY 6

More than our Bodies

For I rejoiced greatly when the brothers came and testified to your truth, as indeed you are walking in the truth. I have no greater joy than to hear that my children are walking in the truth.

3 JOHN 3-4

From our first coming into the world until our passing out of it to "the spirits of just men made perfect," all the Lord's children have found, some more, and others less, that they have had dreadful as well as blessed times, and all has been over-ruled to bring them nearer unto God. But I believe, I am sure, I speak to some this night, that if it were put to their choice, had rather know that their souls prospered, than to have ten thousand pounds left them; and it is supposed that we may not only know it ourselves, but that others may know it, that our profiting may appear to all. Because John says, "I pray that all may go well with you and that you may be in good health, as it goes well with your soul." O may all that converse with us see it in us! We may frequently sit under the gospel, but if we do not take a great deal of care, however orthodox we are, we shall fall into practical Antinomianism, and be contented that we were converted twenty or thirty years ago, and learn, as some Antinomians, "to live by faith." Thank God, say some, we met with God so many months ago, but are not at all solicitous whether they meet with him any more; and there is not a single individual here that is savingly acquainted with Jesus Christ but wishes his soul prospered more than his body.

FEBRUARY 7

Riches of Free Grace

From that time Jesus began to preach, saying, "Repent, for the kingdom of heaven is at hand."

MATTHEW 4:17

When we consider how heinous and aggravating our offenses are in the sight of a just and holy God, that they bring down his wrath upon our heads, and occasion us to live under his indignation, how ought we thereby to be deterred from evil, or at least engaged to study to repent thereof, and not commit the same again. But man is so thoughtless of an eternal state, and has so little consideration of the welfare of his immortal soul, that he can sin without any thought that he must give an account of his actions at the Day of Judgment; or if he, at times, has any reflections on his behavior, they do not drive him to true repentance. He may, for a short time, refrain from falling into some gross sins which he had lately committed; but then, when the temptation comes again with power, he is carried away with the lust. Thus, he goes on promising and resolving, and in breaking both his resolutions and his promises, as fast almost as he has made them. This is highly offensive to God; it is a mocking of him. My brethren, when grace is given us to repent truly, we shall turn wholly unto God. Let me beseech you to repent of your sins, for the time is hastening when you will have neither time nor call to repent; there is none in the grave, whither we are going. Do not be afraid, for God often receives the greatest sinner to mercy through the merits of Christ Jesus. This magnifies the riches of his free grace; and should be an encouragement for you, who are great and notorious sinners, to repent, for he will have mercy upon you, if you, through Christ, return to him.

FEBRUARY 8

The Glass of His Word

This Book of the Law shall not depart from your mouth, but you shall meditate on it day and night …

JOSHUA 1:8

Believers maintain their walk with God by reading his Word. "Search the scriptures," says our Lord, "for in them ye think ye have eternal life: and they are they which testify of me" (John 5:39, KJV). The Psalmist tells us that God's word "is a lamp to my feet and a light to my path" (Ps. 119:105), and states of a good man, "his delight is in the law of the Lord, and on his law he meditates day and night." … If we cease making the written word of God our rule for faith and practice, we shall soon lie open to all manner of delusion, and be in great danger of making shipwreck of faith and a good conscience … The Scriptures are called the lively oracles of God, not only because they are generally used to beget in us new life, but also to increase it in the soul. The Apostle Peter, in his second epistle, prefers it even to seeing Christ transfigured. For after he had said in 2 Peter 1:18, "we ourselves heard this very voice borne from heaven, for we were with him on the holy mountain," he adds in verse 19, "And we have something more sure, the prophetic word, to which you will do well to pay attention as to a lamp shining in a dark place, until the day dawns and the morning star rises in your hearts." Until we shake off these bodies, and see Jesus face to face, we must see and converse with him through the glass of his Word. We must make his testimonies our counselors, and daily, with Mary, sit at Jesus' feet, by faith hearing his word. We shall then by happy experience find that they are spirit and life, meat and drink indeed, to our souls.

FEBRUARY 9

Our Great Glory

Behold, the Lord our God has shown us his glory and greatness, and we have heard his voice out of the midst of the fire. This day we have seen God speak with man, and man still live.

DEUTERONOMY 5:24

Dare you say that your God is your glory, and do you aim at glorifying the Lord your God? If your God is your glory, then say, "But far be it from me to boast except in the cross of our Lord Jesus Christ, by which the world has been crucified to me, and I to the world" (Gal. 6:14). What do you say now? Do not talk of God being your glory if you do not love his cross. If God is our glory, we shall glory not only in doing, but in suffering for him; we shall glory in tribulation, and count ourselves most highly honored when we are called to suffer most for his great name's sake. I might enlarge, but you may easily judge, by my poor feeble voice this last week, that neither my strength of voice or body will permit me to be long tonight, and yet I will venture to give you your last parting salutation; and though I have been dissuaded from getting up to preach this night, yet I thought, as my God was my glory, I should glory in preaching till I died. O that God may be all our glory! All our own glory fades away, there is nothing will be valuable at the great day but this, "You are my God, and you are my glory!"

FEBRUARY 10

Sabbath Rest

It is good to give thanks to the Lord, to sing praises to your name, O Most High.

PSALM 92:1

This is the Day the Lord has made,
He calls the Hours his own:
Let Heav'n rejoice, let Earth be glad,
And Praise surround the Throne.

To-day Christ rose, and left the Dead,
And Satan's Empire fell;
To-day the Saints his Triumphs spread,
And all his Wonders tell.

Hosanna to th' anointed King,
To David's holy Son;
Help us, O Lord, descend, and bring
Salvation from your Throne.

Hosanna, in the highest Strains
The Church on Earth can raise!
The highest Heav'ns in which he reigns
Shall give him nobler Praise.

FEBRUARY 11

Wings of Prayer

But I, O L*ORD, cry to you; in the morning my prayer comes before you.*

PSALM 88:13

The spirit of grace is always accompanied with the spirit of supplication. It is the very breath of the new creature, the fan of the divine life, whereby the spark of holy fire, kindled in the soul by God, is raised into a flame. Neglect of secret prayer has been frequently an inlet to many spiritual diseases, and has been attended with fatal consequences .... Prayer is one of the noblest parts of the believer's spiritual armor. Ephesians 6:18 reads "Praying at all times in the Spirit, with all prayer and supplication." Our Lord says, "Watch and pray, that you may not enter into temptation" (Mark 14:38). Not that our Lord would have us always upon our knees, or in our closets, to the neglect of our other relative duties. But he means, that our souls should be kept in a praying frame, so that we might be able to say, as a good man in Scotland once said to his friends on his deathbed, "Could these curtains, or could these walls speak, they would tell you what sweet communion I have had with my God here." O prayer! Prayer! It brings and keeps God and man together. It raises man up to God, and brings God down to man. If you would therefore, O believers, keep up your walk with God, pray. Pray without ceasing. Be much in secret, set prayer. And when you are about the common business of life, be much in ejaculatory prayer, and send, from time to time, short letters post to heaven upon the wings of faith. They will reach the very heart of God, and return to you again loaded with spiritual blessings.

FEBRUARY 12

Jesus Loved Lazarus

Now Jesus loved Martha and her sister and Lazarus.

JOHN 11:5

Jesus loved Lazarus, and yet Lazarus was sick. And what do his sisters do for him, now that he is sick? No doubt they consulted a physician, for it is tempting God to neglect making use of means for the recovery of our health. But then they were not guilty of Asa's crime, who sought physicians but not the Lord. No, they knew the most skilful prescriptions would be of no effect, unless attended with a blessing from Jesus, the great and Almighty Physician; and, therefore, his sisters sent to him, probably at the beginning of their brother's illness. How unlike is their conduct to that of the generality of people, especially the rich and great! How unfashionable is it today for persons to send to Jesus on behalf of their sick relations! It is so very uncustomary, that in some places, if a minister be sent for to a sick person, it is a sad symptom that the patient is almost past hopes of recovery. But Martha and her sister Mary did not do this; they sent for Jesus, though he was now beyond the Jordan. Hence it was that they knew where to send for him. But what kind of message did they send? A very humble and suitable one: "Lord, the one whom you love is sick." They might have said, "Lord, he who loves you is sick." But they knew that our love was not worth mentioning, and that we love Jesus only because he first loved us. There is no prescribing to our Lord what he should do, or what means he should make use of … they simply tell Jesus the case, knowing it was sufficient barely to lay it before an infinitely compassionate Redeemer and to leave it to him to act according to his own sovereign good-will and pleasure.

FEBRUARY 13

Our God

Your God will be your glory.

ISAIAH 60:19C

What signifies saying, "This is mine, and that is mine," if you cannot say, "God is mine." The best thing that God has left in the New Testament is himself: "I will be their God;" that is one of the legacies; and "a new heart also will I give them;" that is another. "I will put my laws in their mind, and write them in their hearts;" that is another; but all that is good for nothing, comparatively speaking, unless God has said at the same time, for they are all inseparable, "I will be their God, and they shall be my people." Now, how shall I know that God is my God? I am afraid that some people think there is no knowing. Well then, if you think so, you set up a worship, and go, and erect an altar, and instead of receiving God in the sacrament as yours, go and worship an unknown God. I am so far from believing that we cannot know that God is ours, that I am fully persuaded of it, and would speak it with humility, and I would not choose to leave you with a lie in my mouth, that I have known it for about thirty-five years, as clear as the sun is in the meridian, that God is my God … I would ask you this question, "Did you ever feel the want of God to be your God?" Nobody knows God to be his or her God that did not feel him to be his God in Christ; out of Christ, God is a consuming fire. I know there are a great variety of ways in people's conversions, but still, my brothers, we must all feel our misery, we must all feel our distance from God, all feel that we are estranged from God … we cannot be said to believe that God is our God, till we are brought to be reconciled to him through his Son.

FEBRUARY 14

The Greatest Pleasure

And you show that you are a letter from Christ delivered by us, written not with ink but with the Spirit of the living God, not on tablets of stone but on tablets of human hearts.

2 CORINTHIANS 3:3

The examples of our blessed Lord and his apostles are the grand patterns whereby we are to form the conduct of our lives. It is true, indeed, that instances of an exalted piety are rarely to be met with in the present age, and one would think, if we were to take an estimate of our religion, from the lives of most of its professors, that Christianity was nothing but a dead letter. But then it is not our religion, but we ourselves are to be blamed. Would we live as the primitive Christians did, we might no doubt have the same assistance given to us, as they had. God's grace is never restrained, and though we should not arrive at those heights of heavenly-mindedness as some of the primitive Christians were eminent for, yet, I think, we should imitate them as far as we can, and rely on the divine goodness for grants of such a supply of grace, as he, in his good pleasure, shall judge most convenient for us…see how dangerous it is to be a lukewarm Christian, and that there is nothing to be done without breaking from the world, denying ourselves daily, taking up our cross, and following Jesus. These things may seem a little terrible at first, but believe me, they are nothing but suggestions of our enemy to deter us from getting out; and if you can credit me, mortification itself, when once practiced, is the greatest pleasure in the world.

FEBRUARY 15

Christ's Fools

We are fools for Christ's sake, but you are wise in Christ. We are weak, but you are strong. You are held in honor, but we in disrepute.

1 CORINTHIANS 4:10

Woe to you who have no marks of being beloved of the Lord. Have we any profane Esaus here tonight, that are saying, "Do not tell me of your being beloved of the Lord; if I can have the love of such a person, I do not care whether God loves me or not. You may tell me God loves people when they are afflicted, I want none of these marks, I think God loves me because I am a good person; I think God loves me because I prosper; I think God loves me because I am very healthy and strong. I do not care whether I wait upon God or not, or give to the poor or not." I will not soften the matter; there is no going to heaven without wearing a fool's coat – Oh, you may say, that is your impudence; you make people uneasy, and set them upon a false scent, and make them their own persecutors ... There are few that have the courage that the gentleman had who loved God and went to see some carnal relations after he became a fool for Christ's sake. Says one of his relatives, "It is always our custom after dinner to sing a song," and asked him to sing. He said that he would in his turn; two of them sang; his relation said to him, "Come, cousin, sing." Says he, "I have not sung a song a good while, but, if you please, I will sing a hymn." He sung it out but they never asked him to sing again, nor did they sing afterwards. How sweet it is to go through boldly with a thing for Christ!

FEBRUARY 16

Faith's Grammar

O you who love the L*ORD, hate evil! He preserves the lives of his saints; he delivers them from the hand of the wicked.*

PSALM 97:10

The grand inquiry, then, is how shall I know that I am one of Lord's beloved? The natural man never minds the love of God; he flatters himself he loves God naturally, that the love of God is a plant that grows in nature's garden; but a spiritual person does not so … therefore the grand inquiry, and one proof of a person's being awakened, is, how shall I know whether God loves me, or not? … I am persuaded that we may as well know that God loves us, and we love God, as we may know that the sun shines at noon-day. How shall I know it but by the effects of this love, by the fruits of it? That great man, Dr. Watts, who was called the sweet singer of Israel, says, "We should go first to the grammar school of faith and repentance before we go to the university of predestination." Whereas the devil would have them go first to the university, to examine whether they were elected or rejected, or no. They should do as a good woman once did, when Satan tempted her, and wanted to distress her, that there were but few to be saved; she said, if there were but two to be saved, she would strive to be one of them. Surely, I am beloved of the Lord, if my natural enmity against the Lord is slain. How do I know I love a person? How can you prove that you love me? ... when your former enmity is removed, and you are reconciled to the one you used to hate, cannot you know that you love them? And if God has removed that enmity to Christ out of your hearts, surely you are one of his.

FEBRUARY 17

God's Special Love

For God so loved the world, that he gave his only Son, that whosoever believes in him should not perish but have eternal life.

JOHN 3:16

Here is a dispute between the Arminians and the Calvinists: ask an Arminian what is meant by "beloved of the Lord," and they will say that there is meant the *general redemption*, and so the "beloved of the Lord" signifies all the men that were ever born into the world; so, they say, God loves all. That is a good broad bridge to take them in, but broad bridges are not always the strongest bridges in the world. The Arminians will assert Judas was as much beloved of God as Peter, or any of the other apostles. And those who are not Arminians, but are what you call Quakers, and there are a good many, I believe, among them, that have better hearts than heads; they say that we are all alike, that we all come into the world with a seed of grace, and shall be happy according to the improvement of that grace. Hence they talk nothing of a Christ *without* but only *within*; happy are they that experience Christ within! God's mercy is sure, and over all his works; and in one sense our Lord Jesus is the Savior of all men; that is, *all sorts of men*. Even the wicked are beholden to Jesus, whom they despise, for every worldly comfort they enjoy. In this sense we should learn to love as our Lord loved the young man. But we must go more to what we call Calvinism, which I call Scripture truth. The love Jesus bore for the rich young ruler was quite different from that love which with he loved Martha, Mary, and their brother, Lazarus.

FEBRUARY 18

Prosperous Souls

Beloved, I pray that all may go well with you and that you may be in good health, as it goes well with your soul.

3 JOHN 2

That great and sweet singer of Israel, Dr. Isaac Watts, I remember, about two and thirty years ago told me that he had got no sleep for three months, but what was procured by the most exquisite art of the most eminent physicians; and, my dear hearers, none but those that have such habits of body can sympathize with those that are under them. When we are in high spirits we think people might do if they would, but when brought down ourselves we cannot; but notwithstanding his body was in this condition, his soul prospered so eminently, so very eminently, that the apostle could not think it a greater mercy, or the church a greater blessing, than that his bodily health might be as vigorous as the health of his soul. I remember the great colonel Gardiner, who had the honor of being killed in his country's cause, closes one of his last letters to me, with wishing I might enjoy a thriving soul in a healthy body; but this is peculiar to the followers of Jesus, that they find the soul prospers most when the body is worst; and observe, he wishes him a prospering body above all things, that he might have joy and health with a prosperous soul; for if we have a good heart, and good health at the same, and our hearts are alive to God, we go on with a fresh gale. I observe, that the soul of man in general must be made a partaker of a divine life, before it can be said to prosper at all.

FEBRUARY 19

Divine Meditation

You keep him in perfect peace whose mind is stayed on you...
Isaiah 26:3

Holy and frequent meditation is a blessed means of keeping up a believer's walk with God. "Prayer, reading, temptation, and meditation," says Luther, "make a minister." And they also make, and perfect, a Christian. Meditation to the soul is the same as digestion to the body. Holy David found it so, and therefore he was frequently employed in meditation, even in the night season. We read also of Isaac's going out into the fields to meditate and pray in the evening. Meditation is a kind of silent prayer, whereby the soul is frequently carried out of itself to God, and is in a degree made like unto those blessed spirits, who by a kind of immediate intuition always behold the face of our heavenly Father. None but those happy souls that have been accustomed to this divine employ, can tell what a blessed promoter of the divine life meditation is. "As I mused," says *David*, "the fire burned" (Ps. 39:3). And while the believer is musing on the works and word of God, especially that work of works, that wonder of wonders, that mystery of godliness, "God manifest in the flesh," the Lamb of God slain for the sins of the world, he frequently feels the fire of divine love kindle, so that he is obliged to speak with his tongue, and tell of the loving kindness of the Lord to his soul. Be frequent therefore in meditation, all you who desire to keep up and maintain a close and uniform walk with the most high God.

FEBRUARY 20

Christ's Feast

The kingdom of heaven may be compared to a king who gave a wedding feast for his son, and sent his servants to call those who were invited to the wedding feast, but they would not come.

MATTHEW 22:2-3

Poor souls! Many of you are not hungry. You do not feel yourselves halt, maimed, or blind, and therefore you have no relish for Christ's spiritual feast. Well, be not angry with me for calling you; be not offended if I weep over you. You know not the day of your visitation. If I must appear in judgment as a swift witness against you, I must. But that thought chills my blood! And I cannot bear it; I feel that I could lay down my life for you. But I am not willing to go without you. What say you, my dear friends? I would put the question to you once more, will you taste Christ's Supper, or will you not? You shall all be welcome. There is milk at this feast for babes, as well as meat for strong men, and for persons of riper years. There is room and provision for high and low, rich and poor, one with another; and our Savior will thank you for coming. Amazing condescension! Astonishing love! The thought of it quite overcomes me. Help me, help me, O believers, to bless and praise him. And O! that his love may excite us to come afresh to him, as though we had never come before! For, though we have been often feasted, yet our souls will starve unless we renew our acts of faith, and throw ourselves, as lost, undone sinners, continually at his feet. Feeding upon past experiences will not satisfy our souls, any more than what we did eat yesterday will sustain our bodies today. No, believers must look for fresh influences of divine grace, and beg the Lord to water them every moment.

FEBRUARY 21

Hoping in God

Why are you cast down, O my soul, and why are you in turmoil within me? Hope in God; for I shall yet praise him, my salvation and my God.

PSALM 43:5

A never-failing maxim is here proposed, "Hope in God," trust in God, believe in God; for I am sure, and all of you that know Jesus Christ are persuaded of it too, that all our troubles arise from our unbelief…"Put your trust in God; hope in God, for I shall yet praise him." The devil tells me my trouble is so great, I shall never lift up my head again; but unbelief and the devil are liars; "I shall yet praise him;" my God will carry me through all; I shall yet praise him, even for casting me down … though my afflictions have now made my body low, suck up my spirits, and hurt my animal frame, "he will be the help of my countenance." I shall by and by see him again, and be favored with those transforming views, which my God has favored me with in times past; though the devil tempts me, and my evil neighbors say, "Where is your God now?" – yet he shall be "the health of my countenance." Do you think you are a child of God, and your Father suffers you to be cast down? I tell you, I tell you, O Satan, that God who I have been so vilely tempted as to believe has forsaken me, will come over the mountains of my guilt, will forgive my backslidings against himself. My unbelief shall not make his promises of none effect; I shall praise him even while I live, I shall praise him before I die, I shall praise him for ever in heaven, where he will be, after death, "the health of my countenance, and my God;" thus faith will get the better in a saint.

FEBRUARY 22

Return to Him

No, I tell you; but unless you repent, you will all likewise perish.

LUKE 13:3

When we consider how heinous and aggravating our offenses are in the sight of a just and holy God, how they bring down his wrath upon our heads, and occasion us to live under his indignation, how ought we, then, to be deterred from evil, or at least engaged to study to repent thereof and not commit the same sin again – but man is so thoughtless of an eternal state and has so little consideration of the welfare of his immortal soul that he can sin without any thought that he must give an account of his actions at the Day of Judgment. Or, if he, at times, has any reflections on his behavior, they do not drive him to true repentance. Indeed, he may, for a short time, refrain from falling into some gross sins which he had lately committed; but then, when the temptation comes again with power, he is carried away with the lust; and thus he goes on promising and resolving, and in breaking both his resolutions and his promises, as fast almost as he has made them. This is highly offensive to God, and it is a mocking of him. My brothers, when grace is given us to repent truly, we shall then turn wholly unto God. And let me beseech you to repent of your sins, for the time is hastening when you will have neither time nor call to repent; there is none in the grave, whither we are going; but do not be afraid, for God often receives the greatest sinner to mercy through the merits of Christ Jesus. This magnifies the riches of his free grace and should be an encouragement for you who are great and notorious sinners, to repent; for he will have mercy upon you, if you, through Christ, return to him.

FEBRUARY 23

Faith's Feast

I delight to do your will, O my God; your law is within my heart.

PSALM 40:8

If we believe the Scriptures, we must believe what our Lord has declared therein, that the very hairs of his disciples' heads are all numbered; and that a sparrow does not fall to the ground, (either to pick up a grain of corn, or when shot by a fowler) without the knowledge of our heavenly Father (Luke 12:6-7). Every cross has a call in it, and every particular dispensation of divine providence has some particular purpose to fulfill in those to whom it is sent. If it is of an afflictive nature, God says, "Keep yourself from idols." If it is of a prosperous nature, he says, as it were by a small still voice, "My son, give me your heart." If believers, therefore, will keep up their walk with God, they must from time to time hear what the Lord has to say concerning them in the voice of his providence. Thus we find that Abraham's servant watched the providence of God when he went to fetch a wife for his master Isaac, and by that means he found the person that was designed to be his master's wife. "For a little hint from providence," says pious Bishop Hall, "is enough for faith to feed upon." And as I believe it will be one part of our happiness in heaven, to take a view of, and look back upon, the various links of the golden chain which drew us there; so those that enjoy most of heaven below, I believe, will be the most minute in remarking God's various dealings with them, with respect to his providential dispensations here on earth.

FEBRUARY 24

Temples of God

For we are the temple of the living God; as God said, "I will make my dwelling among them and walk among them, and I will be their God, and they shall be my people."

2 CORINTHIANS 6:16

Christians are "the temple of the living God," of Father, Son, and Holy Ghost. They who once held a consultation to create, are all equally concerned in making preparations for, and effectually bringing about the redemption of man. The Father creates, the Son redeems, and the Holy Ghost sanctifies all the elect people of God. Being loved from eternity, they are effectually called in time, they are chosen out of the world, and not only by an external formal dedication at baptism, or at the Lord's Supper, but by a free, voluntary, unconstrained oblation, they devote themselves, spirit, soul, and body, to the entire service of him who has loved and given himself for them. This is true and undefiled religion before God our Heavenly Father. This is the real Christian's reasonable service, or, as some think the word imports, this is the service required of us in the word of God. It implies no less than a total renunciation of the world; in short, it turns the Christian's whole life into one continued sacrifice of love to God, so that, "whether he eats or drinks, he does all to his glory." Not that I would hereby insinuate that to be Christians, or, to keep the words of our text, in order to be temples of the living God, we must become hermits, or shut ourselves up in nunneries or cloisters; this be far from me! No. The religion, which this Bible in my hand prescribes, is a social religion, a religion equally practicable by high and low, rich and poor, and which absolutely requires a due discharge of all relative duties, in whatsoever state of life God shall be pleased to place and continue us.

FEBRUARY 25

Christ's Rays

The heavens declare the glory of God, and the sky above proclaims his handiwork.

PSALM 19:1

If you were all up this morning before the sun arose at five o'clock, how beautiful was the appearance … how pleasant to behold the flowers opening to the rising sun! I appeal to you yourselves, when you were looking out at the window, or walking about, or opening your shop, if in a spiritual frame, whether you did not say, "Arise, Sun of righteousness, with healing in your wings, on me" – all that the natural sun is to the world, so Jesus Christ is, and more, to his people. Without the sun, we should have no corn, or fruit of any kind. What a dark place would the world be without the sun, and how dark would the world be without Jesus Christ; and as the sun does really communicate its rays to the earth, the plants, and to all this lower creation, so the Son of God does really communicate his life and power to every new-created soul, otherwise Christ is but a painted sun. And is Christ nothing but a painted Christ to us, while we receive heat and benefit by the Holy Ghost, on account of the virtue of his blood? Sometimes the sun shines brighter than at other times, and does not always appear alike; clouds intervene, and interrupt its rays; so it is between a renewed soul and the Lord Jesus, the Sun of righteousness. O my brothers, I believe you know it by fatal experience: hold but your hand now, when the sun shines in its meridian, between it and you, and if by the breadth of that you can keep the sun from you, ah! How very little earth will keep off your heart from Jesus Christ! It was a very excellent saying of one of the ancients, that God never leaves a person until he first leaves him.

FEBRUARY 26

Christ's Wandering Sheep

I am the good shepherd. The good shepherd lays down his life for the sheep.

JOHN 10:11

You all know that sheep, of all creatures in the world, are the most apt to stray and be lost. Christ's people may justly, in that respect, be compared to sheep; therefore, we say, "We have erred and strayed from your ways like lost sheep." Turn out a horse, or a dog, and they will find their way home, but a sheep wanders about, he wanders here and there, as much as to say, "Dear stranger, show me my way home again;" thus Christ's sheep are too apt to wander from the fold; having their eye off the great Shepherd, they go into this field and that field, over this hedge and that, and often return home with the loss of their wool. But at the same time sheep are the most useful creatures in the world; they manure the land and thereby prepare it for the seed; they clothe our bodies with wool, and there is not the least part of a sheep but is useful to man. Oh, my brethren, God grant that you and I may, in this respect, answer the character of sheep. The world says because we preach faith we deny good works; this is the usual objection against the doctrine of imputed righteousness, but it is a slander, an impudent slander. It was a maxim in the first reformers' time, that though the Arminians preached up good works, you must go to the Calvinists for them. Christ's sheep study to be useful, and to clothe all they can; we should labor with our hands that we may have to give to all those that need.

FEBRUARY 27

Reading God's Word

Come, O children, listen to me; I will teach you the fear of the LORD.

PSALM 34:11

Reading the word of God is a duty incumbent on every private person. "Search the scriptures; for in them ye think ye have eternal life" (John 5:39, KJV) is a precept given by our blessed Lord indifferently to all; but much more so ought every head of a family to think of it in a peculiar manner to be spoken to himself. He ought to look upon himself as a prophet, and as therefore bound to instruct those under his charge in the knowledge of the word of God. This we find was the order God gave to Israel, for thus speaks his representative Moses in Deuteronomy 6:6,7: "And these words that I command you today shall be on your heart. You shall teach them diligently to your children, and shall talk of them when you sit in your house, and when you walk by the way, and when you lie down, and when you rise." From this we may infer that the only reason why so many neglect to read the words of Scripture diligently to their children is because the words of Scripture are not in their hearts. For if they were, out of the abundance of the heart their mouths would speak. How shall children know the laws of God, unless someone teach them? What is more proper to teach them by, than the lively oracles of God, "which are able to make [them] wise for salvation through faith in Christ Jesus" (2 Tim. 3:15)? And who is more proper to instruct them by these lively oracles than parents, who should be as much concerned to feed them with spiritual, as with bodily bread, day by day.

FEBRUARY 28

Suffering Persecution

...my persecutions and sufferings that happened to me at Antioch, at Iconium, and at Lystra—which persecutions I endured; yet from them all the LORD rescued me.

2 TIMOTHY 3:11

When our Lord was pleased to take upon himself the form of a servant, and to go about preaching the kingdom of God, he took all opportunities in public, and more especially in private, to caution his disciples against seeking great things for themselves and also to forewarn them of the many distresses, afflictions, and persecutions, which they must expect to endure for his name's sake. The great Apostle Paul, following the steps of his blessed Master, takes particular care, among other apostolical admonitions, to warn Timothy of the difficulties he must expect to meet with in the ministry: "But understand this, that in the last days there will come times of difficulty. For people will be lovers of self, lovers of money, proud, arrogant, abusive, disobedient to their parents, ungrateful, unholy, heartless, unappeasable, slanderous, without self-control, brutal, not loving good, treacherous, reckless, swollen with conceit, lovers of pleasure rather than lovers of God ... " (2 Tim. 3:1-4). But, in order to keep him from sinking under their opposition, he tells him, that though God, for wise ends, permitted these false teachers to oppose for some time, yet they should now proceed no farther: "But they will not get very far, for their folly will be plain to all, as was that of those two men" (2 Tim. 3:9). Then, to encourage Timothy more, he shows to him his own example: "You, however, have followed my teaching, my conduct, my aim in life, my faith, my patience, my love ... " (2 Tim. 3:10a). And then, lest Timothy might think that this was only the particular case of Paul, he writes, "Indeed, all who desire to live a godly life in Christ Jesus will be persecuted" (2 Tim. 3:12).

FEBRUARY 29

Beyond Sects

I appeal to you, brothers, by the name of our LORD Jesus Christ, that all of you agree, and that there be no divisions among you, but that you be united in the same mind and the same judgment.

1 CORINTHIANS 1:10

True and undefiled religion does not consist in being of this or that particular sect or communion … perhaps you could say no more for yourselves than this, namely, that you belong to such a church, and worship God in the same way in which your fathers and mothers worshipped God before you; and perhaps, at the same time, you are so narrow in your thoughts, that you think none can worship God but those that worship God just in your way. It is certainly a blessing to be born as you are, in a reformed church; it is certainly a blessing to have the outward government and discipline of the church exercised; but then, if you place religion merely in being of this or that sect – if you contend to monopolize or confine the grace of God to your particular party – if you rest in that you place the kingdom of God in something in which it does not consist – you had as good place it in meat and drink. There are certainly Christians among all sects and communions that have learned the truth as it is in Christ Jesus. I do not mean that there are Christians among Arians, Socinians, or those that deny the divinity of Jesus Christ – I am sure the devil is priest of such congregations as these; but I mean there are Christians among other sects that may differ from us in the outward worship of God. Therefore, my dear friends, learn to be more catholic, more unconfined in your notions; for if you place the kingdom of God merely in a sect, you place it in that in which it does not consist.

MARCH 1

A Divine Light

But we walk in the light, as he is in the light, we have fellowship with one another, and the blood of Jesus his Son cleanses us from all sin.

1 JOHN 1:7

In a short time, [Charles Wesley] let me have another book, entitled, *The Life of God in the Soul of Man*. Though I had fasted, watched and prayed, and received the sacrament for so long, yet I never knew what true religion was until God sent me that excellent treatise by the hands of my never-to-be-forgotten friend. At my first reading it, I wondered what the author meant by saying, "That some falsely placed religion in going to church, doing hurt to no one, being constant in the duties of the closet, and now and then reaching out their hands to give alms to their poor neighbors." Alas! thought I, if this be not true religion, what is? God soon showed me; for in reading a few lines further that "true religion was union of the soul with God, and Christ formed within us," a ray of divine light was instantaneously darted in upon my soul, and from that moment, but not till then, did I know that I must be a new creature. Upon this, like the woman of Samaria, when Christ revealed himself to her at the well, I had no rest in my soul until I wrote letters to my relations, telling them there was such a thing as the new birth. I imagined they would have gladly received it. But, alas! my words seemed to them as idle tales. They thought that I was going beside myself.

MARCH 2

Light Bread

I will make it a waste; it shall not be pruned or hoed, and briers and thorns shall grow up; I will also command the clouds that they rain no rain upon it.

ISAIAH 5:6

Is there a child of God who, when convicted of his sins, does not have a drooping heart? Who does not love sincerity and truth? I do not speak that you may think me humble. I love sincerity, inward and outward, and hate guile. When I consider what God has done for me, how often he has pruned and hedged me, and dug deep into my soul; when I think about how little I have done for God, it makes me to weep; yea, it makes me to weep, if possible, tears of blood … You see manna poured out round about the camp, and I am afraid that you consider it "light" bread – you have bad digestion and do not so well digest the word of God. Consider this and tremble for fear, for God has threatened to remove his candlestick from those who are lukewarm, those who do not study and ready themselves. The laborers are sick; those that did once labor are almost worn out, and others only bring themselves into a narrow sphere, and so confine their usefulness. There are few that like to go out in the fields; broken heads and dead cats are no more the ornaments of a Methodist, but silk scarves. Those honorable badges are now no more: the languor has got from the ministers to the people, and if you do not take care, we shall all fall dead together. May the Lord Jesus rouse us! May the Son of God rouse us all!

MARCH 3

Motions of God's Spirit

Beloved, do not believe every spirit, but test the spirits to see whether they are from God, for many false prophets have gone out into the world.

1 JOHN 4:1

In order to walk closely with God, his children must not only watch the motions of God's providence about them, but also the motions of his blessed Spirit in their hearts. Romans 8:14 says, "For all who are led by the Spirit of God are sons of God." His children must give up themselves to be guided by the Holy Ghost, as a little child gives his hand to be led by a nurse or parent. It is no doubt in this sense that we are to be converted, and to become like little children. And though it is the quintessence of enthusiasm to pretend to be guided by the Spirit without the written word, yet every Christian is duty-bound to be guided by the Spirit in conjunction with the written Word of God. Watch, therefore, I pray you, O believers, the motions of God's blessed Spirit in your souls, and always try the suggestions or impressions that you may at any time feel, by the unerring rule of God's most holy Word. If they are not found to be agreeable to that, reject them as diabolical and delusive. By observing this caution, you will steer a middle course between the two dangerous extremes that many of this generation are in danger of running into. I refer to enthusiasm on the one hand, and deism, and downright infidelity, on the other.

MARCH 4

Warning against Idleness

...My chosen shall long enjoy the work of their hands.

ISAIAH 65:22

There is no license given by the blessed Jesus for idleness; for in the very infancy of the world, idleness was not allowed. In Paradise, Adam and Eve dressed the garden, Cain was a tiller of the ground, and Abel was a keeper of sheep. Labor, my brethren, is imposed on all mankind, as part of the divine curse, and you are called to be useful in the society to which you belong. Take care first for the kingdom of God, and all necessary things shall be added. To labor for the meat that perishes, is your duty. Only take care that you do not neglect getting the meat for the soul; that is of the greatest consequence, for this plain reason, the things of this life are temporal, but those of the next are eternal. I would have rich men to work as well as poor. It is because of idleness that the devil hurries one to his diversions. You have two callings: a general one, and a special one. As we are to regard the one with respect to our bodies, so we are to regard the other on account of our souls. Take heed my brethren, I beseech you, lest you labor for the meat that perishes, and forget that meat which endures forever. Seek the things of God first. Look well to obtain oil in your lamps, grace in your hearts. I am not persuading you to take no care about the things of the world, but only not to be encumbered with them, so as to neglect your duty towards God and a proper concern for your souls. It is fitting, it is right, and it is your bound duty, to mind the callings wherein God has placed you.

MARCH 5

Love not the World

Therefore, my beloved, as you have always obeyed, so now, not only as in my presence but much more in my absence, work out your own salvation with fear and trembling.

PHILIPPIANS 2:12

Most of your own experiences will confirm the truth that the spirit of the world is hatred and that of Christ is love; for are not you reproached and slandered, and does not the world say all manner of evil against you, merely because you follow Jesus Christ, and because you will not go to the same excess with them? While they are singing the songs of the drunkard, you are singing psalms and hymns. While they are at a playhouse, you are hearing a sermon. While they are drinking, reveling, and misspending their precious time, and hastening on their own destruction, you are reading, praying, meditating, and working out your salvation with fear and trembling. This is matter enough for the world to reproach you; you are not polite and fashionable enough for them. If you will live godly, you must suffer persecution; you must not expect to go through this world without being persecuted and reviled. If you were of the world, the world would love you; for it always loves its own. But if you are not of the world, it will hate you; it has done so in all ages; it has never loved any but those who were pleased with its vanities and allurements. It has been the death of many a lover of Jesus merely because they have loved him; and, therefore, my brethren, do not be surprised if you meet with a fiery trial, for all those things will be a means of sending you to your Master the sooner.

MARCH 6

Invisible Worlds

Come to me, all who labor and are heavy laden, and I will give you rest.

MATTHEW 11:28

"Come to me," says Jesus, "and I will give you rest." This speaks encouragement to all that are weary and heavy laden; but the promise of rest is made to them only upon their coming and believing, and taking him to be their God and their portion. Before we can ever have peace with God, we must be justified by faith through our Lord Jesus Christ; we must be enabled to apply Christ to our hearts; we must have Christ brought home to our souls, so as his righteousness may be made our righteousness, so as his merits may be imputed to our souls. My dear friends, were you ever married to Jesus Christ? Did Jesus Christ ever give himself to you? Did you ever close with Christ by a lively faith, so as to feel Christ in your hearts, so as to hear him speaking peace to your souls? Did peace ever flow in upon your hearts like a river? Did you ever feel that peace that Christ spoke to his disciples? I pray God he may come and speak peace to you. These things you must experience. I am now talking of the invisible realities of another world, of inward religion, of the work of God upon a poor sinner's heart. I am now talking of a matter of great importance, my dear hearers; you are all concerned in it, your souls are concerned in it, your eternal salvation is concerned in it. You may be all at peace, but perhaps the devil has lulled you asleep into a carnal lethargy and security, and will endeavor to keep you there, till he get you to hell, and there you will be awakened; but it will be dreadful to be awakened and find yourselves so fearfully mistaken.

MARCH 7

Death's Sting

O death, where is your victory? O death, where is your sting?
1 CORINTHIANS 15:55

We are to be saved from the fear of death...There are a great many good souls that at times may doubt of the reality of this work upon their souls; a relaxed habit of body, a nervous disorder, you may say what you please, will make a weak child of God doubt of what he has done in them, and that hurts the mind, as it has such a close connection with the body; but then a believer is low...But this I stand to, it is our privilege to live above the fears of death. We do not live up to our dignity until every day we are waiting for the coming of our Lord from heaven. I am persuaded of this – that the reason why we do not live more above the fear of death is because we keep in so much with these nasty earthly things. You may have the best eyes in the world, and only put your hands before them, you will find the sun hid from you...And how can people have much of God or heaven when they have so much of the earth in their hearts? It is our privilege to live above the fear of death, though we are not to be saved from dying; and I am sure a believer would not be saved from dying for a million of worlds; it would be death to him not to die; but a soul touched with the love of God, even in sickness, in the midst of a burning fever, in the midst of a fire that will burn a thousand bodies up ... is enabled to say, "O my God, you are love; I am ready to come to you in the midst of all!"

MARCH 8

Safe and Secure

And this is the will of him who sent me, that I should lose nothing of all that he has given me, but raise it up on the last day.

JOHN 6:39

God will take particular care of securing his own; and when the wicked are all destroyed, the Christians shall go to a little city, and there shall dwell in Goshen, until God shall call home his ancient people the Jews. So God will take care of his people, that they shall be safe … and at the great day, when Jesus Christ pronounces the wicked damned, "Depart from me, you cursed," God's people will then lift up their voices with majesty and triumph. Which made a good man say to his son, just before he died, I am afraid I shall never see thee any more until I hear Jesus Christ say unto thee, "Depart, you cursed!" Some years ago, being present at the trial of a very vile person and being in suspense whether he would be brought in guilty or no, when the word "guilty" came, and the people heard of it, they did in effect give an éclat to it. Whether just or unjust, I thought it was an emblem of that awful day, when all the angels of God and his saints shall say, "Amen," when God consigns the wicked to hell. May God grant this may not be any of your case! Says the prophet, "They shall cry aloud from the sea:" some of them may be on the other side of the water, gone abroad, while others stay at home; but whether at home or abroad, though they have been banished by persecution, though they have been driven to the other side of the water, which has been the case of many persons before now, "yet they shall cry aloud;" they shall find the same God abroad as they did at home.

MARCH 9

Coming to Jesus

From that time Jesus began to preach, saying, "Repent, for the kingdom of heaven is at hand."

MATTHEW 4:17

I see you are all silent, and well you may; for if you will not be drawn by the cords of infinite and everlasting love, what will draw you? I could urge many terrors of the Lord to persuade you; but if the love of Jesus Christ will not constrain you, your case is desperate. This day I have invited all, even the worst of sinners, to be married to the Lord Jesus. If you perish, remember you do not perish for lack of invitation. You yourselves shall stand forth at the Last Day, and I here give you a summons to meet me at the judgment-seat of Christ, and to clear both my Master and me. Would weeping, would tears prevail on you, I could wish my head were waters, and my eyes fountains of tears, that I might weep out every argument, and melt you into love. Would anything I could do or suffer, influence your hearts, I think I could bear to pluck out my eyes, or even to lay down my life for your sakes. Or, were I sure to prevail on you by importunity, I could continue my discourse till midnight, and I would wrestle with you even till the morning watch … but such power belongs unto the Lord. I can only invite; only he can work in you both to will and to do after his good pleasure … it is his Spirit that must convince you of unbelief; and of the everlasting righteousness of his dear Son; it is he alone must give faith to apply his righteousness to your hearts; it is he alone can give you a wedding garment, and bring you to sit down and drink new wine in his kingdom.

MARCH 10

Fellowship with the Saints

I was glad when they said to me, 'Let us go to the house of the Lord!'

PSALM 122:1

All rightly informed Christians will be glad when they hear others say, "Come, let us go up to the house of the Lord." They will delight to visit the place where God's honor dwells, and be very eager to embrace all opportunities to show forth the Lord's death till he come. If you want to walk with God, you will associate and keep company with those that walk with him. David says in Psalm 16:3: "As for the saints in the land, they are the excellent ones, in whom is all my delight." The Christians of the early church no doubt kept up their vigor and first love by continuing in fellowship one with another. The Apostle Paul knew this well, and therefore exhorts the Christians to see to it that they did not forsake the assembling of themselves together. For how can one be warm alone? And has not the wisest of men told us that, "Iron sharpens iron, and one man sharpens another." (Prov. 27:17)? If we look, therefore, into church history, or make a just observation of our own times, I believe we shall find, that as the power of God prevails, Christian societies and fellowship meetings prevail proportionately. And as one decays, the other has insensibly decayed and dwindled away at the same time. So necessary is it for those that would walk with God, and keep up the life of religion, to meet together as they have opportunity, in order to provoke one another to love and good works.

MARCH 11

The Breath of Prayer

Therefore let everyone who is godly, offer prayer to you at a time when you may be found; surely in the rush of great waters, they shall not reach him.

PSALM 32:6

If we inquire why there is so little love to be found amongst Christians, why the very characteristic, by which everyone should know that we are disciples of the holy Jesus, is almost banished out of the Christian world, we shall find it, in a great measure, owing to a neglect, or superficial performance, of that excellent part of prayer, intercession, or imploring the divine grace and mercy on behalf of others. Some forget this duty of praying for others because they seldom remember to pray for themselves; and even those who are constant in praying to their Father who is in heaven, are often so selfish in their addresses to the throne of grace, that they do not enlarge their petitions for the welfare of their fellow Christians as they ought. Thereby, they fall short of attaining that Christian charity, that unfeigned love to their brothers and sisters, which their sacred profession obliges them to aspire after, and without which, though they should bestow all their goods to feed the poor, and even give their bodies to be burned, yet it would profit them nothing...It is every Christian's duty to pray for others as well as for himself. Now, prayer is a duty founded on natural religion; the very heathens never neglected it, though many Christian heathens among us do. It is so essential to Christianity that you might as reasonably expect to find a living man without breath as a true Christian without the spirit of prayer and supplication.

MARCH 12

Perfected Praise

I call upon the Lord, *who is worthy to be praised.*
Psalm 18:3

Those who are redeemed by the blood of Christ never lack matter for praise and adoration; those who have such continual scenes of his infinite goodness presented to their view so that their souls are duly affected with a sense of his universal love, cannot cease to call on heaven and earth, men and angels, to join with them in praising and blessing that high and lofty One, who inhabits eternity, and daily pours down his blessings on the whole race of mankind. But few have arrived to such a degree of love as to rejoice with those that do rejoice, and to be as thankful for others' mercies as their own. This part of Christian perfection, though begun on earth, will be consummated only in heaven, where our hearts will glow with such fervent love towards God and one another that every fresh degree of glory communicated to our neighbor will also communicate to us fresh thankfulness and joy. That which has the greatest tendency to generally excite fallen men to praise and thanksgiving, is a sense of God's private mercies and particular benefits bestowed upon us. As these come nearer our own hearts, they affect us more, and as they are proofs of God's special favor, so they cannot but sensibly touch us; and if our hearts are not quite frozen, like coals of a refiner's fire they melt us down into thankfulness and love. It was a consideration of the distinguishing favors God had shown to his chosen people Israel, and the frequent and remarkable deliverances wrought by him on their behalf, that made the holy Psalmist break out as frequently as he does in Psalm 107, in this moving exclamation, "Oh that men would praise the Lord for his goodness, and for his wonderful works to the children of men!"

MARCH 13

New Birth

Therefore, if anyone is in Christ, he is a new creation. The old has passed away; behold, the new has come.

2 CORINTHIANS 5:17

The doctrine of our regeneration, or new birth in Christ Jesus, though one of the most fundamental doctrines of our holy religion; though so plainly and often pressed on us in sacred writ; no, though it is the very hinge on which the salvation of each of us turns, and a point too in which all sincere Christians, of every denomination, agree; yet it is so seldom considered, and so little experimentally understood, by the generality of professors, that were we to judge of the truth of it by the experience of most who call themselves Christians, we should be apt to imagine they had "not so much as heard" whether there be any such thing as regeneration or not. It is true, men for the most part are orthodox in the common articles of their creed; they believe "For there is one God, and there is one mediator between God and men, the man Christ Jesus" (1 Tim. 2:5), and that there is no other name given under heaven whereby they can be saved besides his. But tell them they must be regenerated, they must be born again, they must be renewed in the very spirit, in the inmost faculties of their minds, before they can truly call Christ "Lord, Lord," or have an evidence that they have any share in the merits of his precious blood; and they are ready to cry out with Nicodemus, "How can these things be?" (John 3:9) or with the Athenians, on another occasion, "'What does this babbler wish to say?' Others said, 'He seems to be a preacher of foreign divinities'" (Acts 17:18) – because we preach to them Christ and the new birth.

MARCH 14

The Gospel Minister

Preach the word; be ready in season and out of season; reprove, rebuke, and exhort, with complete patience and teaching.
2 TIMOTHY 4:2

I would endeavor to show you that every minister, before he undertakes to preach the gospel of the Lord Jesus Christ, from a full evidence of a work of conversion, ought to be enabled to say, "The Spirit of the Lord is upon me, because he has anointed me to proclaim the good news to the poor" (Luke 4:18). It is certain there is now a great degeneracy through all the Christian world, and though there may be many reasons assigned for that deadness, that lukewarmness, both in their principle, discipline, and practice, yet I am persuaded one great reason is this: many pretend to preach the Lord Jesus Christ who are strangers to the power of Jesus Christ upon their own hearts. There are many who run before they are called of God; therefore, it is no wonder they do not profit the people at all. A dead clergy will make a dead people. It is absolutely necessary, before a minister undertakes to preach the gospel, that he should have an experimental acquaintance with the Lord Jesus Christ. A man when he comes out to preach should preach so feelingly that all who hear him might take notice of him…that he has been with Jesus. It is a shocking question which Jesus put to Nicodemus: "Are you the teacher of Israel"—Do you pretend to be a teacher of others, a guide to those who are blind, to instruct others in true religion, and "yet you do not understand these things?"—are not acquainted with the new birth yourself? If Christ were to come to preach the gospel, how many ministers must he be obliged to put this question to!

MARCH 15

My Love and Happiness

My flesh and heart may fall, but God is the strength of my heart and my portion forever.

PSALM 73:26

My God, my Portion, and my Love,
My everlasting All;
I've none but you in Heav'n above,
Or on this Earthly Ball.

What empty Things are all the Skies,
And this inferior Clod!
There's nothing here deserves my Joys,
There's nothing like my God.

In vain the bright, the burning Sun,
Scatters his feeble Light: 'Tis your sweet Beams create my Noon,
If you withdraw, 'tis Night.

And whilst upon my restless Bed,
Amidst the Shades I roll;
If my Redeemer shows his Head,
'Tis Morning with my Soul.

To you we owe our Wealth and Friends,
And Health, and safe Abode;
We Praise your Name for all these Things,
But they are not my God.

MARCH 16

A Warning to the Unconverted

This is the one to whom I will look: he who is humble and contrite in spirit and trembles at my word.

Isaiah 66:2

Those of you that are yet strangers to Christ, what can I say to excite you to come and walk with God? If you love honor, pleasure, and a crown of glory, come and seek it where it alone can be found. Come, put on the Lord Jesus. Come, haste away and walk with God, and make no more provision for the flesh, to fulfill the lusts thereof. Stop, stop, O sinner! Turn, for the end of that way you are now walking in, however right it may seem in your blinded eyes, will be eternal destruction of body and soul. Make no tarrying…step not one step further on in your present walk. For how do you know the next step you take will not be into hell? Death may seize you, judgment may find you, and then the great gulf will be fixed between you and endless glory forever and ever. Lay these things to heart. In the strength of Jesus say, "Farewell lust of the flesh, I will no more walk with thee! Farewell lust of the eye, and pride of life! Farewell carnal acquaintance and enemies of the cross, I will no more walk and be intimate with you! Welcome Jesus, welcome thy word, welcome thy ordinances, welcome thy Spirit, welcome thy people, I will henceforth walk with you." O that there may be in you such a mind! God will seal it with the broad seal of heaven, even the signet of his Holy Spirit. Yes, he will, though you have been following after the desires of your desperately wicked hearts ever since you have been born. The precious blood of Jesus Christ, if you come to the Father in and through him, shall cleanse you from all sin.

MARCH 17

Casting Crowns

And when the chief Shepherd appears, you will receive the unfading crown of glory.

1 PETER 5:4

Resolve to cast yourself at the feet of Christ, in subjection to him, and throw yourself into the arms of Christ, for salvation by him. Consider, my dear brothers, the many invitations he has given you to come to him, to be saved by him. God has "laid on him the iniquity of us all." O let me prevail with you, above all things, to make choice of the Lord Jesus Christ, and to resign yourselves unto him, and take him. Oh, take him upon his own terms! Whosoever you are, how great a sinner soever you have been, in the name of the great God do I offer Jesus Christ to you; as you value your life and soul, refuse him not, but stir up yourself to accept the Lord Jesus. Take him wholly as he is, for he will be applied wholly unto you, or else not at all. Jesus Christ must be your whole wisdom, Jesus Christ must be your whole righteousness, Jesus Christ must be your whole sanctification, or he will never be your eternal redemption. What though you have been ever so wicked and reckless, yet if you will now abandon your sins and turn unto the Lord Jesus Christ, you shall have him given to you, and all your sins shall be freely forgiven. O why will you neglect the great work of your repentance? Do not defer the doing of it one day longer, but today, even now, take that Christ who is freely offered to you.

MARCH 18

Things not Seen

Though you have not seen him, you love him. Though you do not now see him, you believe in him and rejoice with joy that is inexpressible and filled with glory,

1 PETER 1:8

Though some modern preachers do not actually deny the Spirit of God, yet they say, "Christians must not feel him," which is in effect to deny him. When Nicodemus came to Christ, and the Lord Jesus was instructing him concerning the new birth, he said to our Lord, "How can these things be?" The answer that Christ gave Nicodemus should stop the mouths of our letter-learned Pharisees: "The wind blows where it wishes, and you hear its sound, but you do not know where it comes from or where it goes. So it is with everyone who is born of the Spirit" (John 3:8). Now, until the Spirit of God is felt on our souls, as the wind on our bodies, indeed, my dear brethren, you have no interest in him. Religion consists not in external performance; it must be in the heart, or else it is only a name, which cannot profit us, a name to live while we are dead. A late preacher upon this text seems to laugh at us for talking of the Holy Spirit in a sensible manner, and talks to us as the Jews did to Christ. They questioned, "How can this man give us his flesh to eat?" so he asked, "What sign or proof do we give of it?" We do not imagine that God must appear to us, and give it to us; but there is a frequent receiving without seeing it. It is as plainly felt in the soul, as any impression can be upon the body.

MARCH 19

Comforting Grace

And I will ask the Father, and he will give you another Helper, to be with you forever …

John 14:16

What do you think, my brothers, of our Redeemer's comforting grace? What can you do without it? ... It is commendable to strive, but we shall never be content, we shall never be cheerful under sufferings, but through the assistance of the Redeemer. Even now, in respect of parting from one another, what can comfort friends, when separated, but the Spirit of God? Paul, when going away for Jerusalem, said, "What are you doing, weeping and breaking my heart? For I am ready not only to be imprisoned but even to die in Jerusalem for the name of the Lord Jesus" (Acts 21:13). Paul could not have said this had he not felt the comforting grace of Jesus Christ. Our Lord, when going away says, "And I will pray the Father, and he shall give you another Comforter, that he may abide with you for ever; even the Spirit of truth; whom the world cannot receive … I will not leave you comfortless: I will come to you" (John 14:16-17a) … We can easily, my brothers, talk when not under the rod ourselves. There is not a physician or apothecary in London but can give good advice; yet when they are sick themselves, poor souls, they are just like their patients and many times more impatient than those whom they used to preach patience to … It is so with the greatest Christian; we are all men of like passions; there is none of us who, when under the rod, if left to ourselves, would but curse God … and say to the Redeemer, "What do you do?" … if it were not for the Lord Jesus Christ's comfortings, no flesh could bear them.

MARCH 20

Law and Gospel

For I am not ashamed of the gospel, for it is the power of God for salvation to everyone who believes, to the Jew first and also to the Greek.

ROMANS 1:16

First, we hear Moses' voice, we hear the voice of the law; there is no going to Mount Zion but by the way of Mount Sinai, that is the right straight road. I know some say, they do not know when they were converted; those are, I believe, very few; generally, no, I may say almost always, God deals otherwise. Some are, indeed, called sooner by the Lord than others, but before they are made to see the glory of God, they must hear the voice of the law; so you must hear the voice of the law before ever you will be savingly called unto God. You never throw off your cloak in a storm, but you hug it the closer; so the law makes a man hug close his corruptions (Rom. 7:7-9), but when the gospel of the Son of God shines into their souls, then they throw off the corruptions which they have hugged so closely. They hear his voice saying, "Son, daughter, be of good cheer, your sins, which are many, are all forgiven." ... The wicked hear the voice of the devil, the lusts of the flesh, the lusts of the eye, and the pride of life. Christ's sheep themselves attended to them before conversion. But when called afterwards by God, they hear the voice of a Redeemer's blood speaking peace to them; they hear the voice of his word and of his Spirit. The consequence of hearing his voice, and the proof that we do hear his voice, will be – to follow him.

MARCH 21

Seeing Jesus

Beloved, we are God's children now, and what we will be has not yet appeared; but we know that when he appears we shall be like him, because we shall see him as he is. And everyone who thus hopes in him purifies himself as he is pure.

1 John 3:2-3

I shall mention but one thing more, though I might mention twenty. If we have the love of God in our hearts, though we cannot get over the fears of death at all times, yet I think the bent of the mind of such a person will be, "When shall I see the object of my love, 'him whom my soul loves?'" They sit at ordinances, and long to be led to the fountainhead. "I am hard pressed between the two," says Paul; the word signifies a strong and intense desire to be with Christ; he does not say to be "in heaven" but "to be with Christ, for that is far better." But to stay here was better for his hearers; therefore, you should be content to stay in the world, not because you love the world or the things of the world, but because you wait for your Master's call home. I could not help admiring while I was reading it that when Christ ascended into heaven, one angel left those who were attending Christ into glory, and stopped to preach to the disciples who were gazing into heaven. He does not go to heaven to wait for Christ to come but comes down to earth to preach to some poor fishermen – may Almighty God help us to see if we are the beloved of the Lord or no.

MARCH 22

The Son's Submission

Father, if you are willing, remove this cup from me. Nevertheless, not my will, but yours, be done.

LUKE 22:42

In the story of Abraham traveling up Mount Moriah to offer his son Isaac, do you read of Isaac carrying the wood upon his shoulders up the mountain? Let this lead you to Mount Calvary (this very mountain of Moriah where Isaac was offered, as some think) and take a view of the antitype, Jesus, the Son of God, bearing and ready to sink under the weight of that cross on which he was to hang for us. Do you admire Isaac for so freely consenting to die, though a creature, and therefore obliged to go when God called? Do not forget to admire infinitely more the dear Lord Jesus, who willingly said, "Behold, I have come," though under no obligation to do so, "to do your will," to obey and die for men, "O God," (Heb. 10:7)! Look by faith at our all-glorious Emmanuel, unbound, but nailed on an accursed tree; see how he hangs, crowned with thorns, enduring derision of those around him; see how the thorns pierce him, and how the blood in purple streams trickles down his sacred temples! Hark how the God of nature groans! See how he bows his head, and at length humanity gives up the ghost! Isaac is saved, but Jesus, the God of Isaac, dies. A ram is offered up in Isaac's place, but Jesus has no substitute. Jesus must bleed; Jesus must die. God the Father provided this Lamb for himself from all eternity. We have been the betrayers and the murderers of this Lord of glory. Having been so much forgiven, shall we not love much? O, let us love him with all our hearts, minds, and strength, and glorify him in our souls and bodies, for they are his.

MARCH 23

Fools in Heart

Say to God, "How awesome are your deeds! So great is your power that your enemies come cringing to you"...in the pride of his face the wicked does not seek him; and all his thoughts are, "There is no God."

PSALM 66:3; 10:4

Whenever God intends to bring about any great thing, he generally begins with a day of small things. As a proof of this, I will not lead you so far back as to the beginning of time, when the Everlasting "I am" spoke all things into existence by his almighty will; and out of a confused chaos, "without form and void," produced a world worthy of a God to create, and of his favorite creature, man, his vicegerent and representative here below, to inhabit, and enjoy in it both himself and his God. And yet, though the heavens declare his glory, and the firmament shows his handy work, though there is no speech nor language where their voice is not heard, and their line is gone out through all the earth; and by a dumb, yet persuasive language, proves the hand that made them to be divine; yet there have been, and are now, such fools in the world that say in their hearts, "There is no God" (Ps. 14:1; 53:1); or so wise, as by their wisdom, not to know God or own his divine image to be stamped on that book, wherein these grand things are recorded, and that in such legible characters, that he who runs may read...And yet, though God himself has become an author among us, we will not condescend to give his book one thorough reading! Be astonished, O heavens, at this!

MARCH 24

In all our Afflictions

And the angel of the Lord appeared to him in a flame of fire out of the midst of a bush. He looked, and behold, the bush was burning, yet it was not consumed.

Exodus 3:2

Learn that in all our afflictions God is concerned. He is in the midst of the bush; and oh, it is a sweet time with the soul when God speaks to him out of the bush, when he is under affliction, and talks to him all the while. Though the bush was threatened by fire, which surrounded it with immediate and total desolation, yet it burned and was not consumed … every Christian has a coat of arms and…that is the burning bush; every Christian is burned but not consumed. But how is it that the saint is held up? Where does he get his strength? Or, how is this strength, this supporting, comforting strength, conveyed to his heart? You shall find David say that there is a river, mind that, there is a river, the streams whereof make glad the city of God, the holy place of the tabernacles of the Most High. Need I tell you, that probably here is an allusion to the situation of Jerusalem, and the waters of Shiloah, that flowed through the city of Jerusalem, which the people found sweet and refreshing in the time of its being besieged. So, too, the rivers run through most of the cities in Holland, and bring their commodities even to the doors of the inhabitants. Pray, what do you think this river is? Why, I believe it means the covenant of grace. O, that is a river, the springs of which first burst out in Paradise, when God said the seed of the woman shall bruise the serpent's head; then God made this river visit the habitation of man, as the first opening of his everlasting covenant.

MARCH 25

Our Great Burden

To me, though I am the very least of all the saints, this grace was given ...

EPHESIANS 3:8

When the sinner is first awakened, he begins to wonder – How did I come to be so wicked? The Spirit of God then strikes in and shows him that he has no good thing by nature; then he sees that he is altogether gone out of the way, that he is altogether become abominable, and the poor creature is made to lie down at the foot of the throne of God, and to acknowledge that God would be just to damn him, just to cut him off, though he never had committed one actual sin in his life. Did you ever feel and experience this, any of you – to justify God in your damnation – to own that you are by nature children of wrath, and that God may justly cut you off, though you never actually had offended him in all your life? If you were ever truly convicted, if your hearts were ever truly cut, if self were truly taken out of you, you would be made to see and feel this. And if you have never felt the weight of original sin, do not call yourselves Christians. I am verily persuaded original sin is the greatest burden of a true convert; this ever grieves the regenerate soul, the sanctified soul. The indwelling of sin in the heart is the burden of a converted person; it is the burden of a true Christian. He continually cries out, "O! who will deliver me from this body of death," this indwelling corruption in my heart? This is that which disturbs a poor soul most. And, therefore, if you never felt this inward corruption, if you never saw that God might justly curse you for it, indeed, my dear friends, you may speak peace to your hearts, but I fear, no, I know, there is no true peace.

MARCH 26

Glorifying God

I will give thanks to you, O LORD my God, with my whole heart, and I will glorify your name forever.

PSALM 86:12

When do we glorify God? When we endeavor to get such grace from the Lord that we may not dishonor him when we are under the cross, and therefore we glorify God in the fire when we quietly endure it as a chastisement for our sins. If you keep watch now, and live near to God, you will never find that you are put into a fire, but you first brought yourselves into it; and I do verily believe from my heart, that our sin is always to be seen in our punishment … you will find in all the Old and New Testament that the afflictions of God's people were suitable to their faults. Jacob was over-persuaded by his mother to get the blessing by a lie; but he was a simple-hearted poor creature. Some persons think nothing of a lie; if they can but get by it, they do not mind it; but an honest man will shun it. Jacob argues with his mother against it; O, says she, "the curse is on me, my son!" Oh, how dreadful, for a good woman to say so! Doubtless, she was persuaded God would give Jacob the blessing, but she took a wrong way to obtain it; she might have waited for the blessing to come with a blessing. How did God punish Jacob? Why, in a night afterwards poor Jacob was imposed upon by a wrong wife, he got a Leah instead of a Rachel; the poor creature was imposed upon there, and so all along almost to the end of his life, he had a furnace of affliction. Happy they who pray in the furnace, Lord, let me know why thou dost contend with me.

MARCH 27

Grace and Supplication

Praying at all times in the Spirit, with all prayer and supplication.

EPHESIANS 6:18A

The Lord has said that he will pour out his Spirit of grace and supplication; and I will venture to say that if the Spirit of grace resides in our hearts, the Spirit of supplication will not be wanting. Persons under their first love dare not go without God. They go to God, not as the formalist does, not for fear of going to hell, or being damned. It is a mercy anything drives to prayer; and a person under the spirit of bondage, which has been just brought to the liberty of the sons of God, goes freely to his Heavenly Father under the discoveries and constraints of divine love. Come, I will appeal to you – did you not do as a dear fond mother did, if the child, the beloved child, made but the least noise in the world – O says the mother, the dear child cries, I must go and comfort him. So, time was when many hearkened to the call of God and could no more keep from the presence of God in secret than a fond mother from the presence of her dear child. Now, if your souls do prosper, this connection between you and God will be kept up. I do not say that you will always have the same fervor as when you first set out. I do not say you will always be carried up into the third heavens; the animal spirits possibly will not admit of such solace; but you should inquire with yourselves whether you would be easy to be out of God's company? Take time from your daily labors and go and converse with God.

MARCH 28

Clear Heads, Warm Hearts

Older men are to be sober-minded, dignified, self-controlled, sound in faith, in love, and in steadfastness.

TITUS 2:2

Therefore, you need not be afraid of our destroying inward holiness by preaching the doctrine of the imputation of Christ's righteousness, that one is the foundation and the other the superstructure. To talk of my having the righteousness of Christ imputed to my soul, without my having the holiness of Christ imparted to it, and bringing forth the fruits of the Spirit, as an evidence of it, is only a deceiving ourselves. I would never preach upon imputed righteousness without speaking of inward holiness, for if you do not take a great deal of care, you will unawares, under a pretence of exalting Christ, run into Antinomianism – depths that Calvin never went into. Probably, you will embitter other spirits that do not agree with you, and at the same time hurt the fruits of the Spirit. May God give you clear heads, and at the same time warm hearts…I pray to God we may all die singing that anthem, and sing it to all eternity. After his temptation, they came and ministered to him, as some think, food for his body, and wished him joy and comfort in his soul: and in his agonies in the garden, an angel strengthened him. After his resurrection, two appeared again, one at the head and another at the foot of his sepulcher, to let those that looked into the sepulcher know, that they would not only wait upon the head, but the foot; and the angels are glad to wait upon the meanest of the children of God. When our Lord departed, a cloud received him out of their sight, which probably was a cloud of angels. Having led his disciples out of the city, he blessed them, and then away he went to heaven; may that blessing rest upon you and your children!

MARCH 29

Washing Our Duties

And if it is evil in your eyes to serve the Lord, choose this day whom you will serve, whether the gods your fathers served in the region beyond the River, or the gods of the Amorites in whose land you dwell. But as for me and my house, we will serve the Lord.

JOSHUA 24:15

They that love the Lord will study to keep from offending God, not for fear of being damned but because sin murdered his dear Son. There are a great many people abstain from sin for fear of punishment; but hear what Joseph said, "Behold, because of me my master has no concern about anything in the house, and he has put everything that he has in my charge. He is not greater in this house than I am, nor has he kept back anything from me except yourself, because you are his wife. How then can I do this great wickedness and sin against God?" (Gen. 39:8-9) – that is, against my God that loves me? ... If we are the beloved of the Lord, we shall be willing to work for the Lord. Indeed, faith without works is the religion of every carnal man. Make an end of one good work, and then begin another, and lay it down, and wonder that Jesus Christ should accept anything at your hands. I knew a lady some time ago, that wanted more sun to be the more employed for God; says she, "If Jesus Christ would but help me to do such and such a thing I have in view, Oh, I would kiss his feet, and dedicate myself more and more to his honor." A true Christian loves to be thus employed, but, above all, he is glad he has the blood of Christ to wash his duties in.

MARCH 30

Abundant Joy

You make known to me the path of life; in your presence there is fullness of joy; at your right hand are pleasures forevermore.
PSALM 16:11

It is a pleasing thing to walk with God. The wisest of men has told us in Proverbs 3:17, "Her ways are ways of pleasantness, and all her paths are peace." I have been listed under Jesus' banner only for a few years, but I have enjoyed more solid pleasure in one moment's communion with my God, than I could have enjoyed in the ways of sin, even if I had continued to go on in them for thousands of years. And may I not appeal to all you that fear and walk with God, for the truth of this? Has not one day in the Lord's courts been better to you than a thousand? In keeping God's commandments, have you not found a present, and very great reward? Has not his word been sweeter to you than the honey, or the honeycomb? O what have you felt, when, Jacob-like, you have been wrestling with your God? Has not Jesus often met you when meditating in the fields, and been made known to you over and over again in breaking of bread? Has not the Holy Spirit frequently shed his divine love abroad in your hearts abundantly, and filled you with joy unspeakable, even joy that is full of glory? I know you will answer all these questions in the affirmative, and freely acknowledge the yoke of Christ to be easy, and his burden light. What motives do we then further need to excite us to walk with God?

MARCH 31

The Father's Love

In this the love of God was made manifest among us, that God sent his only Son into the world, so that we might live through him.

1 JOHN 4:9

Who can hear the story of Abraham preparing to offer his son Isaac and not have his heart affected? But … If you admire Abraham offering up Isaac, how much more ought you to extol, magnify, and adore the love of God, who so loved the world as to give his only begotten Son Christ Jesus our Lord, "that whosoever believes in him should not perish but have eternal life." (John 3:16)! May we not cry out, "Now know we, O Lord, that thou hast loved us, since thou hast not withheld thy Son, your only Son, from us?" Abraham was God's creature, and therefore under the highest obligation to surrender up Isaac. But O stupendous love! While we were his enemies, "God sent forth his Son, made of a woman, made under the law, To redeem them that were under the law" (Gal. 4:4). O the freeness and infinity of the love of God our Father! It is unsearchable. Think, O believers, of the love of God in giving Jesus Christ to be a propitiation for our sins. And when you hear how Abraham built an altar, laid the wood in order, bound Isaac his son, and laid him on the altar upon the wood, think how your heavenly Father bound Jesus Christ his only Son, offered him upon the altar of his justice, and laid upon him the iniquities of us all (Isa. 53:6). When you read of Abraham's stretching forth his hand to slay his son, think of how God actually suffered his Son to be slain, that we might live for evermore.

APRIL 1

Family Prayer

But as for me and my house, we will serve the Lord.
JOSHUA 24:15

Family prayer is a duty, though much neglected, that is absolutely necessary. Reading is a good preparation for prayer, as prayer is an excellent means to render reading effectual. And the reason why every head of a family should join both these exercises together is plain, because he cannot perform his priestly office without performing this duty of family prayer. We find, when mention is made of Cain and Abel's offering sacrifices, that they brought them. But to whom did they bring them? In all probability, to their father Adam, who, as priest of the family, was to offer sacrifices in their names. So ought every spiritual son of the second Adam, who is entrusted with the care of a household, offer up the spiritual sacrifices of supplications and thanksgivings, acceptable to God through Jesus Christ, in the presence and name of all who eat meat at his table.When our blessed Lord was among us, it is said often that he prayed with his twelve disciples, which was then his little family. And he himself has promised a particular blessing to joint supplications: "For where two or three are gathered in my name, there am I among them" (Matt. 18:20). Add to this the words of the apostle: "Praying always, with all prayer and supplication" (Eph. 6:18), which doubtless includes family prayer. When Joshua resolved that he and his household would serve the Lord, he certainly resolved to pray with his family, which is one of the best testimonies they could give of serving him. All families have common blessings to give thanks for, common crosses and afflictions to pray against, and common sins to lament and bewail; but how this can be done, without joining together in one common act of humiliation, supplication, and thanksgiving?

APRIL 2

Be not Righteous over much

So we, though many, are one body in Christ, and individually members one of another.

ROMANS 12:5

When we confine the Spirit of God to this or that particular church, and are not willing to converse with any but those of the same communion, this is to be righteous over much with our witness. So it is, to confine our communion within church walls, and to think that Jesus could not preach in a field as well as on consecrated ground, this is bigotry. This is like Peter, who would not go to preach the gospel to the Gentiles, until he had a vision from God, and when the disciples blamed his conduct, he could not satisfy them until he had acquainted them with the vision he had seen. Therefore, we may justly infer that the Spirit of God is the center of unity, and wherever I see the image of my Master, I never inquire of them their opinions; I do not ask them what they are; if they love Jesus Christ in sincerity and truth, I embrace them as my brother, my sister, and my spouse. This is the spirit of Christianity. Many people, who are bigots to this or that opinion, when one of a different way of thinking has come where they were, have left the room or place on the account; this is the spirit of the devil, and if it were possible that these persons could be admitted into heaven with such tempers, that very place would be hell to them. Christianity will never flourish until we are all of one heart and of one mind; and this would be the only means of seeing the gospel of Jesus to flourish, much more than by persecuting those who differ from us.

APRIL 3

On Drunkenness

And do not get drunk with wine, for that is debauchery, but be filled with the Spirit.

EPHESIANS 5:18

What renders drunkenness more inexcusable is that it robs a man of his reason. Reason is the glory of a man; it is the chief thing whereby God has made us to differ from the brute creation. And our modern unbelievers have exalted it to such a high degree, as even to set it in opposition to revelation, and so deny the Lord that bought them. But though, in doing this, they greatly err, and while they profess themselves wise, they become real fools. We must acknowledge that reason is the candle of the Lord, and whosoever puts it out, shall bear his punishment, whosoever he be. This the drunkard does. Nebuchadnezzar's curse he makes his choice, and his reason departs from him; and then what is he better than a brute? The very heathen kings were so sensible of this, that, in order to deter their young princes from drinking, they used to make their slaves get drunk, and be exposed before them. Did you but see your own picture, O drunkard, when, after having drowned your reason, you, staggering to and fro, as one of the fools in Israel; did you but see your companions making songs about you, surely you would not return to your vomit again, but rather would abhor yourself in dust and ashes … May not every one that meets a drunkard justly say, "How glorious does he that was made a little lower than the angels look today, when, unmindful of his dignity, he has by drinking robbed himself of his reason, and reduced himself to a level with the beasts that perish!"

APRIL 4

The Great Redeemer

Behold, I have refined you, but not as silver; I have tried you in the furnace of affliction.

ISAIAH 48:10

Gracious words indeed! Words worthy of a God! Who has promised that he will not always chastise, that he will not keep his anger forever, but, on the contrary, will take care in the midst of judgment to remember mercy. If he strikes with one hand, he will uphold with the other. I hope I need not tell you, my dear hearers, that these words were spoken to comfort the captives in Babylon, who, for their various sins and great backslidings, constrained the God of love, the God of mercy, their covenant God, to send them captives into a foreign soil. Upon this, their enemies take occasion to insult them, "Where now are your songs?" – give us one of your temple songs, with which you used to pour out your hallelujahs; let us see now whether you can praise him in a strange land – "Has God forgotten to be gracious? Has he in anger shut up his compassion?" (Ps. 77:9) – that the darkness in which they were now involved would not be a temporary, but a perpetual one; and notwithstanding the prophets were sent in mercy of God to comfort them in their trouble, yet many of them were tempted to say, "All men were liars." It is very well if they stopped there, and did not say, God is a liar too. The enemy being thus suffered to break in upon them like a flood, it was high time for the blessed God to lift up a standard against him; and therefore the great Redeemer, the angel of the everlasting covenant, lets them know that he would some time or other, no, very speedily, appear, to relieve his afflicted people.

APRIL 5

Mercy's Doors

Surely goodness and mercy shall follow me all the days of my life.

PSALM 23:6A

Your Mercy, my God, is the Theme of my Song,
The Joy of my Heart, and the Boast of my Tongue:
Your free Grace, alone, from the first to the last,
Has won my Affections, and bound my Soul fast.

Without your sweet Mercy, I could not live here;
Sin soon would reduce me to utter Despair:
But, thro' your free Goodness, my Spirits revive,
And he that first made me, still keeps me alive.

Whene'er I mistake, your kind Mercy begins
To melt me, and then I can mourn for my Sins
And, led by your Spirit, to Jesus's Blood,
My Sorrows are dry'd, and my Strength is renew'd.

Your Mercy is more than a Match for my Heart
Which wonders to feel its own Hardness depart:
Dissolv'd by your Presence I fall to the Ground,
And weep to the Praise of the Mercy I found.

The doors of your Mercy stand open all Day,
To the poor and the needy who knock by the Way:
Your Mercy is endless, most tender, and free;
No Sinner need doubt, since 'tis given to me.

APRIL 6

Divine Life

In this the love of God was made manifest among us, that God sent his only Son into the world, so that we might live through him.

1 JOHN 4:9

As Christ was born of the Virgin's womb, so must he be spiritually formed in our hearts. As he died for sin, so must we die to sin. And as he rose again from the dead, so must we also rise to a divine life. None but those who have followed him in this regeneration, or new birth, shall sit on thrones as approvers of his sentence, when he shall come in terrible majesty to judge the twelve tribes of Israel. It is true, as for the outward work of our redemption, it was a transient act, and was certainly finished on the cross; but the application of that redemption to our hearts, is a work that will continue always, even to the end of the world. So long as there is an elect man breathing on the earth, who is naturally engendered of the offspring of the first Adam, so long must the quickening Spirit, which was purchased by the resurrection of the second Adam, that Lord from heaven, will be breathing upon his soul. For though we may exist by Christ, yet we cannot be said to exist in him, till we are united to him by one spirit, and enter into a new state of things, as certainly as he entered into a new state of things after that he rose from the dead. We may throng and crowd round about Christ, and call him, "Lord, Lord," when we come to worship before his footstool. But we have not effectually touched him until, by a lively faith in his resurrection, we perceive a divine virtue coming out of him, to renew and purify our souls.

APRIL 7

Instructing Children

Hear, O sons, a father's instruction, and be attentive, that you may gain insight, for I give you good precepts; do not forsake my teaching.

PROVERBS 4:1-2

Parents are commanded in the New Testament to bring up their children "in the discipline and instruction of the Lord" (Eph. 6:4). The psalmist acquaints us with the one great reason why God did such great wonders for his people, namely, to "tell to the coming generation the glorious deeds of the Lord, and his might," (Ps. 78:4). In Deuteronomy 6:20 and following, God strictly commands his people to instruct their children in the true nature of the ceremonial worship, when they would inquire about it, as he supposed they would do, in time to come. And if servants and children were to be instructed in the nature of Jewish rites, much more now they ought to be initiated and grounded in the doctrines and first principles of the gospel of Christ, not only because it is a revelation, which has brought life and immortality to a fuller and clearer light, but also because many seducers are gone abroad into the world, who try their utmost not only to destroy the superstructure, but also to sap the very foundation of our most holy religion. Oh that the present generation's posterity would truly love and honor God! Parents must take Solomon's good advice, and train up and catechize their households in the way that they should go.

APRIL 8

Human Companionship

Two are better than one, because they have a good reward for their toil.

ECCLESIASTES 4:9

Man could not be fully happy, even in paradise, without companionship of his own species, much less now that he has been driven out. Let us view him a little in his natural estate now, as since the fall his understanding is darkened and his mind is alienated from the life of God. He is no more able to see the way wherein he should go than a blind man to describe the sun. Besides this, he must receive his sight in order to see God, and if he never sees him, he never can be happy. Let us view him in this light (or rather this darkness) and deny the necessity of society if we can. A divine revelation we find is absolutely necessary, as we are by nature unable to know how to do our duty. And how shall we learn, except one teaches us? But if God were to do this himself, we, with Moses, would exceedingly quake and fear! Nor would the ministry of angels in this affair be without much terror. It is necessary therefore, (at least God's dealing with us has shown it to be so) that we should be drawn with the cords of a man, and that a divine revelation being granted, we should use one another's assistance, under God, to instruct each other in the knowledge, and to exhort one another to the practice, of those things which belong to our everlasting peace. This is undoubtedly the great end of society intended by God since the fall, and a strong argument why "two are better than one," and why we should "not forsake the assembling of ourselves together."

APRIL 9

Faith's Sight

Jesus said to him, "Have you believed because you have seen me? Blessed are those who have not seen and yet have believed."

JOHN 20:29

We might think ourselves happy if we had seen the holy Jesus after he was risen from the dead and our hands had handled that Lord of life. But happier are they who have not seen him and yet, having felt the power of his resurrection, believe in him. For many who were not saved by him saw our divine Master; but whosoever has thus felt the power of his resurrection, has the earnest of his inheritance in his heart, and has passed from death to life, and shall never fall into final condemnation. I am very sensible that this is foolishness to the natural man, as were many such-like truths to our Lord's own disciples when only weak in faith, before he rose again. But when these natural men, like them, have fully felt the power of his resurrection, they will then own that this doctrine is from God and say with the Samaritans, "Now we believe," for we ourselves have experienced it in our hearts. O that all unbelievers, all letter-learned masters of Israel, who now look upon the doctrine of the power of Christ's resurrection, or our new birth, as an idle tale, and condemn the preachers of it as enthusiasts and madmen, did but thus feel the power of it in their souls, they would no longer ask, how this thing could be? But they would be convinced of it, as much as Thomas was, when he saw the Lord's Christ; and like him, when Jesus bid him reach out his hands, and thrust them into his side, then would they cry out, "My Lord, and my God!"

APRIL 10

To Honor Jesus

In whose eyes a vile person is despised, but who honors those who fear the LORD; who swears to his own hurt and does not change.

PSALM 15:4

Jesus Christ will not be behind-hand with those who receive him or his followers, for his name's sake. Those who thus honor him, he will honor. A cup of cold water given in the name of a disciple shall in no wise lose its reward. He will turn water into wine. Though those who abound in alms-deeds, out of a true faith in, and love for Jesus, may seem as it were to throw their bread upon the waters, yet they shall find it again after many days. For they who give to the poor out of this principle, lend unto the Lord; and look, whatsoever they lay out, it shall be repaid them again. Even in this life, God often orders good measure, pressed down and running over, to be returned into his servants' bosoms. It is the same in spirituals. To him that has and improves what he has, for the sake of Christ and his disciples, shall be given, and he shall have abundance. Brothers, I would not boast but to my Master's honor … When I have considered that I am a child, and cannot speak, and have seen so many of you come out into the wilderness to be fed, I have often said within myself, what can I do with my little stock of grace and knowledge among so great a multitude? But, at my Lord's command, I have given you to eat of such spiritual food as I had, and, before I have done speaking, have had my soul richly fed with the bread which cometh down from heaven. Thus shall it be done to all such who are willing to spend and be spent for Christ or his disciples – for there is no respect of persons with God.

APRIL 11

How many Hells?

But I say to you that everyone who is angry with his brother will be liable to judgment.

MATTHEW 5:22A

If one evil thought, if one evil word, if one evil action, deserves eternal damnation, how many hells, my friends, do every one of us deserve whose whole lives have been one continued rebellion against God? Before ever, therefore, you can speak peace to your hearts, you must be brought to see, brought to believe, what a dreadful thing it is to depart from the living God. And now, my dear friends, examine your hearts, for I hope you came here with a design to have your souls made better. Give me leave to ask you, in the presence of God, whether you know the time, and if you do not know exactly the time, do you know there was a time, when God wrote bitter things against you, when the arrows of the Almighty were within you? Was ever the remembrance of your sins so grievous to you? Was the burden of your sins intolerable to your thoughts? Did you ever see that God's wrath might justly fall upon you, on account of your actual transgressions against God? Were you ever in all your life sorry for your sins? Could you ever say that your sins are gone over your head and as a burden too heavy for you? Did you ever experience any such thing as this? Did ever any such thing as this pass between God and your soul? If not, for Jesus' sake, do not call yourselves Christians; you may speak peace to your hearts, but there is no peace – May the Lord awaken you, may the Lord convert you, may the Lord give you peace, if it be his will, before you sleep!

APRIL 12

A most Deceitful Delusion

And he marveled because of their unbelief.

Mark 6:6a

The Bible is a sacred depository. What thanks have we to give to God for these lively oracles! But yet we may have these, and not believe in the Lord Jesus Christ. My dear friends, there must be a principle wrought in the heart by the Spirit of the living God. Did I ask you how long it is since you believed in Jesus Christ, I suppose most of you would tell me, you believed in Jesus Christ as long as ever you remember – you never did misbelieve. Then, you could not give me a better proof that you never yet believed in Jesus Christ, unless you were sanctified early, as from the womb; for, they that otherwise believe in Christ know there was a time when they did not believe in Jesus Christ. You say you love God with all your heart, soul, and strength. If I were to ask you how long it is since you loved God, you would say, As long as you can remember; you never hated God, you know no time when there was enmity in your heart against God. Then, unless you were sanctified very early, you never loved God in your life. My dear friends, I am more particular in this because it is a most deceitful delusion whereby so many people are carried away, that they believe already. Therefore, it is remarked of Mr. Walter Marshall, giving account of his experiences, that he had been working for life and he had arranged all his sins under the Ten Commandments, and then coming to a minister, asked him the reason why he could not get peace. The minister looked to his catalogue. "Away," says he, "I do not find one word of the sin of unbelief in all your catalogue."

APRIL 13

Heaven and Hell

The men of Nineveh will rise up at the judgment with this generation and condemn it, for they repented at the preaching of Jonah, and behold, something greater than Jonah is here.

LUKE 11:32

If it is asked why you should repent and be converted, I answer, because otherwise you can never be happy in the life hereafter. What do you think heaven is? The covetous man thinks heaven is a place full of gold. Others would like heaven very well if there were a gaming table there, a place to play cards and chance with dice … so the gamester will ask, where is the backgammon table? Where is the box? He will want to shake his ungodly hand in heaven; he will say, let us have a gaming table in heaven, where as he will find, he has lost the game – indeed, that God has damned him without an interest in Christ. "Can two walk together unless they are agreed?" If you die, and do not love God here, if you cannot love praying to God here, and cannot watch one hour, suppose you were to be struck by death and be taken to heaven, there is no such language and amusement there, what would you do? ... one Godly minister said, "Christ is heaven, if I worship God here and do all to God and for God, without any hopes of reward upon the earth." My dear brothers, the devils would never be troubled with such a wretch in hell; he would set all hell in an uproar. If a true Methodist were to go to hell, the devil would say, "Turn that Methodist out, he is come to torment us;" therefore you must he converted if you will go to heaven. Dr. Thomas Scott says that if a natural man were to be put into heaven it would be such a hell to him that he would be glad to go to hell for shelter.

APRIL 14

Above all Worlds

Do not love the world or the things in the world. If anyone loves the world, the love of the Father is not in him.

1 John 2:15

If I am beloved of the Lord, I really shall live above the world. You may say what you will, and you may bring the Scriptures as low as you think proper, but the friendship of the world is hatred to God; and if any man loves the world, the love of the Father is not with him. Now, by not loving the world, I do not mean that you should shut up your shops, and run into a convent; or, that you should hide yourselves from the world; how idle for persons to say they love God that hide themselves from the world – this is no religion at all. But the greatest proof of a Christian's loving God is, "I am in the world, but not of it;" I work with my hands all the day, but my heart is from it. I remember a dear friend once sent me word, many years ago, how busy he was morning and night, up early and late; "perhaps," says he, "you will think by this account, I am worldly;" he said, "No, sir, I thank God that my heart is above the world." God grant we may thus prove we love God! I do not say, but many that love the Lord may be in another situation; but when persons are enabled to leave all for Christ, it is a great mercy. God be praised, we have some such; God add to their happiness!

APRIL 15

Hated by the World

If the world hates you, know that it has hated me before it hated you.

John 15:18

If we are beloved of the Lord, we shall be hated by the world. "If you were of the world, the world would love you, but because you are not of the world, but I have chosen you out of the world, therefore the world hateth you" (John 15:19, KJV). Will you make me believe that any of you who are beloved of the Lord never lost your good worldly reputation by it? Why, you may as well make me believe that you are emperors of the world. Where is the blessing the Sermon on the Mount speaks of? Where is the blessing of persecution? Where is the blessing of being hated of all men? Where is the blessing of being hated for the cross? You love the Lord, and not carry the cross after you! You love the Lord, and will not be hated as your Lord was! I do not say all are hated alike; poor ministers are set in the front of the battle; in proportion to our successes we shall be hated. There are numbers of ministers now asleep in whole skins, that were formerly in a worse plight; the devil disturbs them not because they are quite civil and do not trouble and contradict him; but if you oppose the world and the devil, the world will hate you. There is no greater proof of being beloved of the Lord, than the world hating you. But it must be for Christ's sake. So Ahab said of the prophet, "all his prophesying is against me" (Neh. 6:12) … for it is a blessed mark of our belonging to God that when we are honored to suffer for him, we are never right until we are bearing his cross.

APRIL 16

Union with Christ

To him who loves us and has freed us from our sins by his blood … to him be glory and dominion forever and ever.
Revelation 1:5-6

What must you do that your soul may be joined unto Christ? You must be sensible of your need of him. You must cry mightily unto him to espouse you to himself. Put off the filthiness of sin, and all its defilements, and then, put on the white raiment, and clean garments, which Christ has provided for you, the robes of his righteousness; in these garments you shall be beautiful, and in these garments you shall be accepted. You must have the wedding garment on; you must put off all your own good works, for they will be but a means to keep you from Christ; no, you must come as not having your own righteousness, which is of the law, but you must have the righteousness of Christ (Gal. 2:16). Therefore, come unto the Lord Jesus Christ, and he will give it to you; he will not send you away without it. Receive him upon his own terms, and he is yours forever. But if any of you die before this espousal unto the Lord Jesus Christ, then woe, woe unto you, that ever you had a being in life. But if you go to Christ, you shall be espoused unto him. Though your sins have been ever so great, yea, the blood of Christ will cleanse you from them. The marriage covenant between Christ and your souls will dissolve all your sins; you will then be weary of your old ways, for all things will become new in your souls.

APRIL 17

Christ Rose for us

If you confess with your mouth that Jesus is Lord and believe in your heart that God raised him from the dead, you will be saved.

ROMANS 10:9

Christ is indeed risen; that Jesus should rise from the dead was absolutely necessary. He had often appealed to this as the last and most convincing proof he would give them that he was the true Messiah. His words his enemies remembered and urged it as an argument to induce Pilate to grant them a watch, to prevent his being stolen out of the grave. "We know what the deceiver said while he was alive, 'After three days I will rise again.'" They said this so that, had he not risen again, they might have justly said, "We know this man was an imposter." But more, Christ's resurrection was necessary on our account. "He rose again for our justification;" or, for the debt we owed to God for our sins – that our debt might be fully satisfied and discharged. It had pleased the Father (for ever adored be his infinite love and free grace!) to wound his only Son for our transgressions, and to arrest and confine him in the prison of the grave, as our surety, for the guilt we had contracted by disobeying his commandments. Now, had Christ continued always in the grave, we could have had no more assurance that our sins were satisfied for, than any common debtor can have of his creditor's being satisfied, whilst his surety is kept confined. But he being released from the power of death, we are thereby assured, that with his sacrifice God was well pleased, that our atonement was finished on the cross, and that he has made a full, perfect, and sufficient sacrifice, oblation, and satisfaction for the sins of the world.

APRIL 18

The Lord our Light

The sun shall be no more your light by day, nor for the brightness shall the moon give you light; but the Lord *will be your everlasting light and your God will be your glory. Your sun shall no more go down, nor your moon withdraw itself; for the* Lord *will be your everlasting light, and your days of mourning shall be ended.*

Isaiah 60:19-20

Upon reading these words I cannot help thinking of what the royal psalmist said, "Glorious things of you are spoken, O city of God" (Ps. 87:3). I am afraid, my dear hearers, that even believers themselves, who have tasted of the grace of God, reflect not and meditate as they ought, on the glorious and amazing felicity they are called by the Spirit of God to experience in this life. We content ourselves too much with our hopes, and if we attain to "a good hope through grace," we are ready to think we have got up to the last step of the gospel ladder, and have nothing more to do but to rest in that hope, without ever attaining to an abiding, full assurance of faith. If we would examine the Scriptures, and not choose to bring them down to us, but beg of God to raise our hearts up to them, we shall find the believer is made partaker of the grace of life, as well as an heir of it; the one is on earth, the other in heaven, and one is only a predication of the other. This blessed prophet Isaiah, speaking of the privileges of the children of God says, "What no eye has seen, nor ear heard, nor the heart of man imagined, what God has prepared for those who love him" (1 Cor. 2:9). God grant that we may be of that happy number!

APRIL 19

Strength in Numbers

And though a man might prevail against one who is alone, two will withstand him – a threefold cord is not quickly broken.

Ecclesiastes 4:12

Another excellent blessing arising from religious society is that friends can secure each other from those who oppose them. The devil is fully aware of this, and therefore he has always done his utmost to suppress, and put a stop to, the communion of saints. This was his grand artifice at the first planting of the gospel, to persecute the professors of it, in order to separate them. Which, though God overruled for the better, shows what an enmity he has against Christians assembling themselves together. Nor has he yet left off his old strategy (it being his usual way to entice us by ourselves) in order to tempt us, where, by being destitute of one another's help, he hopes to lead us captive at his will. But, on the contrary, knowing his own interest is strengthened by society, he would first persuade us to neglect the communion of saints, and then to "stand in the way of sinners" (Ps. 1:1), hoping thereby to put us into the seat of the scornful. Judas and Peter are melancholy instances of this. The former had no sooner left his company at supper, but he went out and betrayed his Master, and the dismal downfall of the latter, when he would venture himself among a company of enemies, plainly shows us what the devil will endeavor to do when he gets us by ourselves. Had Peter kept his own company, he might have kept his integrity, but a single cord, alas! How quickly was it broken! Our blessed Savior knew this full well, and therefore it is very observable, that he always sent out his disciples two by two.

APRIL 20

As Sparks Fly Upwards

And to put on the new self, created after the likeness of God in true righteousness and holiness.

EPHESIANS 4:24

Though there are some who dare to deny the Lord Jesus and disbelieve the revelation he has been pleased to give us, and thereby bring upon themselves swift destruction, yet I would charitably hope there are but few, if any such among you, to whom I am now to preach the kingdom of God. If I were to ask you how you expect to be justified in the sight of an offended God? I suppose you would answer, "Only for the sake of our Lord Jesus Christ." But, were I to come more home to your consciences, I fear that most would make the Lord Jesus but in part their Savior and go about as it were to establish a righteousness of their own. And this is not thinking contrary to the rules of Christian charity, for we are all self-righteous by nature; it is as natural for us to turn to a covenant of works, as for the sparks to fly upwards. We have had so many legal, and so few free-grace preachers, for these many years, that most professors now seem to be settled upon their lees, and rather deserve the title of Pharisees than Christians. Thus it was with the generality of the people during the time of our Lord's public ministration; and, therefore, in almost all his discourses, he preached the gospel to poor sinners and denounced terrible woes against proud self-justiciaries. The parable to which the words of the text belong, looks both these ways, for the evangelist informs us that our Lord, "spoke it to certain who trusted in themselves that they were righteous and despised others." And a notable parable it is; a parable worthy of your most serious attention. "He who has ears to hear, let him hear" what Jesus Christ speaks to all visible professors in it.

APRIL 21

Fellow Soldiers

Iron sharpens iron, and one man sharpens another.
PROVERBS 27:17

It is an observation that if kindled coals are placed apart they soon go out, but if heaped together they quicken and liven each other, and give a lasting heat. The same will hold true with Christians. If Christians kindled by the grace of God unite, they will quicken and liven each other, but if they separate and keep asunder, it is no marvel if they soon grow cool or tepid. An excellent benefit flowing from religious society is that it will keep us zealous and steady in the ways of godliness. Let us illustrate this a little farther by a comparison. Let us look upon ourselves as soldiers listed under Christ's banner. And then tell me, all ye that fear God, if it is not an invaluable privilege to have a company of fellow soldiers continually about us, animating and exhorting each other to stand our ground, to keep our ranks, and to manfully follow the Captain of our salvation, though it be through a sea of blood? Let us consider ourselves in another view, as persons travelling to a long eternity, as rescued by the free grace of God, in some measure, from our natural Egyptian bondage, and marching under the conduct of our spiritual Joshua, through the wilderness of this world, to the land of our heavenly Canaan. How prone we are, with the foolish Israelites, to long again for the fleshpots of Egypt, and to return to our former natural state of bondage. Consider this, and see what a blessed privilege it is to have a set of Israelites about us, always reminding us of the folly of any such cowardly design, and of the intolerable misery we shall run into, if we fall in the least short of the promised land.

APRIL 22

Sanctified by God's Spirit

Therefore put away all filthiness and rampant wickedness and receive with meekness the implanted word, which is able to save your souls.

James 1:21

By receiving the Spirit of God, it is not to be understood that we are to be inspired to show outward signs and wonders, to raise dead bodies, to cure leprous people, or to give sight to the blind; these miracles were only of use in the first ages of the church. Therefore Christians (nominal Christians) may have all the gifts of the Spirit, and yet none of the graces of it. You may be enabled by faith to remove mountains; you, by the power of God, may cast out devils; you, by that power, may speak with the tongues of men and angels; yes, you may, by that power, hold up your finger, and stop the sun in the firmament; but if all these are unsanctified by the Spirit of God, they would be of no service to you, but would hurry you to hell with the greater solemnity. Saul received the spirit of prophesying, but was probably a castaway. We must receive the Spirit of God in its sanctifying graces upon our souls. We are all by nature born in sin, and as though at as great a distance from God as the devils themselves. We cannot recover ourselves from the state wherein we have fallen, and therefore must be renewed by the Holy Spirit. By the Holy Spirit, I mean the third person of the ever-blessed Trinity, co-equal, co-essential, co-eternal, and consubstantial with the Father and the Son. Therefore, when we are baptized, it is into the nature of the Father, into the nature of the Son, and into the nature of the Holy Ghost and we are not true Christians until we are sanctified by the Spirit of God.

APRIL 23

Abstaining from Evil

So, whether you eat or drink, or whatever you do, do all to the glory of God.

1 CORINTHIANS 10:31

We are commanded to "abstain from the appearance of evil" (1 Thess. 5:22) and that "whatsoever we do, whether we eat or drink, we shall do all to the glory of God" (1 Cor. 10:31). We must take care to avoid the appearance of sin. One can talk of innocent diversions and recreations; for my part, I know of no diversion but that of doing well. If you can find any diversion which is not contrary to your baptismal vow of renouncing the pomp and vanity of this wicked world; if you can find any diversion which tends to the glory of God; if you can find any diversion which you would be willing to be found at by the Lord Jesus Christ; I give you free license and welcome to go to them. But on the contrary, if they are found to keep sinners from coming to the Lord Jesus Christ; if they are a means to harden the heart, and such as you would not willingly be found in when you come to die; then, my dear brethren, keep from them. For indeed the diversions of this age are contrary to Christianity. Many of you may think I have gone too far, but I will attack the devil in his strongest holds, and bear my testimony against our fashionable and polite entertainments. Whatsoever is not done in faith, to the glory of God, is sin.

APRIL 24

Christ's Righteousness

He must increase, but I must decrease.

JOHN 3:30

Salvation is the free gift of God. It is God's free grace that I preach unto you, not of works, lest any one should boast (Eph. 2:9). Jesus Christ justifies the ungodly. Jesus passed by, saw you polluted with your blood, and bid you live. It is not of works; it is of faith. We are not justified for our faith, for faith is the instrument, but by our faith. The active and the passive obedience of Christ must be applied to us. Jesus Christ has fulfilled the law and made it honorable. He has made full and complete satisfaction to his Father's justice; God will not demand it again. Jesus Christ is the way; Jesus Christ is the truth; and Jesus Christ is the life. His righteousness, my friends, must be imputed to you, or you can never have any interest in his blood; your own works are but as filthy rags, for you are justified before God, without any respect to your works past, present, or to come. If any deny these truths of the gospel, they must not be offended, though a child dare, by the Spirit of God, speak in vindication of the cause of Jesus Christ. If I had a voice so great, and could speak so loud, so that the whole world could hear me, I would cry, "Be not righteous over much," by bringing your own righteousness to Christ, and by being righteous in your own eyes. Man must be abased, so that God may be exalted.

APRIL 25

New Desires

Bear fruits in keeping with repentance. And do not begin to say to yourselves, "We have Abraham as our father." For I tell you, God is able from these stones to raise up children for Abraham.

LUKE 3:8

A man that has truly repented is truly regenerated … there is, as it were, a new creation wrought in your hearts. If your repentance is true, you are renewed throughout, both in soul and body; your understandings are enlightened with the knowledge of God and of the Lord Jesus Christ; and your wills, which were stubborn, obstinate, and hated all good, are obedient and conformable to the will of God. Indeed, our deists tell us, that man now has a free will to do good, to love God, and to repent when he will; but indeed, there is no free will in any of you but to sin; no, your free will leads you so far that you would, if possible, pull God from his throne. This may, perhaps, offend the hypocrites, but (it is the truth in Christ which I speak) every man by his own natural will hates God. "You adulterous people! Do you know that friendship with the world is enmity towards God? Therefore whoever wishes to be a friend of the world makes himself an enemy of God" (James 4:4). But when you are turned to the Lord by evangelical repentance, your will is changed; your consciences, now hardened and benumbed, shall then be quickened and awakened; your hard hearts shall then be melted, and your unruly affections shall be crucified. Thus, by that repentance, the whole soul will be changed. You will have new inclinations, new desires, and new habits.

APRIL 26

Our Sovereign God

Our God is in the heavens; he does all that he pleases.

PSALM 115:3

At sundry times and in divers manners, God spoke to the fathers by the prophets before he spoke to us in these last days by his Son; "but in these last days he has spoken to us by his Son, whom he appointed the heir of all things, through whom also he created the world" (Heb. 1:2). And as God is a sovereign agent, and his sacred Spirit blows when and where he wills, surely he may reveal and make known his will to his creatures, when, where, and how he pleases; "whatever the Lord pleases, he does, in heaven and on earth, in the seas and all deeps" (Ps. 135:6). Indeed, this seems to be one reason, to display his sovereignty, why he chose, before the canon of Scripture was settled, to make known his mind in such various methods, and to such a variety of his servants and messengers. Hence it is that we hear he talked with Abraham as a man talks with a friend. To Moses, he spoke "face to face." And to others, he spoke by dreams or visions imposed strongly upon their imaginations. This seems to be frequently the happy lot of the favorite evangelical prophet, Zechariah. I call him an "evangelical" prophet because his predictions, however they pointed at some approaching or immediate event, ultimately terminated in him who is the Alpha and Omega, the Beginning and the End, of all the lively oracles of God.

APRIL 27

For Themselves

For where jealousy and selfish ambition exist, there will be disorder and every vile practice.

JAMES 3:16

I see Zechariah, this man of God, starting out of his sleep, and being all attention. Indeed, the angel asked him, "What do you see?" He answers, "I have looked, and behold, a candlestick all of gold" – an emblem of the church of God, "with a bowl upon the top of it, and seven lamps thereon, and seven pipes to the seven lamps, which were upon the top thereof." He implies that the church, however reduced to its lowest ebb, should still be preserved and kept supplied and shining through the invisible aids and operations of the blessed Spirit of God. The occasion of such an extraordinary vision, if we compare this passage with the second chapter of Haggai, seems to be this: it was now near eighteen years since the Jewish people had been delivered from their long and grievous captivity; and being so long deprived of their temple and its worship, one would have imagined, that immediately upon their return, they should have postponed all private works, and with their united strength have first set about rebuilding that once stately and magnificent structure. But they, like so many Christians of a lukewarm stamp yet put themselves and others off, with this godly pretence, "The time is not yet come that the Lord's house should be built." The time is not yet come? What, not in eighteen years! For so long had they been returned from their state of bondage. Why has the time not come? The prophet Haggai tells them: their whole time was so taken up in building for themselves that they had no time left to build a habitation for their great and glorious Benefactor, the mighty God of Jacob.

APRIL 28

Looking to Jesus

In my distress I called upon the LORD; to my God I cried for help. From his temple he heard my voice, and my cry to him reached his ears.

PSALM 18:6

O that Bethesda's God may make this day, though but a day of small things, productive of great things to the souls of all who hear. A great and good day will it be indeed if Jesus Christ should, by the power of the eternal Spirit, bless these words and cause every mountain of difficulty that lies in the way of your conversion to become a plain. What are you, O Great Mountain, whether it is the lust of the flesh, the lust of the eye, the pride of life, sin, or self-righteousness? Before our God you shall become a plain. Brethren, my heart is enlarged towards you; it is written (and blessed be God that it is written), "As I live, says the Lord, every knee shall bow to me, and every tongue shall confess to God" (Rom. 14:11). O that we may be made a willing people in the day of his power! Look, look to him, all who live in these ends of the earth … Come to him all you who are weary and heavy laden, and he will give you rest. He will give you rest from the guilt, rest from the power, rest from the punishment of sin; he will give rest from the fear of divine judgments here, and rest with himself eternally hereafter. Fear not, though your beginnings are but small, Christ will not despise the day of small things. A bruised reed will he not break, and the smoking flax will he not quench, until he bring forth judgment unto victory. His hands that laid the foundation shall finish it; yet a little while and the top-stone shall be brought forth with shouting.

APRIL 29

Overcoming the World

Do not marvel that I said to you, 'You must be born again.'
JOHN 3:7

I shall not speak to the Pharisees or to any except to you who have experienced the pangs of the new birth, or are at present under them, and who know what it is to love the Lord Jesus in sincerity and truth. Do not be discouraged or think hard of the ways of God because the people of this world do not love you. If you were of the world, it would love you; it would then be pleased with your company; it would not thrust you from a tavern, or an alehouse; it would not dislike you for singing the songs of the drunkard, or for going to plays, balls, or other polite and fashionable entertainments, as they are called; no, these the children of the world like; but if you will sing hymns and psalms, and go to hear what God has to say unto your souls, and spend your time in reading, praying, and frequenting religious assemblies, then it is that they dislike you, and thrust you out of their company, as unworthy thereof. Do not let any of these things move you, for the rest that Jesus Christ has prepared for you is an ample recompense for all you may meet with here. This rest is the fruit of the blood of the Lord Jesus Christ: O how will it fill our souls with love, to think that through the streams of this blood, we have overcome the violence of the world, and the snares of the devil. My dear brethren, be not discouraged at the treatment you meet with here, but let it be a means to stir you up to advance in the love of the Lord who has prepared a rest for you.

APRIL 30

Loving our Neighbors

While Ezra prayed and made confession, weeping and casting himself down before the house of God, a very great assembly of men, women, and children, gathered to him out of Israel, for the people wept bitterly.

EZRA 10:1

For in the heart of every true believer there is a heavenly tendency, a divine attraction, which as sensibly draws him to converse with God as the loadstone attracts the needle. A deep sense of their own weakness, and of Christ's fullness; a strong conviction of their natural corruption, and of the necessity of renewing grace; will not let them rest from crying day and night to their almighty Redeemer that the divine image, which they lost in Adam, may, through his all-powerful mediation and the sanctifying operations of his blessed Spirit, be begun, carried on, and fully perfected both in their souls and bodies. Thus earnest, thus importunate, are all sincere Christians in praying for themselves. But then, not having so lively, lasting, and deep a sense of the wants of their Christian brethren, they are for the most part too remiss and defective in their prayers for them. Were the love of God shed abroad in our hearts and did we love our neighbor in the manner in which the Son of God our Savior loved us, we could not but be as importunate for their spiritual and temporal welfare, as we are for our own. Do not let anyone think that this is an uncommon degree of charity – a high pitch of perfection to which not everyone can attain. For, if we are all commanded to love our neighbors as we do ourselves (and even to lay down our lives for our brothers), then it is the duty of all to pray for their neighbors as much as for their own needs.

MAY 1

What is Grace?

Grace to you and peace from God our Father and the Lord Jesus Christ.

1 CORINTHIANS 1:4

The word "grace" is a very complex word and takes in all that the blessed Spirit of God does for a poor sinner, from the moment he first draws his breath, and brings him to Jesus Christ, until he is pleased to call him by death. And as it is begun in grace, it will be swallowed up in an endless eternity of glory hereafter; this is called "the grace of our Lord Jesus Christ." Why so? It is because the Lord Jesus Christ purchases this gift for us. Moses gave the Law, but grace and truth came by Jesus Christ, the Son of God. If it were not for the purchase of a Mediator's blood, if it were not that Jesus Christ had bought us with a price, even with the price of his own blood, you and I should never have had, you and I could never have had, the grace of God manifested at all to our souls. The covenant of works being broken, our first parents stood convicted before God: they were criminals, though they did not care to own it; condemned before God, and in themselves, so that like their children they make excuses for their sin. Man by nature had but one neck, and, if God had pleased to have done it, he might justly have cut it off at one blow; but no sooner had man incurred the curse of the law, but behold a Mediator is provided, under the character of the seed of the woman, which should bruise the serpent's head: implying what the Redeemer was first to do without, and afterwards to do in the hearts of all his people. Well, therefore, are we taught in our church collects to end all our prayers with the words, "through Jesus our Lord."

MAY 2

Restraining Grace

But by the grace of God I am what I am ...
1 Corinthians 15:10

If it were not for God's restraining grace, God's people would be just as weak and wicked as other folks are ... we may talk what we please and build upon our own reputation, but we are just like little children that wish to walk by themselves. Well, says the father, walk alone then – they tumble down, get a broken brow, and then are glad to take hold of their father again. Thus Jesus Christ is always acting in a restraining way to his people. If it were not so, by the blindness of their understandings, the corruptions of their hearts and affections, together with the perverseness of their will, alas!, alas!, there is not a child of God that would not run away every day – that is, if Christ did not restrain him! And there is a convicting grace, which from the Lord Jesus Christ acts every day and hour. It is a blessed thing to be under the Redeemer's convicting grace! A man may speak to the ear, but it is the Spirit of God alone who can speak to the heart. I am not speaking of the convicting grace that comes before conversion, and gives us a sense of our sin and misery. Rather, I mean the convicting grace that follows the believer from time to time. If a heathen, Socrates, could say that he always had a monitor with him to check him when he did amiss, and direct him to when he went right, surely the Christian may say (and blessed be God for it!) that he has Jesus Christ who kindly shows him when he goes astray, and by his grace puts him in the path of righteousness, that his feet may not slip.

MAY 3

Converting Grace

For it is all for your sake, so that as grace extends to more and more people it may increase thanksgiving, to the glory of God.
2 CORINTHIANS 4:15

There is the converting grace of our Lord Jesus Christ. Oh! What poor unhappy creatures are they that think they can turn to God when they please, that they leave it till they cannot turn in their beds. Satan tells them, then, it is too late, and their consciences are filled with horror; they go off in a whirlwind; may this be the case of none here! There is a most excellent prayer in our form for Communion, "Turn us, O good Lord, and we shall be turned." We can no more turn our hearts than we can turn the world upside-down. It is the Redeemer by his Spirit who must take away our heart of stone, and by the influence of the Holy Spirit give us a heart of flesh. I might as well attempt to reach the heavens with my hand; I might as well go to some churchyard and command the dead to rise. I might as soon shake my handkerchief and bid the streams divide and they give way as to expect a soul to turn to God without the grace of the Mediator. Come, my dear hearers, I am of a good man's opinion that prayed he might be converted every day. In the divine life, not to go forwards is to go backwards; it is one great part of the work of the Spirit of God to convert the soul from something that is wrong to something that is right, every day, hour, and moment of the believer's life – so that, in short, his life is one continued act of converting grace.

MAY 4

Establishing Grace

Do not lie to one another, seeing that you have put off the old self with its practices.

COLOSSIANS 3:9

Then there is establishing grace. David prays, "Create in me a clean heart, O God, and renew a right spirit within me" (Ps. 51:10). In the margin of our text it reads, "renew a constant spirit within me." You hear of some that are rooted and grounded in the love of God, and the apostle prays that they may always abound in the work of the Lord. Again, it is good to have one's heart established with grace; there are a good many people who have some religion in them but they are not so established. Hence they are mere weathercocks, fickle and changing, turned about by every wind of doctrine; and you may as soon measure the moon for a suit of clothes as some people that are always changing. This is for want of more grace, more of the Spirit of God; and, as children grow that are got stronger and riper, so as people grow in grace and in the knowledge of the Lord Jesus Christ, they will be more settled, and more confirmed in their faith. On first setting out they prattle but they will become more adult-like, firmer, steadier. Young Christians are like rivulets that make great noise and have shallow water. Old Christians are like deep water that makes little noise, carries a good load and gives not away … What do you think, my brothers, of the Redeemer's comforting grace? What can you do without it? "In the multitude of my thoughts within me," says the psalmist, "your comforts have refreshed my soul" (Ps. 94:19, KJV).

MAY 5

Grace to All

And behold, I am with you always, to the end of the age.
MATTHEW 28:20

I do not have time to show you in how many ways the Redeemer's grace is displayed; but wherever this grace is, what reason have you that are partakers of it, and I, to pray that it may be with us all. The grace of our Lord Jesus Christ, says John, be with you all; it is not said to be with all ministers; it is not said to be with this or that particular people, but with all believers. Remember, my friends, what Matthew Henry said, that he desired to be a Catholic but not a Roman Catholic. I have often thought since I went to see the waterworks that it was an emblem of Christ; there is a great reservoir of water from which this great city is supplied; but how is it supplied from that reservoir? Why, by hundreds and hundreds of pipes: but where does this water go, does it go only to the dissenters or to the church people, or only to this or that people? No, the pipes convey waters to them all; and I remember when I saw it, it put me in mind of the great reservoir of grace, that living water that is in Christ Jesus, and the pipes are ordinances by which his grace is conveyed to believing souls. God grant that we may be of that happy number! O, what a mercy it is that Christ has said, "I am with you always, to the end of the age" (Matt. 28:20). And therefore we must look upon this prayer to be as efficacious now as it was the moment the words dropped from the Apostle's pen.

MAY 6

Hearing the Word

If I speak in the tongues of men and of angels, but have not love, I am a noisy gong or a clanging cymbal.

1 Corinthians 13:1

Can any man understand the Scriptures without the Spirit of God who helps him? Jesus Christ must open our understanding to understand the Scriptures, and the Spirit of God must take of the things of Christ and show them unto us … what signifies my preaching, and your hearing, if the Spirit of God does not enlighten? Formal ministers can steal a sermon, and add a little out of their own heads, but a minister of the gospel cannot preach to purpose without the assistance of the Spirit of God no more than a ship can sail without wind. As for a carnal man, he may take his sermon in his pocket, and you will find his sermons always the same; but spiritual preachers are seldom so. Sometimes they are in darkness, so as to speak to those that are in darkness; sometimes they are tempted, so as to speak to those that are tempted; sometimes they have a full gale, and go before the wind, and this is all by the assistance of the Spirit of God. Without this, a man may preach like an angel, and do no good at all. So, in respect to hearing the word of God, I declare I would not preach again, if I did not think that God would accompany the word by his Spirit. What are we but as sounding brass and tinkling cymbals? If the word is preached in the strength of the Spirit, it will be attended with convictions and conversions, and the grace of God will be both with preacher and hearer.

MAY 7

Eyeing God's Providence

Great are the works of the LORD, studied by all who delight in them. Full of splendor and majesty in his work, and his righteousness endures forever. He has caused his wondrous works to be remembered; the LORD is gracious and merciful. He provides for those who fear him; he remembers his covenant forever.

PSALM 111:2-5

The grace of God is with us in his providence. Oh, says Bishop Joseph Hall, a little aid is not enough for me! I will comment on what I have seen many times—if the sailors perceive a storm coming, they do not choose to speak to the passengers, for fear of frightening them; rather, they will go quietly on deck and give orders for proper care to be taken; and if a sailor can tell of storms approaching, by the clouds, why cannot God's people tell why God does so and so with them? The people of God eye him in his providence; the very hairs of their heads are all numbered, and the grace of God is with them in the common business of life. Some people think that the Methodists preach so and so, to make them neglect their business, and we preach at unseasonable times. We would not preach at this time, but that we are going to part from one another. No, we preach that the grace of God may attend them in their counting houses, and woe be to those persons that do not take the grace of God with them into their counting houses, and in their common business! O, what blessed times would it be, if every one made the grace of God their employ, that when the Lord comes he may say, "Lord, here I am waiting for you."

MAY 8

One Faith

Only let your manner of life be worthy of the gospel of Christ, so that whether I come and see you or am absent, I may hear of you that you are standing firm in one spirit, with one mind striving side by side for the faith of the gospel …

PHILIPPIANS 1:27

Though we all profess to own one Lord, one faith, one baptism; though Jesus Christ never was, and never will be, divided in himself, yet the followers of Jesus Christ have in all ages been sadly divided among themselves, and what has rendered the case the more to be pitied, is, that they have generally been divided about the circumstantials of religion, they have generally received one another to doubtful disputation and embittered one another's hearts by talking about those things which they might either do or not do, either know or not know, and yet at the same time be the true followers of the meek and lowly Jesus. I am persuaded that this is the great artifice and engine of the devil. He knows if he can divide Christians, he will get the better of them; and therefore he endeavors to sow the tares of division among them, in order to make them a common prey to their enemies. And, indeed, God has permitted this in all ages of the church. In consequence of this, the early ages of Christianity were not altogether free of it. No, there is pregnant and sufficient proof of it … There are two things which those who call themselves Christians want much to be convinced of: first, what religion is not; second, what religion positively is. The kingdom of God is not meat and drink, but righteousness, and peace, and joy in the Holy Spirit.

MAY 9

Stand Firm

Therefore, take up the whole armor of God, that you may be able to withstand in the evil day, and having done all, to stand firm.

EPHESIANS 6:13

The devil will give you leave to amuse yourselves; you may have your choice of diversions, only take care to be diverted from God, and the devil is sure of you; but the believer has something better: faith sweeps away the refuge of lies, and the believer turns to his God, and says, "O, my God; you shall be my refuge! The devil pursues me, my false friends have designs against me, my own wicked heart itself molests me, my foes are those of my own house; but do, O God, be my refuge, I will fly there." By these it may be said that God is our refuge. The question is, "What shall I do to make him my refuge? How shall I be helped to do so? You bid me fly; you say, I may fly there, but where shall I get wings? How shall I be supported?" Here is a blessed word – God shall not only be our refuge, but God shall be our strength also. What strength? – to make every day of trouble so easy to us by his power, as to carry us through it. God has said, and will stand to it, "As your day is, so shall your strength be." Afflictions even at a distance will appear very formidable, when viewed by unbelief. Our fears say, "O God, if I come to be tried this or that way, how shall I bear it?" But we do not know what we can bear till the trial comes; and we do not know what strength God can give us, or what a strong God he will be, until he is pleased to put us into a furnace of affliction ... he will never leave us till we are helped quite over and quite through it.

MAY 10

Mushroom Converts

Peter answered him, "Though they fall away because of you, I will never fall away."

MATTHEW 26:33

Now the gospel signifies good news and glad tidings: "Fear not, for behold," said the angel, "I bring you good news of great joy that will be for all the people." Mean and contemptible as the office of a preacher may be thought now, the angels were glad of the commission to preach this gospel; and Dr. Thomas Goodwin, that learned pious soul, says in his familiar way, and that is the best way of writing, "God had but one Son, and he made a minister of him;" and, I add, he made an itinerant minister of him too. Well, and some say, you must not preach the law; you cannot preach the gospel without preaching the law; for you shall find, by and by, we are to preach something that the people must be saved by; it is impossible to tell them how they are to be saved, unless we tell them what they are to be saved from. The way the Spirit of God takes, is like that we take in preparing the ground; do you think any farmers would have a crop of corn next year unless they plough now? And you may as well expect a crop of corn on un-ploughed ground, as a crop of grace until the soul is convinced of its being undone without a Savior. That is the reason we have so many mushroom converts, so many persons that are always happy! happy! happy! and never were miserable – why? Because their stony ground is not ploughed up; they have not got a conviction of the law; they are stony ground hearers; they hear the word with joy and in a time of temptation, which soon come after a seeming or real conversion, they fall away.

MAY 11

Refusing Life

Yet you refuse to come to me that you may have life.
John 5:40

Christ is the treasure hid in that field, yet, as there are equal proofs of the divinity of the New Testament, the word Holy Scriptures include both, especially as Christ is the antitype of all the types, the Alpha and Omega, the beginning and the end, of all divine revelation: would to God he were your Alpha and Omega too! Now, says Christ, you pretend to reverence the Scriptures; you that are set apart as persons learned in the Scriptures, you scribes, you lawyers, such as were mentioned in the gospel today. I fancy some people think that when we read of lawyers in the Scriptures, that we mean such lawyers as ours, who deal only in the civil and common law; but they were those that opened and explained the law to the people; these were the persons who thought and professed, that in them they had eternal life, that they testify of Christ the great Prophet that was promised in the Scriptures to come into the world. Yet says our divine Master to these very professors, these masters in Israel, "Yet you refuse to come to me that you may have life;" that is, though I am now present with you, though I am now come to explain the Scriptures, and fulfill them, am now come to proclaim to you that life, that eternal life, which the Scriptures declare was to be published and proclaimed by me, yet "you refuse to come to me that you may have life." By eternal life, we are to understand all the blessings of a converted state, particularly the pardon of sins, not only before conversion but also forever after.

MAY 12

Haste to the Feast

Then I saw an angel standing in the sun, and with a loud voice he called to all the birds that fly directly overhead, "Come, gather for the great supper of God … "

REVELATION 19:17

Haste, therefore, and away to the supper of the Lamb. If you do not come, I know the Master will be angry. And who can stand before him when he is angry? "Do not harden your hearts as in the rebellion, on the day of testing in the wilderness" (Heb. 3:8). Do not provoke the Lord to say, "None of those that were bidden shall taste of my supper." O dreadful words! Much more is implied in them than is expressed. It is the same with that in the psalms, "I swore in my wrath, that they should not enter into my rest." And if you do not enter into God's rest, nor taste of Christ's supper, you must lift up your eyes in torments, where you will have no rest, and must sup with the damned devils forever more. Knowing therefore the terrors of the Lord, we persuade you to haste away, and make no more frivolous excuses: for there is no excuse against believing. Perhaps you say, "You call to the halt, and maimed, and blind, and poor. But if we are halt, and maimed, how can we come? If we are blind, how can we see our way? If we are poor, how can we expect admission to so great a table?" But happy are you if you are sensible that you are halt and maimed; for if you feel yourselves so, and are lamenting it, who knows but while I am speaking, God may send his Spirit with the word, and fetch you home?

MAY 13

Oracles of God

But whoever keeps his word, in him truly the love of God is perfected.

1 JOHN 2:5A

The Scriptures are given to us for no other end but to show us our misery, our happiness, our fall, our recovery; or, in one word, after what manner we died in Adam, and how in Christ we may again be made alive. Hence then arises the necessity of searching the scriptures: for since they are nothing else but the grand charter of our salvation, the revelation of a covenant made by God with men in Christ, and a light to guide us in the way of peace; it follows, that all are obliged to read and search them, because all are equally fallen from God, all equally stand in need of being informed how they must be restored to and again united with him. How foolishly, then, do the disputing infidels of this generation act who are continually either calling for signs from heaven or seeking for outward evidence to prove the truth of divine revelation! Whereas what they so earnestly seek for is nigh unto, no, within them. For let them but consult their own hearts, they cannot but feel what they want. Let them but consult the lively oracles of God and they cannot but see a remedy revealed for all their wants, and that the written word does as exactly answer the wants and desires of their hearts, as face answers to face in the water. Where then is the scribe, where is the wise, where is the solidity of the reasoning of the disputers of this world? Has not God revealed himself unto them as plain as their own hearts could wish? And yet they require a sign; but there shall no other sign be given them. For if they believe not a revelation that is every way so suited to their wants, neither will they be persuaded, though one should rise from the dead.

MAY 14

Heart-Work

This is true religion, pure and undefiled in the sight of God, to look after widows and orphans in their time of need.

James 1:27 KJV

I take it for granted you believe religion to be an inward thing; you believe it to be a work in the heart, a work wrought in the soul by the power of the Spirit of God. If you do not believe this, you do not believe your Bibles. If you do not believe this, though you have got your Bibles in your hand, you hate the Lord Jesus Christ in your heart, for religion is everywhere represented in Scripture as the work of God in the heart. "The kingdom of God is within us," says our Lord; and, "He is not a Christian who is one outwardly; but he is a Christian who is one inwardly." If any of you place religion in outward things, I shall not perhaps please you this morning; you will understand me no more when I speak of the work of God upon a poor sinner's heart, than if I were talking in an unknown tongue. I would further premise a caution, that I would by no means confine God to one way of acting. I would by no means say that all persons, before they come to have a settled peace in their hearts, are obliged to undergo the same degrees of conviction. No; God has various ways of bringing his children home; his sacred Spirit blows when and where and how he wills … Before you can speak peace to your hearts, you must be made to see, made to feel, made to weep over, made to bewail, your actual transgressions against the law of God.

MAY 15

God's Justice

What shall we say then? Is there injustice on God's part? By no means!

ROMANS 9:14

Before you can speak peace to your hearts, you must not only be troubled for the sins of your life, the sin of your nature, but likewise for the sins of your best duties and performances. When a poor soul is somewhat awakened by the terrors of the Lord, then the poor creature, being born under the covenant of works, flies directly to a covenant of works again. And as Adam and Eve hid themselves among the trees of the garden, and sewed fig leaves together to cover their nakedness, so the poor sinner, when awakened, flies to his duties and to his performances, to hide himself from God, and goes to patch up a righteousness of his own … But before you can speak peace to your heart, you must be brought to see that God may damn you for the best prayer you ever put up; you must be brought to see that all your duties – all your righteousness – as the prophet elegantly expresses it – put them all together, are so far from recommending you to God, are so far from being any motive and inducement to God to have mercy on your poor soul, that he will see them to be filthy rags … God hates them and cannot do with them if you bring them to him in order to recommend you to his favor. My dear friends, what is there in our performances to recommend us to God? Our persons are in an unjustified state by nature, we deserve to be damned ten thousand times over; and what must our performances be? We can do no good thing by nature: "Those who are in the flesh cannot please God" (Rom. 8:8).

MAY 16

The Reigning Sin

They were broken off because of their unbelief, but you stand fast through faith. So do not become proud, but fear.
ROMANS 11:20

Before you can speak peace to your souls, there is one particular sin you must be greatly troubled for, and yet I fear there are few of you think what it is; it is the reigning, the damning sin of the Christian world, and yet the Christian world seldom or never think of it. And what is that? It is what most of you think you are not guilty of – and that is the sin of unbelief. Before you can speak peace to your heart, you must be troubled for the unbelief of your heart. But, can it be supposed that any of you are unbelievers here in this church-yard, that are born in Scotland, in a Reformed country, that go to church every Sabbath? Can any of you that receive the sacrament once a year – O that it were administered oftener! – can it be supposed that you who had tokens for the sacrament, that you who keep up family prayer, that any of you do not believe in the Lord Jesus Christ? I appeal to your own hearts, if you would not think me uncharitable, if I doubted whether any of you believed in Christ; and yet, I fear upon examination, we should find that most of you have not so much faith in the Lord Jesus as the devil himself. I am persuaded the devil believes more of the Bible than most of us do. He believes the divinity of Jesus Christ; that is more than many who call themselves Christians do; no, he believes and trembles, and that is more than thousands amongst us do.

MAY 17

Strangers to Jesus

Take care, brothers, lest there be in any of you an evil, unbelieving heart, leading you to fall away from the living God.

HEBREWS 3:12

You may be convicted of your actual sins so as to be made to tremble, and yet you may be strangers to Jesus Christ. You may have no true work of grace upon your hearts. Before ever, therefore, you can speak peace to your hearts, conviction must go deeper; you must not only be convinced of your actual transgressions against the law of God but likewise of the foundation of all your transgressions. And what is that? I mean original sin – that original corruption each of us brings into the world with us, which renders us liable to God's wrath and damnation. There are many poor souls that think themselves reasonable, yet they pretend to say there is no such thing as original sin; they will charge God with injustice in imputing Adam's sin to us; although we have got the mark of the beast and of the devil upon us, yet they tell us we are not born in sin. Let them look abroad into the world and see the disorders in it, and think, if they can, if this is the paradise in which God did put man. No! Everything in the world is out of order. I have often thought, when I was abroad, that if there were no other argument to prove original sin, the rising of wolves and tigers against man, no, the barking of a dog against us, is a proof of original sin. Tigers and lions dare not rise against us, if it were not for Adam's first sin … If we look inwardly, we shall see enough of lusts, and man's temper contrary to the temper of God. There is pride, malice, and revenge, in all our hearts; and this temper cannot come from God.

MAY 18

The God-Man

In the beginning was the Word, and the Word was with God, and the Word was God.

JOHN 1:1

The deists, who own a God but deny his Son, dare go to God outside of Christ. But Jacob was taught better. God soon reveals the gospel unto him. Here is a ladder by which God preaches to us; if you have a mind to climb from earth to heaven, you must get up by the Son of God. No one ever pointed out a proper way to heaven for us, but himself. When Adam and Eve fell from God, a flaming sword turned every way to keep them from the tree of life. But Jesus alone is a new and living way, not only to the holy of holies below, but into the immediate presence of God. And that we might know that he was a proper Savior, the top of it reached to heaven. If it had stopped short, Jacob might have said, ah! the ladder is within a little way of heaven, but does not quite reach it; if I climb to the top, I shall not get there, after all. But the top reached to heaven, to point out the divinity and exaltation of the Son of God. Such a Savior became us; he who was God, God over all, blessed for evermore! Therefore, the Arian scheme is most uncomfortable and destructive – to talk of Christ as if he were a Savior who is not God is no Christ at all. I would turn deist tomorrow if I did not know that Christ was God. "Cursed is the man who builds his faith upon an arm of flesh." If Christ is God, the Arians and Socinians, by their own thoughts, are undone forever. But Jesus Christ is very God and very man, begotten (and not made) of the Father. May God, of his infinite mercy, write his divinity deep in our hearts!

MAY 19

Jacob's Ladder

And he dreamed, and behold, there was a ladder set up on the earth, and the top of it reached to heaven.

GENESIS 28:12

I cannot help admiring that part of the Litany in which we pray that God would take care not only of the grown people, but also of children: God take care of yours both in body and soul. But what gave the greatest comfort to Jacob was that the Lord was on the top of the ladder, which I do not know whether it would have been so, if Jacob had not seen God there. It comforts me, I assure you, to think that whenever God shall call for me, I shall be carried by angels into Abraham's bosom. I have often thought that whenever that time comes, that blessed, long longed-for moment comes, as soon as ever they have called upon me, my first question will be to them, "Where is my dear Master? Where is Jesus? Where is that dear Emanuel, who has loved me with an everlasting love, and has called me by his grace, and has sent you to fetch me home to see his face?" But I believe you and I shall have no occasion to ask where he is, for he will come to meet us, he will stand at the top of his ladder, to take his pilgrims in; so God was at the top of the ladder … He appears not sitting, as he is often represented in heaven, but standing: as much as to say, "Here, here, Jacob; your brother wants to kill you … but here I am ready in order to preserve you. I stand above, and I see your weariness; I see the fatigue and hardships you have yet to undergo, though you do not see it yourself. You have thrown yourself upon my providence and protection, and I will give you my word that I will stand by you.

MAY 20

Your Glory

Light is sweet, and it is pleasant for the eyes to see the sun.
Ecclesiastes 11:17

A great many good and great men have gathered what they call the millennium, that Jesus Christ is to come and reign a thousand years on earth; but I must acknowledge that I have always rejected a great many good men's positive opinion about the season when this state commences, and I would warn you all against fixing any time; for what signifies whether Christ comes to reign a thousand years, or when he comes, since you and I are to die very soon? And therefore instead of puzzling our heads about it, God grant we may live so that we may reign with him for ever, and it seems to me, that whatsoever is said of this state on earth, that the millennium is to be understood in a spiritual sense, as an emblem of a glorious, eternal, beatific state in the kingdom of heaven. "The sun shall be no more your light by day, nor for brightness shall the moon give you light; but the Lord will be your everlasting light, and your God will be your glory" (Isa. 60:19). In order to prepare us for that light, and show us the nature of it, while we speak of it, may it come with light and power to our souls! "And your God shall be your glory." This is spoken to all fearful believers in particular … what has been my comfort this day in the meditation on this passage may be yours and mine to all eternity. He who has an ear to hear, let him hear what the evangelical prophet says to you, "Your God your glory."

MAY 21

A Sinner's God

To the one who conquers I will grant to eat of the tree of life, which is in the paradise of God.

REVELATION 2:7B

My dear Christians … you that can go and call God your God … Go and beg of God … pray to heaven … pray for those that are in the gall of bitterness, that have no God, no Christ, to go to, and if they were to die tonight, would be damned for ever. O, poor sinner, where is your glory then? Where is your purple and fine linen? Your purple robes will be turned into purple fire, and instead of calling God your God, you will be damned with the devil. O, think of your danger! "O earth, hear the word of the Lord!" If you never were awakened before, may the arrows of God, steeped in the blood of Jesus Christ, reach your hearts now! Think how you live at enmity with God; think of your danger every day and every hour, your danger of dropping into hell. Think how your friends in glory will leave you; and may this consideration, under the influences of the Holy Spirit, excite you to choose God for your God! Though the sun is going down, though the shadow of the evening is coming on, God is willing, O man, God is willing, O woman, to be a sinner's God; he has found out a way whereby he can be reconciled to you. I remember, when I saw a nobleman condemned to he hanged, the lord high steward told him that however he was obliged to pass sentence on him, and did not know that justice would be satisfied but by the execution of the law in this world, yet there might be a way whereby justice might be satisfied and mercy take place in another – "Truly, I say to you, today you will be with me in Paradise" (Luke 23:43).

MAY 22

Poor, Blind, Naked

For you say, I am rich, I have prospered, and I need nothing, not realizing that you are wretched, pitiable, poor, blind, and naked. I counsel you to buy from me gold refined by fire, so that you may be rich, and white garments so that you may clothe yourself and the shame of your nakedness may not be seen, and salve to anoint your eyes, so that you may see.

REVELATION 3:17-18

Remember when you say, "you are rich, and increased in goods," that you know not, says Christ, that "you are poor, and miserable, and blind, and naked." We do not see ourselves fallen creatures, we do not know that. May God give you to know and feel that "there is no name given under heaven whereby we can be saved, but Jesus Christ." Must I have inward feeling? What would the polite world do without feeling? Do you think they would go to the playhouse, and places of public diversion, without feeling? If I can feel other things that do not concern religion, how can I come to God until I feel a need of him? We do not choose to come to Christ because we do not choose to have him as a free gift; we do not like to come to him as poor and needy. I remember I heard an excellent minister of Christ in Scotland preaching upon these words, "Behold, I stand at the door and knock." He says, "Christ comes knocking at the door to come into your houses, but you will not come down to accept of his mercy."

MAY 23

Sagely Counsel

But as for you, continue in what you have learned and have firmly believed, knowing from whom you learned it and how from childhood you have been acquainted with the sacred writings, which are able to make you wise for salvation through faith in Christ Jesus.

2 TIMOTHY 3:14-15

Catch an old Christian without profound humility – if you can. Believe me … it is nothing but this flesh of ours, those cursed seeds of the proud apostate, which lie lurking in us, that make us to think ourselves worthy of the very air we breathe. When our eyes are opened by the influences of divine grace, we then shall begin to think of ourselves, as we ought to think, even, that God is all, and we are less than nothing. Well, you may cry … could I but learn of Christ to be meek and lowly in heart, I should certainly find rest to my soul … Our Savior learned obedience by the things which he suffered – so must we. Pain, if patiently endured and sanctified to us, is a great purifier of our corrupted nature. It will teach us excellent lessons … Never despair when God acts upon the soul, for he makes quick work of it … Oh, let us young, inexperienced soldiers, be always upon our guard; the very moment we desert our post, the enemy rushes in; and if he can but divert our eyes from looking heavenward, he will soon so blind us, that we shall not look towards it at all. A great deal may be learned from a little fall … It must be confessed that we must make a great progress in religion, and be inured by frequent prayer and meditation, to the ecstatic contemplation of heavenly objects before we can arrive at true heavenly-mindedness; and, perhaps, after all our endeavors, while our souls are immersed in these fleshly tabernacles, we shall make but very small advances in so delightful and glorious an undertaking.

MAY 24

Guards of Angels

And he will send out his angels with a loud trumpet call, and they will gather his elect from the four winds, from one end of heaven to the other.

MATTHEW 24:31

Perhaps the deists would say, Jacob, our patriarch, was tired and dreamed among other things of a ladder. Yes, he did, but this dream was from God; and how kind God was to meet him at the end of his first day's journey, to strengthen and animate him to go forward in this lonesome pilgrimage! This ladder is reckoned by some to denote the providence of God. It was let down as it were from heaven, particularly at this time, to poor Jacob, that he might know that, however he was become a pilgrim, and left his all, all for God's glory, that God would take care for his comfort, and give his angels charge over him, to keep him in all his ways, which was denoted by the angels ascending and descending upon the ladder. Some think that particular saints and countries have particular guardian angels, and therefore that the angels that ascended were those that had the particular charge of that place, so far as Jacob had come; that the angels that descended were another set of angels, sent down from heaven to guard him in his future journey; perhaps this is more a fancy, than the word of God. However, I very much like the observation of one: "Why should we dispute whether every individual believer has got a particular angel, when there is not one believer but has got guards of angels to attend him."

MAY 25

Dreams and Visions

For a dream comes with much business, and a fool's voice with many words.

ECCLESIASTES 5:3

The wise man observes that "in the multitude of dreams there are many vanities," being often the effects of a peculiar disorder of body, or owing to some disturbance of the mind. They whose nervous system has been long relaxed, who have had severe domestic trials, or have been greatly affected by extraordinary occurrences, know this to be true by their own experience. But however this may be, there have been, and possibly may be still, dreams that have no manner of dependence on the indisposition of the body, or other natural cause, but seem to bring a divine sanction with them, and make peculiar impressions on the party though this was more frequent before the canon of Scripture was closed than now. God spoke to his people in a dream, in a vision of the night. Witness the subject of our present meditation, a dream of the patriarch Jacob's, when going forth as a poor pilgrim with a staff in his hand, from his father's house, deprived of his mother's company and instruction, persecuted by an elder brother, without attendants or necessaries, only leaning on an invisible power. I need not inform you in how extraordinary a way he got the blessing, which provoked his brother to such a degree, as determined him to be the death of Jacob, as soon as ever his aged father dropped. To what a height did this wicked man's envy rise when he said, "The days of mourning for my father will soon come;" and what then? Why, though I have some compassion for the old man, and therefore will not lay violent hands upon my brother while my father is alive, yet I am resolved to kill him before my father is cold in his grave.

MAY 26

Liberty to Captives

He has sent me to proclaim liberty to the ...

LUKE 4:18B

We are "to preach liberty to the captives, to proclaim the acceptable year of the Lord; sound the jubilee trumpet, and tell them the year of release is come;" we are to tell them that Jesus can make them happy –But, pray, if we are to preach, what are the creatures to do that see their need of this salvation? I will tell you – they are to believe. "He who believes and is baptized" – The grand topics Christ's ministers are to preach are repentance towards God and faith in our Lord Jesus Christ. The men of the world fancy they have believed already, and some of them lift up their heads and say, "Thank God, we have believed ever since we were born;" and in one sense many people believe, but in what sense? Just as the devil believes; they believe and until continue devils in their carnal state; that is, they assent to the gospel, they assent to it as a thing that is credible. This is our school definition of faith – and I believe there are thousands that call themselves Christians who do not believe a thousandth part of what the devil does. The devil believes more than an Arian, for the Arian does not believe Christ to be God. The devil says, "I know who you are, the holy one of God." The devil will rise up in judgment against him. He believes more than a Socinian, who believes Jesus Christ to be no more than an extraordinary man; and he believes more of Jesus Christ than thousands of professors do, who are neither Arians nor Socinians. There are a thousand things in the Bible they are ashamed to own it. The furthest that they go is to assent to the creed, to the Lord's Prayer or the Ten Commandments.

MAY 27

From the Gallows

So faith comes from hearing, and hearing through the word of Christ.

ROMANS 10:17

When we are once convinced of our need and helplessness and of Jesus being a Redeemer that is mighty and willing to save, a poor soul then throws himself upon this Jesus, receives him, ventures upon him, believes the word, and by thus venturing on the promise, receives the thing promised. But then, where there is true faith that will, my dear hearers, be attended with salvation … He receives everything that God can give to complete his whole salvation. What is it a poor sinner wants to be saved from? O, sin, sin, the guilt of sin. The first conviction brings the creatures to God by force; there are very few that are drawn by love entirely and I seldom find any of those that have been drawn by love, but have had dreadful conflicts afterwards for either before or after conversion; our hearts must be ploughed up, or we shall never be prepared for the kingdom of heaven. You shall be saved from the painful guilt of sin – what is that? Why, the common prayer book will tell you, in the communion office: "the remembrance of our sins is grievous to us, and the burden of them is intolerable" … No matter where we preach, so that sinners feel Christ's power in delivering them from this burden, which certainly implies a consciousness of pardon. I do not think any poor creatures who were freed from their bonds would have believed it had they not seen the king's pardon – Why, they say, here is his majesty's pardon, he takes and receives it with joy, and is now freed from the gallows.

MAY 28

Fresh Winds

The elder to the beloved Gaius, whom I love in truth ... that you may be in good health.

3 JOHN 1-2A

When we are in high spirits we think people might do what they would, but when brought down ourselves we cannot; but notwithstanding, even though Gaius's body was in this condition, his soul prospered so eminently, so very eminently, that the apostle could not think it a greater mercy, or the church a greater blessing, than that his bodily health might be as vigorous as the health of his soul. I remember the great colonel Gardiner, who had the honor of being killed in his country's cause, closes one of his last letters to me with wishing I might enjoy a thriving soul in a healthy body; but this is peculiar to the followers of Jesus; they find the soul prospers most when the body is worst; and observe, he wishes him a prospering body above all things that he might have joy and health with a prosperous soul; for if we have a good heart, and good health at the same, and our hearts are alive to God, we go on with a fresh gale. The soul of man in general must be made a partaker of a divine life, before it can be said to prosper at all. The words of our text are particularly applicable to a renewed heart, to one that is really alive to God. When a tree is dead, we do not so much as expect leaves from it, nor to see any beauty at all in a plant or flower that we know is absolutely dead; and therefore the foundation of the apostle's wish lies here, that the soul of Gaius, and consequently the souls of all true believers, have life communicated to them from the Spirit of the living God – such a life may God of his infinite mercy impart to each of us!

MAY 29

Be not Murderers

Do not give dogs what is holy, and do not throw your pearls before pigs, lest they trample them underfoot and turn to attack you.

MATTHEW 7:6

O, my dear hearers, let me plead and entreat you. If that would do, I would go down on my knees. If that would do, I would come down from the pulpit, I would hang on your necks, I would not let you go, I would offer myself to be trodden under your feet … Use me as you will, I am a poor sinner; and if I were to be killed a thousand ways, I suffer no more than my reward as an unprofitable servant of God. But do not trample the dear Jesus under foot; what has he done to you! Was it any harm to leave his Father's bosom, come down and die, and plead for sinners? See him yonder hang on the tree! Behold him with his arm stretched out! See him all of a bloody gore, and in his last agony preaching love! Would you give him a fresh stab? Are there any of you here that think the sword did not pierce him enough, that they did not knock the briers and thorns into his head deep enough? And will you give him the other slash, the other thorns? Will you pierce him afresh, and go away without believing he is love? I cannot help it – I would be free from the blood of you all – Oh, that you may not damn your own souls! Do not be murderers; nor, like Esau, sell your birthright for a mess of pottage! May God convince and convert you; God help those that never believed, to believe; God help those that have believed, to believe more; that they may experience more and more this salvation, until faith is turned into vision and hope into fruition.

MAY 30

Over Jordan

And they departed and went through the villages, preaching the gospel and healing everywhere.

Luke 9:6

We are to preach the gospel to every creature. Here is our commission – "to every creature." I suppose the apostles were not to see every creature because they did not go into all nations; they had particular districts; but wherever they did go, they preached. Did you ever hear Paul, or any of the apostles send away a congregation without a sermon? No, when turned out of the temple, they preached in the highways, hedges, streets, and lanes of the city; they went to the waterside, where Lydia was caught. My brothers, we have got a commission from Christ; and not only a commission, but we have a command "to preach to every creature;" that is, to all that are willing to hear. "If anyone has ears to hear, let him hear" (Mark 4:23). If some shall say that they will not come if we do preach, would to God we tried to get them – we are to preach glad tidings of salvation; to tell a poor benighted world, lying in the wicked one, the devil, their state and condition. We are to tell them, "God is love;" to tell them that God loves them better than they do themselves. We must preach the law, but not leave the people there. We must tell them how Moses brings them to the borders of Canaan, and then tell them of a glorious Joshua that will carry them over Jordan; first, to show them their wants, all, then point out to them a Jesus that can supply, and more than supply, all their wants. Thus, we are "to tell every creature;" and it is for this that people stone gospel preachers.

MAY 31

Fiery Trials

Beloved, think it not strange concerning the fiery trial which is to try you, as though some strange thing happened to you.
1 PETER 4:12 KJV

O may God put me into one furnace after another, that my soul may be transparent; that I may see God as he is. My brothers, we need to be purged; how apt are we to want to go to heaven upon a feather bed, without any cross or trial. Many go lying upon beds of pain and languishing, which is the King's highway to heaven. You know there are some ways in London called the king's road, and they are finely graveled and well kept, but the King's road to heaven is strewed with crosses and afflictions. We are all apt to think well of being Christians; it is very pretty talking of being Christians until we are put into one furnace after another. We are not to think it a strange thing when we are tried in the fire. What must we do? Well, since we are in the fire, we must thank our corruptions for it. God will not put you or me into the fire were it not for some thing that must be purged away from us; you see, the grand thing is to learn to glorify God in the fire. "The Lord knows how to rescue the Godly from trials, and to keep the unrighteous under punishment until the Day of Judgment" (2 Pet. 2:9).

JUNE 1

All our Faith

But let him ask in faith, with no doubting, for the one who doubts is like a wave of the sea that is driven and tossed by the wind.

JAMES 1:6

All the faith of God's people, says Bishop Hall, is but mere infidelity; and all the love of the people of God is but mere hatred, compared with God's love, or that which his law justly requires. Therefore it is said, "beloved of the Lord," and that because if ever we love God, he first loved us, which is what Moses' very expression means. As streams flow from the fountain, so they shall return to it. Hence the apostle says, "To those who are called, beloved in God the Father and kept for Jesus Christ" (Jude 1). I know very well the mystics talk of loving God with a love for himself only, without any respect to the creature at all; that is, we must love God without any regard at all for what God has done for us. No, some go so far as to say, that if we do not so love God, we are not converted, though we have as much grace as we can have; that we do not love God properly until we love him for what he is, not what he has done for us. I truly believe, the angels do not love God in that manner; and we cannot love God until we are made partakers of a divine nature, and have eyes given us to see his glory. "But you, O Lord, are a shield about me, my glory, and the lifter of my head" (Ps. 3:3).

JUNE 2

Imputed Righteousness

And there is salvation in no one else, for there is no other name under heaven given among men by which we must be saved.

ACTS 4:12

The imputed righteousness of Jesus Christ is a comforting doctrine to all Christians. To you, sinners, who ask what you must do to be saved, how uncomfortable would it be to tell you, by good works, when perhaps you have never done one good work in all your life. This would be driving you to despair. Indeed, no: "Believe in the Lord Jesus, and you will be saved," (Acts 16:31). Come to Jesus by faith, and he will receive you. You have no righteousness of your own to depend on. If you are saved, it is by the righteousness of Christ, through his atonement and sacrifice for sin. His righteousness must be imputed to you, otherwise you cannot be saved. There is no difference between you, by nature, and the greatest criminal; the difference made is all owing to the free, rich, and undeserved grace of God. Come by faith to Christ. Do not come, Pharisee-like, telling God what you have done, how often you have gone to church, received the sacrament, fasted, prayed, or the like; no, come to Christ as poor, lost, undone sinners, and he will accept you. Do not be rich in spirit, proud and exalted, for no blessing attends such; but be poor in spirit, for theirs is the kingdom of God (Matt. 5:3). There is no salvation but by Jesus Christ; there is no other name given under heaven among men whereby we may be saved, but that of the Lord Jesus (Acts 4:12). God outside of Christ is a consuming fire; therefore strive for an interest in his Son. Take him on the terms offered to you in the gospel, and lay hold on him by faith.

JUNE 3

A Call to Christ

Wretched man that I am! Who will deliver me from this body of death? Thanks be to God through Jesus Christ our Lord!"
ROMANS 7:24-25

I do not preach despair; I despair of no one, when I consider that God had mercy on such a wretch as I, who was running in a full career to hell. I was hastening there, but Jesus Christ passed by, and stopped me. Jesus Christ passed by me while I was in my blood, polluted with filth; he passed by me, and bid me live. Thus I am a monument of God's free grace, and therefore, my brethren, I despair of none of you. I am not speaking now out of a false humility, a pretended sanctity, as the Pharisees call it; no, the truth in Jesus Christ I speak. Therefore, men and devils, do your worst; I have a gracious Master who will protect me. It is his work that I am engaged in, and Jesus Christ will carry me above their rage. To those who reject this Master, remember that you have had Jesus Christ offered to you; I offer Jesus Christ to every one of you. Perhaps you may not regard it, but Jesus Christ is wherever his people meet in sincerity and truth to worship him. He is not confined to church walls. Very many of you know this and he has met you. Therefore you may believe on him with greater confidence.

JUNE 4

Wolves in Sheep's Clothing

Vindicate me, O God, and defend my cause against an ungodly people, from the deceitful and unjust man deliver me!

PSALM 43:1

Beloved in the Lord, your most dangerous and formidable enemies are the kind of men who render vice mixed with apparent virtue, and clothe wickedness in the apparel of righteousness. "Beware of false prophets, who come to you in sheep's clothing but inwardly are ravenous wolves" (Matt. 7:15). This perverse generation will ensnare you into ungodliness, by seeming oppositions to vice, and allow you to swallow what seems to be virtue and righteousness like an emetic, only to vomit forth the reality of them. They paint black, white; and the white they convert into black. Not content with seeming what they are not, they labor to make you what they are. Righteousness and wickedness they interweave artfully, capable of deceiving the very elect, and difficult for the most discerning to unravel, as almsgiving and greed, pride and humility, temperance and luxury, are blended together with dexterity. For example, the worldly-minded man, who labors to deceive you, gains credit enough with you to establish this maxim, that all superlative degrees of almsgiving, are great sins, and that a man must never sell all he has and give it to the poor, because some may have families of their own, and ought to make sufficient provision for them, according to that proverb, "Charity begins at home," when no one, at least scarce any one, is wise enough to know when he has a sufficiency. Oh Lord, which are we to believe, these men, or thee? If thou dost deceive us, why dost thou threaten us with punishments if we do not heed thee? And if the world is deceitful, shall we not flee from it, and cleave to thee?

JUNE 5

Undivided Devotion

No one can serve two masters ... You cannot serve God and money.

MATTHEW 6:24

What people does Solomon address when he says, "Be not righteous over much; neither make thyself over wise: why shouldest thou destroy thyself?" (Eccles. 7:16, KJV). Plainly not to the wicked, for besides that it would have been an unnecessary precaution, he turns to these in the next verse with another kind of warning: "Be not over much wicked, neither be thou foolish: why shouldest thou die before thy time?" Was it then to the righteous, in a common way, that is, to such as content themselves with the observance of the absolute essentials of God's laws? It cannot possibly be supposed that the persons spoken to are perfectly righteous men, since we can never be righteous enough, much less perfectly righteous, until we come up to the perfection of our Heavenly Father. The Apostle John says, "If we say we have no sin, we deceive ourselves, and the truth is not in us" (1 John 1:8). It remains, that the persons spoken to in the text, are such, only as persisting steadfastly in a firm adherence to all the essential laws of God, not content themselves with the practice of common virtues in a common degree, but live in a perpetual habit of desires, struggles, and yearnings towards an intimate union with Christ, the perfection of righteousness. They are not of the number of those righteous with indifference, who would blend the service of God and mammon, who would have Christ and the world for their masters, and halting between two, like the children of Israel of old, with their faces to heaven, and their hearts to the earth, are neither hot nor cold. Alas, that they would be cold or hot! But the Lord says, "because you are lukewarm, and neither hot nor cold, I will spit you out of my mouth" (Rev. 3:16).

JUNE 6

Remember your Creator now

But God said to him, "Fool! This night your soul is required of you,"

LUKE 12:20

The wanton prodigal, who is spending his substance in riotous living, cries, "A little more pleasure, a little more sensuality, and then I will be sober in earnest!" The covetous worldly one, that employs all his care and pains in "heaping up riches, though he cannot tell who shall gather them," does not flatter himself that this will do always, but hopes, with the rich fool in the gospel, to lay up goods for a few more years on earth, and then he will begin to lay up treasures in heaven. In short, thus it is that most people are convinced of the necessity of religion some time or another, but then, like Felix, they put it off suitably to their convictions, until what they imagine a more convenient season. If we would be so humble as to be guided by the experience and counsel of the wisest men, we would learn that youth is the fittest season for religion. Solomon says, "Remember also your Creator in the days of your youth" (Eccles. 12:1). By the word remember, we are not to understand a bare, speculative remembrance, or calling to mind, (for that, like a dead faith, will profit us nothing) but such a remembrance as will constrain us to obedience, and oblige us, out of gratitude, to perform all that the Lord our God will require of us. Forgetting God implies a total neglect of our duty, and in like manner, remembering him signifies a perfect performance of it. When Solomon says, "Remember also your Creator in the days of your youth," it is the same as if he had said, "Keep God's commandments," or in other words, "Be religious in the days of your youth," thereby implying that youth is the most proper season for it.

JUNE 7

Receiving Christ's Righteousness

His (Abraham's) faith was "counted to him as righteousness." But the words "it was counted to him" were not written for his sake alone, but for ours also. It will be counted to us who believe in him who raised from the dead Jesus our Lord, who was delivered up for our trespasses and raised for our justification.

ROMANS 4:22-25

Some who at first would appear to be friends of morality say that the doctrine of an imputed righteousness is destructive to good works, and leads to licentiousness. And who are the persons that generally urge this objection? Are they men full of faith, and men really concerned for good works? No, although there are a few or no exceptions, it is notorious that they are generally men of corrupt minds, reprobate concerning the faith. The best title I can give them is that of profane moralists, or moralists falsely so called. I appeal to the experience of the present as well as past ages, whether iniquity did not most abound, where the doctrine of Christ's whole personal righteousness was most seldom mentioned. Arminian principles, being anti-Christian, always did, and always will, lead to anti-Christian practices. Never was there a reformation brought about in the church without preaching the doctrine of an imputed righteousness. This, as that man of God, Martin Luther, calls it, is the article by which the church stands or falls. And though the preachers of this doctrine are generally branded with the names of Antinomians and deceivers by those on the other side, yet, I believe, if the truth of the doctrine, on both sides, was to be judged of by the lives of the preachers and professors of it, on our side the question would have the advantage in every way.

JUNE 8

Followers of Christ

Whoever exalts himself will be humbled, and whoever humbles himself will be exalted.

MATTHEW 23:12

None of us can boast of having attained the summit of perfection, although he who is the farthest from the appetites of the flesh is nearest to it, and he who is the lowliest in his own esteem stands the highest. Wherefore, as many of us as have made any advances towards Christ and his kingdom, "Nevertheless, whereto we have already attained, let us walk by the same rule, let us mind the same thing" (Phil. 3:16, KJV). Brethren and sisters, let us not walk then according to the ways of the world, but let us be followers of Christ together. And if any creature, even an angel of light, should presume to teach you any other gospel than that which I have here taught you, let him be accursed. Scripture says, "For many, of whom I have often told you and now tell you even with tears, walk as enemies of the cross of Christ. Their end is destruction, their god is their belly, and they glory in their shame, with minds set on earthly things. But our citizenship is in heaven, and from it we await a Savior, the Lord Jesus Christ, who will transform our lowly body to be like his glorious body, by the power that enables him even to subject all things to himself" (Phil. 3:18-21), even the stubborn heart of our perverse adversary.

JUNE 9

Partakers of Piety

For a day in thy courts is better than a thousand. I had rather be a doorkeeper in the house of my God, than to dwell in the tents of wickedness.

Psalm 84:10

What! Will not all the arguments I have mentioned, prevail you to leave your husks, and return home to eat of the fatted calf? What! Will you thus requite our Savior's love? That should be far from you! Did he come down and shed his precious blood to deliver you from the power of sin, and will you spend your youthful strength and vigor in the service of it, and then think to serve Christ when you can follow your lusts no longer? Is it right that many who are endowed with excellent gifts, and are thereby qualified to be supports and ornaments of our church, should, notwithstanding, forget the God who gave them these gifts, and employ themselves in things that will not profit? O why will they not arise and be zealous for the Lord of hosts? Doubtless, when death overtakes them, they will wish they had, and what hinders them to begin now! Do you think that anyone has ever yet repented that he began to be religious too soon? But how many, on the contrary, have repented that they began when it was almost too late? We may well imagine that young Samuel now rejoices that he was so soon at the tabernacle of the Lord. And Timothy, that from a young child he knew the Holy Scriptures. If you wish to be partakers of their joy, let me persuade you to be partakers of their piety.

JUNE 10

Be Strong in the Lord

Finally, be strong in the LORD and in the strength of his might.

EPHESIANS 6:10

Be ever mindful of the words that have been spoken to us by the apostles of our Lord and Savior: "Therefore, brothers, be all the more diligent to make your calling and election sure, for if you practice these qualities you will never fall (2 Peter 1:10). "Therefore let anyone who thinks that he stands take heed lest he fall" (1 Cor. 10:12). "Mind not high things, but condescend to men of low estate. Be not wise in your own conceits" (Rom. 12:16). "Yet in your case, beloved, we feel sure of better things – things that belong to salvation. For God is not unjust so as to overlook your work and the love that you have shown for his name in serving the saints … And we desire each of you to show the same earnestness to have the full assurance of hope until the end, (Heb. 6:9-11). It is true that we have many difficulties to encounter and many powerful enemies to overcome before we can receive possession of the Promised Land. We have an artful devil, an ensnaring world, and above all, the treachery of our own hearts, to withstand and strive against. "Because strait is the gate, and narrow is the way, which leadeth unto life" (Matt. 7:14). But wherefore should we fear, since he that is with us is far more powerful than all who are against us? Have we not already experienced his almighty power, in enabling us to conquer some difficulties that seemed as insurmountable then, as those we struggle with now? Cannot he, who delivered us out of the paws of those bears and lions, preserve us also from being hurt by the strongest Goliath?

JUNE 11

Renouncing our own Righteousness

And be found in him, not having a righteousness of my own that comes from the law, but that which comes through faith in Christ ...

PHILIPPIANS 3:9

In all lawful marriages, it is absolutely necessary that the parties to be joined together be legally freed from all pre-engagements. The same is true with respect to the man. So if either party is betrothed and promised, though not actually married to another, the marriage is not lawful until that pre-engagement is fairly and mutually dissolved. It is also this way between Jesus and us. For, we are all by nature born under and wedded to the law as a covenant of works. This is why we are so fond of trying to establish a righteousness of our own. It is as natural for us to do this, as it is to breathe. Our first parents, Adam and Eve, even after the covenant of grace was revealed to them, reached out their hands, and would again have taken hold of the tree of life, if God had not driven them out of paradise. Even gracious souls, who are inwardly renewed, find a strong propensity this way in their old man. "Do and live," is the native language of a proud self-righteous heart. But we must be divorced from our old husband, the law; we must renounce our own righteousness as dross for the excellence of the knowledge of Christ Jesus our Lord. When Paul began to experience the power of Christ's resurrection, we find him, in his epistle to the Philippians, renouncing all his external privileges, and pharisaical righteousness: "Indeed, I count everything as loss because of the surpassing worth of knowing Christ Jesus my Lord" (Phil. 3:8). We must be dead to the law and count all external privileges and our most splendid performances as "dung and dross, for the excellency of the knowledge of Jesus Christ our Lord."

JUNE 12

Without Spot or Wrinkle

Likewise, my brothers, you also have died to the law through the body of Christ, so that you may belong to another, to him who has been raised from the dead, in order that we may bear fruit for God.

ROMANS 7:4

All hail, those who are the Lamb's bride! For you are all glorious within, and comely, through the comeliness your heavenly Bridegroom has put upon you. Your garment is of wrought gold, and before long the King will bring you forth with a raiment of needlework. He will present you blameless before his Father without spot or wrinkle, or any such thing. Meanwhile, it will be well with you, and you will be happy, you who belong to Jesus Christ, for all that Christ has is yours. He is made of God to you, "wisdom, and righteousness, and sanctification, and redemption" (1 Cor. 1:30, KJV). "Whether Paul or Apollos or Cephas or the world or life or death or the present or the future – all are yours" (1 Cor. 3:22). All his attributes are engaged for your preservation, and all things shall work together for your good, who love God, and by being thus married to the Lord Jesus, give an evident proof that you are called according to his purpose. What do you say? When you meditate on these things, are you not frequently ready to cry out, "What shall I render unto the Lord for all these mercies, which, of his free unmerited grace, he has been pleased to bestow upon me?" For though you are dead to the law as a covenant of works, yet you are alive to the law as a rule of life, and are in or under the law, to your glorious Savior Jesus Christ.

JUNE 13

Marred Clay

For to set the mind on the flesh is death, but to set the mind on the Spirit is life and peace.

Romans 8:6

Being made in the image of God, undoubtedly before the fall man had no other will but his Maker's. God's will and Adam's, were like music in unison. There was not the least disunion or discord between them. But now man has a will directly contrary to God's will, as light is contrary to darkness, or heaven to hell. We all bring into the world a carnal mind, which is not only an enemy to God, but enmity itself, which is not subject to the law of God, neither indeed can it be (Rom. 8:7). Many show much zeal in talking against sin in others, but know that less discerned self-will sits daily in the temple of your heart, exalting itself above God and saying of Christ himself, "We will not have this man to reign over us." God's people, whose spiritual senses are exercised, and whose eyes are opened to see the abominations that are in their hearts, frequently feel this to their sorrow. In spite of all their watchfulness and care, this enmity bubbles up from time to time. When they are under the pressure of some sharp affliction, a long desertion, or a tedious night of temptation, they often find something within rising in rebellion against the all-wise disposals of divine providence, and saying unto God their heavenly Father, "What doest thou?" This makes them to cry, "Wretched man that I am! Who will deliver me from this body of death?" (Rom. 7:24). The renewed soul groans thus, being burdened, but as for the natural and unawakened man, self-will and every other evil reigns in his soul, and proves, whether he knows and will confess it or not, that with respect to the disorders of his will, as well as his understanding, man is only a piece of marred clay.

JUNE 14

Perfect Obedience

Who, being in the form of God, thought it not robbery to be equal with God: But made himself of no reputation, and took upon him the form of a servant ...

PHILIPPIANS 2:6-7

It pleased God to create man after his own image. So infinite was his condescension, that although he might have insisted on the everlasting obedience of man and his posterity, yet he was pleased to oblige himself by a covenant, made with his own creatures, upon condition of an un-sinning obedience, to give them immortality and eternal life. For when it is said, "For in the day that you eat of it you shall surely die" (Gen. 2:17), we may infer that so long as he was obedient, and did not eat thereof, he should surely live. Genesis 3 gives us a mournful account of how our first parents broke this covenant, and therefore needed a better righteousness than their own to procure their future acceptance with God. For what must they do? They were as much under a covenant of works as ever. And though, after their disobedience, they were without strength, yet they were obliged to continue to do all things which the Lord required of them perfectly, and to also make satisfaction to God's infinitely offended justice for the breach of which they were already guilty. Here opens the amazing scene of God's love to man: what man could not do, Jesus Christ, the Son of his Father's love, undertakes to do for him. In his human nature he obeyed and fulfilled the whole moral law in our stead, and also died a painful death upon the cross, becoming a curse instead of those whom the Father had given to him. Being God and man in one person, he wrought out a full, perfect, and sufficient righteousness for all to whom it was imputed.

JUNE 15

One with Christ

I have been crucified with Christ. It is no longer I who live, but Christ who lives in me. And the life I now live in the flesh I live by faith in the Son of God, who loved me and gave himself for me.

GALATIANS 2:20

When God brought Eve to Adam, he received her with joy, and said, "This at last is bone of my bones and flesh of my flesh" (Gen. 2:23). Adam and Eve were one flesh, and were to have one heart. The same terms are used in Scripture to express the believer's union with Jesus Christ. We are called Christians after Christ's name, and made partakers of Christ's nature. Out of his fullness believers receive grace for grace. O infinite condescension! O ineffable union! Hence it is that believers are said to be members of his body, of his flesh, and of his bones. Hence it is, that the apostle, speaking of himself, says, "It is no longer I who live, but Christ who lives in me" (Gal. 2:20). What an expression! How much it comprehends! The question was given to the Corinthians: "Do you not realize this about yourselves, that Jesus Christ is in you? – unless indeed you fail to meet the test!" (2 Cor. 13:5). Agreeable to this is Colossians 1:27: "Christ in you, the hope of glory." Therefore in communion, our church directs the minister to acquaint all those who receive the sacrament worthily, that they are one with Christ, and Christ with them; they dwell in Christ, and Christ in them. These words deserve to be written in letters of gold.

JUNE 16

Change of Nature

For if you live according to the flesh you will die, but if by the Spirit you put to death the deeds of the body, you will live.

ROMANS 8:13

By the word religion, I do not mean a bare, outward profession, or naming the name of Christ. We are told that many who have even prophesied and cast out devils in his name will still be rejected by him in the last day. Nor do I mean being admitted into Christ's church by baptism, for many false believers might pass for religious persons, who were baptized. No, I mean a thorough, real, inward change of nature, wrought in us by the powerful operation of the Holy Spirit, nourished in our hearts by a constant use of the means of grace, evidenced by a good life, and bringing forth the fruits of the Spirit. The attaining of this real, inward religion, is a work of such great difficulty that Nicodemus, a learned doctor and teacher in Israel, thought it impossible, and therefore ignorantly asked Christ, "How can this thing be?" And truly, to rectify a disordered nature, to mortify our corrupt passions, to turn darkness to light, to put off the old man, and put on the new, and thereby to have the image of God re-stamped upon the soul, or, in one word, "to be born again," must be owned by man to be impossible. Indeed, it is true that Christ's yoke is said to be easy or gracious, and his burden light, but it is only for those to whom grace has been given to bear and draw in it. The spiritual birth is attended with its pangs, as well as the natural. For they that have experienced it (and they only are the proper judges), can acquaint you that in all things that are dear to corrupt nature, we must deny ourselves, lest, after all, when we come to the birth, we should lack strength to bring forth.

JUNE 17

Sweet Effectual Persuasion

But the Scripture imprisoned everything under sin, so that the promise by faith in Jesus Christ might be given to those who believe.

GALATIANS 3:22

Before a marriage among us can stand as being lawfully good, both parties must not only be freed from all pre-engagements, but also there must be a mutual consent on both sides; we are not used to marrying people against their wills. This practice is what the Jews called betrothing or espousing, something which occurs previous to the solemnity of marriage. Thus we find that the Virgin Mary was said to be espoused to Joseph, before they actually came together (Matt. 1:18). And thus it is among us. Both parties are previously agreed, and as it were espoused to each other, before we publish an announcement of marriage concerning them. And so it will be in the spiritual marriage between Jesus Christ and our souls. Before we are actually married, or united to him by faith, we must be made willing people in the day of God's power; we must be sweetly and effectually persuaded by the Holy Spirit of God that the glorious Emmanuel is willing to accept us just as we are, and also that we are willing to accept him on his own terms, yes, on any terms. And when once it comes to this, regenerate souls are married by faith to Jesus Christ and partake of a real, vital union with him.

JUNE 18

Fit for Heaven

Therefore, if anyone is in Christ, he is a new creation. The old has passed away; behold, the new has come.

2 CORINTHIANS 5:17

All of us hope after death to go to heaven. My heart's desire and prayer to God is that you all may have mansions prepared there. But let me tell you, if you were to see heaven opened now, and Christ himself giving you an invitation to come to heaven, heaven would be no heaven to you, it would even be a hell to your souls, unless you were first prepared for a proper enjoyment of it here on earth. "For what communion hath light with darkness?" People generally form strange ideas of heaven. And because Scripture, in condescension to the weakness of our capacities, describes it by images taken from earthly delights and human grandeur, therefore they carry their thoughts no higher. But permit me to tell you, and God grant it may sink deep into your hearts! Heaven is rather a state than a place, and consequently, unless you are previously disposed by a suitable state of mind, you could not be happy even in heaven itself. For what is grace, but glory militant? What is glory but grace triumphant? One author said, "Holiness, happiness, and heaven are only three different words for one thing." A great man said on his deathbed, "I am changing my place, but not my company." To make us fit to be blissful partakers of such heavenly company, our depraved natures must undergo a moral change: our understandings must be enlightened; our wills, reason, and consciences must be renewed; our affections must be fixed upon things above; and because flesh and blood cannot inherit the kingdom of heaven, this corruptible must put on incorruption, this mortal put on immortality. Old things must literally pass away, and behold all things, the body as well as the faculties of the soul, must become new.

JUNE 19

Unsearchable Riches

Their Redeemer is strong; the Lord of hosts is his name.
JEREMIAH 50:34

What infinitely great honor and riches has the God and Father of our Lord Jesus conferred on his only Son, to whom I now invite every sinner! To you, therefore, I call, assuring you that there is everything in Jesus that your hearts can desire, or hunger and thirst after. God the Father has given Jesus a name above every name; he has on his vesture and on his thigh a name written, "The King of kings, and the Lord of lords," and we are told, "The Lord of hosts is his name." And he does not have an empty title, but power equivalent, for he is a Prince, as well as a Savior. "All power is given unto him, both in heaven and on earth." "The God of the whole earth he shall be called." The government of men, of the church, and of devils, is put upon his shoulders: "Thrones, principalities, and powers, are made subject unto him; by him kings reign, and princes decree justice; he setteth up one, and putteth down another; and of his kingdom there shall be no end." Will riches induce you to come to Jesus? Why then, I can tell you that the riches of Jesus are infinite. Ephesians 3:8 says, "To me, though I am the very least of all the saints, this grace was given, to preach to the Gentiles the unsearchable riches of Christ." I appeal to you that are his saints, whether you have not found this true by happy experience; and though some of you may have been acquainted with him thirty, forty or fifty years ago, do you not find that his riches are yet unsearchable, and as much past finding out, as they were the very first moment in which you gave him your hearts?

JUNE 20

Delightful Remembrance

Though you have not seen him, you love him.

1 PETER 1:8

Must I tell anyone who is married that they must go to the university and learn the languages, before they can tell whether they are married or not? Or if their marriage was to be doubted could they not bring their certificates to certify the time and place of their marriage, and the minister that joined them together in that holy state? If you are indeed married to Jesus Christ, though you may be unlearned, can you not tell me the rise, progress, and consummation of the spiritual marriage between Jesus Christ and your soul? Do you not know the time when you were first under the drawings of the Father? Tell me, O man or woman, do you not know the time, or at least that there was a time, when the blessed Spirit of God stripped you of the fig-leaves of your own righteousness, hunted you out of the trees of the garden of your performances, forced you from the embraces of your old husband, the law, and made you abhor your own righteousness? Can you not remember when Jesus appeared to you as altogether lovely, mighty and willing to save? Can you not reflect upon a season when your own stubborn heart was made to bend, and you were made willing to embrace him, as freely offered to you in the everlasting gospel? And can you not, with unspeakable pleasure, reflect on a certain point of time that you could say, in a rapture of holy surprise and ecstasy of divine love, "My Lord and my God! My Beloved is mine, and I am his! I know that my Redeemer liveth." These are transactions not able to be forgotten, and the day of our espousals is, generally, a very remarkable day, and a day to be had in everlasting remembrance.

JUNE 21

Freedom in Service

O LORD, I am your servant; I am your servant, the son of your maidservant. You have loosed my bonds.

PSALM 116:16

All believers, whether they are men or women, ought to be subject to Jesus Christ, for he is the Head of the church. He has bought her by his blood. Believers therefore are not their own, but are under the highest obligation to glorify and obey Christ in their bodies and their souls, which are his. But what is more, we find perfect freedom in his service. His commandments are holy, just and good. Therefore it is your highest privilege, O believers, to submit to and obey them. Earthly husbands may be so mean as to impose some things upon their wives, merely to show their authority, but it is not so with Jesus Christ. He can, and does impose nothing except that which is conducive to our present and future good. In suffering for Jesus Christ there is a present and unspeakable reward. Therefore, I may say to believers, as the blessed virgin said to the servants at the marriage in Cana, "Whatsoever he saith unto you, do it" (John 2:5, KJV). Jesus says, "For my yoke is easy, and my burden is light" (Matt. 11:30). I believe that it could easily be proved in a few minutes, that all the problems that are now in the world, whether in church or state, are because of a lack of being universally, unanimously, cheerfully and perseveringly conformed to the laws and example of our Lord and Savior Jesus Christ.

JUNE 22

The Spirit on our Souls

According to the foreknowledge of God the Father, in the sanctification of the Spirit, for obedience to Jesus Christ and for sprinkling with his blood:

1 PETER 1:2

The heavenly potter, this blessed agent, is the Almighty Spirit of God, the third person in the most adorable Trinity, co-essential with the Father and the Son. This is that Spirit which at the beginning of time moved on the face of the waters, when nature lay in universal chaos. This was the Spirit that overshadowed the Virgin Mary before Jesus was born of her, and this same Spirit must come and move upon the chaos of our souls before we can be called the sons and daughters of God. This is what John the Baptist calls being "baptized with the Holy Ghost," without which his and all other baptisms, whether infant or adult, avail nothing. This is that fire which I pray for the Lord to kindle this day in every reader with an un-renewed heart. As for the extraordinary operations of the Holy Spirit such as the working of miracles, or speaking with divers kinds of tongues, they have long ceased. But as for this miracle of miracles, turning the soul to God by the more ordinary operations of the Holy Spirit, this still abides, and will abide until time itself will be no more. It is he that sanctifies all the elect people of God. True believers are born from above, "not of blood nor of the flesh nor of the will of man, but of God" (John 1:13). Their second, as well as their first creation is purely divine. Ephesians 4:24 says, "Put on the new man, which after God is created in righteousness and true holiness".

JUNE 23

Nearness with Christ

No longer do I call you servants, for the servant does not know what his master is doing; but I have called you friends, for all that I have heard from my Father I have made known to you.

JOHN 15:15

Although believers, by nature, are far from God, and are children of wrath even as others, yet it is amazing to think how close they are brought to him again by the blood of Jesus Christ. Eye hath not seen, nor ear heard, neither hath it entered into the heart of any man living, fully to conceive the nearness and dearness of that relation in which they stand to their common Head. He is not ashamed to call them brothers and sisters. "Behold," says the blessed Jesus in his days on earth, "my mother and my brethren." And again, after his resurrection, "Go tell my brethren." Sometimes he is pleased to term believers his friends. "Henceforth call I you no longer servants, but friends." "Our friend Lazarus sleepeth." What is a friend? Why there is a friend that is nearer than a brother, even as near as one's own soul? And "thy friend, (says God, in the book of Deuteronomy) which is as thy own soul." These are kind and endearing appellations that undoubtedly speak of a very near and ineffably intimate union between the Lord Jesus and the true, living members of his mystical body! In respect to nearness and dearness, this relationship exceeds all others. I mean that of a Husband. "For thy Maker is thine husband; the Lord of hosts is his name; and thy Redeemer the Holy One of Israel; the God of the whole earth shall he be called" (Isa. 54:5, KJV).

JUNE 24

Warning against worldliness

But seek ye first the kingdom of God, and his righteousness; and all these things shall be added unto you.

MATTHEW 6:33

Worldly-mindedness, my brothers and sisters, is another rock against which we are in danger of splitting. For, if other sins have slain their thousands of professing Christians, this has slain its ten thousands. I do not need to appeal to past ages; your own experience, no doubt, has furnished you with many unhappy instances of young men, who, "after they had escaped the pollutions which are in the world through lust, and had tasted the good word of life," and endured for a season, while under the tuition and inspection of others, yet when they have come to be their own masters, through a lack of faith, and through too great an earnestness in "laboring for the meat which perisheth," have cast off their first love, been again entangled with the world, and returned like the dog to his vomit, and like the sow that was washed to her wallowing in the mire. You would therefore do well, my brethren, frequently to remind each other of this dangerous snare, and to exhort one another to begin, pursue, and end your Christian warfare, in a thorough renunciation of the world, and worldly tempers; so that, when you are obliged by providence to provide for yourselves and those of your respective households, you may continue to walk by faith, and still "seek first the kingdom of God and his righteousness," not doubting that all other things, upon your honest industry and endeavors, shall be added unto you.

JUNE 25

Glory in Christ Alone

Be not wise in your own eyes; fear the L*ORD, and turn away from evil.*

PROVERBS 3:7

Whoever is acquainted with his own heart must acknowledge that self-righteousness is the last idol that is rooted out. Once born under a covenant of works, it is natural for us all to have recourse to a covenant of works for our salvation. And we have contracted such a devilish pride by our fall that we would glory in being the cause of our own salvation. It is true that we disclaim the doctrine of merit and are ashamed directly to say we deserve any good at the hands of God. But as the apostle well observes, "we go about to establish a righteousness of our own," and like the Pharisees of old, "will not wholly submit to that righteousness which is of God through Jesus Christ our Lord." Alas! This is the sorest and most common evil under the sun. Even many ministers are so sadly degenerated from their pious ancestors that the doctrines of grace, especially the personal, all-sufficient righteousness of Jesus, are too seldom mentioned. Therefore the love of many waxes cold. The righteousness of Christ seems to be one of the first lessons that God taught men after the fall. For what were the coats that God made but types of the application of the righteousness of Christ to believers' hearts? We are told that these coats were made of animal skins, and since animals were not then food for men, we may fairly infer that they were slain in sacrifice, in commemoration of the great sacrifice, Jesus Christ, to be offered. Adam and Eve, and we too, were hereby taught how their nakedness was to be covered with the righteousness of the Lamb of God.

JUNE 26

Safe from Enemy Harm

When my enemies turn back, they stumble and perish before your presence.

PSALM 9:3

"Fear not," says the great Head and King of his church, "For you will not be ashamed (finally or totally); be not confounded (dissipated or dejected, giving up all for gone, as though you should never see better days, or another revival of religion), for you will not be disgraced" (Isa. 54:4), though for a while, for your humiliation, and the greater confusion of your adversaries, I suffer them to triumph over you. "For you will forget the shame of your youth, and the reproach of your widowhood you will remember no more" (Isa. 54:4). In other words, God is saying, "I will vouchsafe you such a glorious gale of my blessed Spirit, that you will quite forget your former troubled state, and give your enemies no more occasion to insult you on account of your condition, but rather they will envy you, gnash their teeth, and melt away at the sight of your glory and prosperity." Why will the infinitely great and condescending Jesus deal in this way with his people? It is because the church is his spouse. Your Maker is your husband, your Redeemer, and the Holy One of Israel, and therefore he loves you too well to let your enemies always trample you under foot. He is the Lord of hosts and the God of the whole earth, and therefore he is armed with sufficient power to relieve his oppressed people and overcome and avenge himself of all their haughty and insulting foes.

JUNE 27

Honoring God early

How then can I do this great wickedness and sin against God?
GENESIS 39:9

There are advantages to remembering our Creator in the days of our youth, which may serve as so many motives to excite and quicken all people immediately to set about it. The first benefit is that it will bring honor and glory to God. This, I suppose every serious person will grant, ought to be the point in which our actions should center, for to this end we were born, and to this end we were redeemed by the precious blood of Jesus Christ, that we should promote God's eternal glory. And as the glory of God is most advanced by paying obedience to his precepts, they that begin soonest to walk in his ways act most to his glory. The common objection against the divine laws in general, and the doctrines of the gospel in particular, is that they are not practicable, that they are contrary to flesh and blood, and that all the precepts concerning self-denial, renunciation of and deadness to the world, are merely arbitrary restraints imposed upon human nature. But when we see others not only practicing, but delighting in such religious duties, and in the days of their youth, and when, if ever, they have a relish for sensual pleasures, subduing and despising the lust of the flesh, the lust of the eye, and the pride of life, this is pleasing to God. This vindicates his injured honor and shows that his service is perfect freedom, that "his yoke is easy, and his burden light" (Matt. 11:30).

JUNE 28

Payment for Debt

The Spirit of the L*ORD* *is upon me, because he has anointed me to proclaim good news to the poor. He has sent me to proclaim liberty to the captives and recovering of sight to the blind, to set at liberty those who are oppressed,"*

LUKE 4:18

Are you poor? If that is all, you may still be welcome to Jesus. "Has not God chosen those who are poor in the world to be rich in faith and heirs of the kingdom?" (James 2:5). What does the Savior, to whom I now invite you, say? "Blessed are the poor in spirit, for theirs is the kingdom of heaven" (Matt. 5:3). And what does the Apostle Paul say? "Though he was rich, yet for your sake he became poor, so that you by his poverty might become rich" (2 Cor. 8:9). But you say, "We are not only poor, but we are in debt; we owe God ten thousand talents, and have nothing to pay." That does not need to keep you back, for God the Father, from the Lord Jesus, his dearly beloved Son, has received double for all believers' sins; the blood of Jesus cleanses from them all. But if you are blind, and miserable, and naked, to whom then should you fly, but to Jesus, who came to open the eyes of the blind, to seek and save the miserable and lost, and to clothe the naked with his perfect and spotless righteousness … For I know my Master will take you into his banqueting-house, and his banner over you shall be love. May the glorious God grant that this may be the happy case of you all, for the sake of Jesus, his dearly beloved Son, the glorious Bridegroom of his church, to whom, with the Father, and the Holy Spirit, be all honor and glory, now and forevermore.

JUNE 29

Grace and Good Works

For we are his workmanship, created in Christ Jesus for good works, which God prepared beforehand, that we should walk in them.

EPHESIANS 2:10

Our Lord does recommend morality and good works, as all faithful ministers will do, and clears the moral law from many corrupt glosses put upon it by the letter-learned Pharisees. But before he comes to this, he talks of inward piety, such as poverty of spirit, meekness, holy mourning, purity of heart, and especially hungering and thirsting after righteousness. He then recommends good works as evidence that we have his righteousness imputed to us, and these graces wrought in our hearts. Matthew 5:16 says, "Let your light shine before others, so that they may see your good works and give glory to your Father who is in heaven." Then Jesus immediately adds in the next verse, "Do not think that I have come to abolish the Law or the Prophets; I have not come to abolish them (to take away the force of it as a rule of life) but to fulfill them (to obey it in its whole latitude, and give the complete sense of it)." Then he goes on to show how broad the moral law is. So our Lord, instead of setting aside an imputed righteousness in his Sermon upon the Mount, confirms it by making good works a proof and evidence of its being imputed to our souls. Anyone who has eyes to see may read this truth plainly.

JUNE 30

Undeniable Divinity

Simon Peter replied, "You are the Christ, the Son of the living God."

MATTHEW 16:16

Let none of you deny the divinity of the Lord who has bought poor sinners with his precious blood. The Person mentioned in Jeremiah 23:5 is Jesus Christ: "Behold, the days are coming, declares the LORD, when I will raise up for David a righteous Branch, and he shall reign as king and deal wisely, and shall execute justice and righteousness in the land. In his days Judah will be saved, and Israel will dwell securely. And this is the name by which he will be called: 'The LORD is our righteousness.'" (Jer. 23:5-6). If there was no other text in the Bible to prove the divinity of Christ, this is sufficient, for if the word "Lord" may properly belong to Jesus Christ, he must be God. And, as you have it in the margin of your Bibles, the word "Lord" is in the original, Jehovah, which is the essential title of God himself. Come then, ye Arians, kiss the Son of God, bow down before him and honor him, even as ye honor the Father. Learn from the angels, and worship him as truly God, for otherwise you are idolaters. And as for you Socinians, who say Christ was a mere man, and yet profess that he was your Savior, according to your own principles you are accursed. For if Christ is a mere man, then he is only an arm of flesh, and it is written, "Cursed is he that trusteth on an arm of flesh." It is plain that by the word "Lord" we are to understand the Lord Jesus Christ, who here takes the title of Jehovah, and therefore must be very God of very God, or as the apostle devoutly expresses it, "God blessed for evermore."

JULY 1

Everlasting Love

Having loved his own who were in the world, he loved them to the end.

JOHN 13:1

The spirits of just men who are made perfect, and the angels in heaven, do not cease day or night saying, "Holy, holy, holy." And his beauty is not inferior to his wisdom or holiness. The seraphs veil their faces when they appear before him. And as he is altogether lovely, he is also altogether loving; his name and his nature is love. God in Christ is love. And in this has he manifested his love, in that while we were yet sinners, even open enemies, Jesus, in his own due time, died for the ungodly (Rom. 5:8). He loved us and gave himself for us. O what manner of love is this! What was Jacob's love to Rachel in comparison to the love that Jesus bore to a perishing world! He became a curse for us. For it is written, "Cursed is everyone who is hanged on a tree" (Gal. 3:13). And having once loved his people, he loves them unto the end. His love, like himself, is from everlasting to everlasting. Though we change, yet he does not change; he abides faithful. In an earthly marriage, there comes a shocking clause, "Till death us do part." But death itself shall not separate a true believer from the love of God, which is in Christ Jesus his Lord; for he will never cease loving his bride, and will love her to heaven, and present her before his Father, without spot or wrinkle. His love will, as it were, be just beginning, through the endless ages of eternity.

JULY 2

The Lord our Righteousness

In those days Judah will be saved, and Israel will dwell securely. And this is the name by which he will be called: "The LORD is our righteousness."

JEREMIAH 23:6

Never did greater or more absurdities flow from the denying any doctrine, than will flow from denying the doctrine of Christ's imputed righteousness. If we deny this doctrine, we turn the truth of God's Word, as much as we can, into a lie, and utterly subvert all the places of Scripture which say that we are saved by grace; that it is not of works, lest any man should boast; that salvation is God's free gift; and that he who glories, must glory only in the Lord. For if the whole personal righteousness of Jesus Christ is not the sole cause of my acceptance with God, if any work done by or foreseen in me, was in the least to be joined with it, or looked upon by God as an inducing, impulsive cause of acquitting my soul from guilt, then I have something wherein I may glory in myself. Now boasting is excluded in the great work of our redemption, but that cannot be, if we are enemies to the doctrine of an imputed righteousness. It would be endless to enumerate how many texts of Scripture must be false, if this doctrine were not true. Let it suffice to affirm in general that if we deny an imputed righteousness, we may as well deny a divine revelation all at once, for it is the alpha and omega, the beginning and the end, of the book of God. We must either disbelieve that, or believe what the prophet hath spoken, that "the LORD is our righteousness."

JULY 3

Sufficient Savior

But when Christ had offered for all time a single sacrifice for sins, he sat down at the right hand of God,

HEBREWS 10:12

Suppose I were to come and tell you that you must intercede with saints, for them to intercede with God for you. What would you think? Would you not then say that I was in error? I suppose you would. And why? Because, you would say, the intercession of Jesus Christ is sufficient of itself, without the intercession of saints, and that it is blasphemous to join theirs with his, as though it was not sufficient. Suppose I went a little more round about, and told you that the death of Christ was not sufficient without our death being added to it, that you must die as well as Christ, join your death with his, and then it would be sufficient. Might you not then, with a holy indignation, throw dust in the air, and justly call me a "setter forth of strange doctrines?" And now then, if it is not only absurd, but blasphemous, to join the intercession of saints with the intercession of Christ, as though his intercession was not sufficient, or our death with the death of Christ, as though his death was not sufficient, judge ye, if it be not equally absurd, equally blasphemous, to join our obedience, either wholly or in part, with the obedience of Christ, as if that were not sufficient. It is absurd to deny that the Lord, in both his active and passive obedience, is our righteousness.

JULY 4

Leaning on the Rock of Ages

And were all baptized unto Moses in the cloud and in the sea; And did all eat the same spiritual meat; And did all drink the same spiritual drink: for they drank of that spiritual Rock that followed them: and that Rock was Christ.

1 CORINTHIANS 10:2-4

I remember a story of a certain prelate, who after many arguments, in vain urged to convince the Earl of Rochester of the invisible realities of another world. He took his leave of his lordship with some such words as these: 'Well, my lord, if there be no hell, I am safe: but if there should be such a thing as hell, what will become of you?' I apply this to those that oppose the doctrine of Christ's imputed righteousness. If there is no such thing as the doctrine of an imputed righteousness, then those who hold it, and bring forth fruit unto holiness, are safe. But if there is such a thing (as there certainly is), what will become of you that deny it? It is no difficult matter to determine. Since you will rely upon your works, then by your works you shall be judged. They shall be weighed in the balance of the sanctuary, and they will be found wanting. By your works, therefore, shall you be condemned, and you, being outside of Christ, shall find God to be a consuming fire to your poor wretched souls. But there is safety in appearing in the righteousness of Christ. For why should I lean upon a broken reed, when I can have the rock of ages to stand upon, that never can be moved?

JULY 5

Only Christ

That as sin hath reigned unto death, even so might grace reign through righteousness unto eternal life by Jesus Christ our Lord.

ROMANS 5:21

Let me ask you one question. Can you say, "The LORD is our righteousness"? For entertaining this doctrine in your heads without receiving the Lord Jesus Christ savingly by a lively faith into your hearts, will only increase your damnation. I tell you that an unapplied Christ is no Christ at all. Can you, with believing Thomas, cry out, "My Lord, and my God?" Is Christ your sanctification, as well as your outward righteousness? For the word righteousness not only implies Christ's personal righteousness imputed to us, but also holiness wrought in us. These two, God has joined together. He never did, he never does, and he never will, put them asunder. If you are justified by the blood of Jesus, then you are also sanctified by the Spirit of our Lord. Can you in this sense say, "The LORD is our righteousness?" Were you ever made to abhor yourselves for your actual and original sins, and to loathe your own righteousness, for, as the prophet expresses it, your righteousness is as filthy rags? Were you ever made to see and admire the all-sufficiency of Christ's righteousness and, excited by the Spirit of God, to hunger and thirst after it? Could you ever say, "My soul is thirsty for Christ, yes, even for the righteousness of Christ?" O, when shall I come to appear before the presence of my God in the righteousness of Christ! Nothing but Christ! Nothing but Christ. Give me Christ, O God, and I am satisfied! My soul shall praise thee forever.

JULY 6

Constraining Love

Therefore I tell you, her sins, which are many, are forgiven – for she loved much. Be he who is forgiven little, loves little.
LUKE 7:47

Have you ever been enabled to reach out the arm of faith and embrace the blessed Jesus in your souls, so that you could say, "My beloved is mine, and I am his?" If so, fear not, whoever you are. The Lord, the everlasting God, is your righteousness. Christ has justified you; who is he that condemns you? Christ has died for you, is risen again, and ever lives to make intercession for you. Being now justified by his grace, you have peace with God, and shall before long be with Jesus in glory, reaping everlasting and unspeakable fruits both in body and soul. All is yours if you are Christ's, for Christ is God's. My brethren, my heart is enlarged towards you! Think of the love of Christ in dying for you! Talk of and recommend the righteousness of Christ, when you lie down and when you rise up, at your going out and coming in! Think of the greatness of the gift, as well as of the Giver! Show to all the world, in whom you have believed! Let all by your fruits know that the Lord is your righteousness, and that you are waiting for your Lord from heaven! Study to be holy, even as he who has called you, and washed you in his own blood, is holy! Let not the Lord's righteousness be evil spoken of through you. Grow in the grace and knowledge of Jesus Christ day by day. Think of his dying love! Let it constrain you to obedience! Having been much forgiven, love much.

JULY 7

A Sober Warning

How shall we escape if we neglect such a great salvation?
HEBREWS 2:3

O sinners, do you think that you will be able to stand in the Judgment Day if Christ is not your righteousness? No, that alone is the wedding garment in which you must appear. O Christ-less sinners, I am distressed for you! O that this may be an accepted time! For where would you flee, if death should find you naked? Indeed, there is no hiding yourselves from his presence. The pitiful fig leaves of your own righteousness will not cover your nakedness, when God shall call you to stand before him. Adam found them ineffectual, and so will you. O think of death! Think of judgment! Yet a little while, and time shall be no more, and then what will become of you, if the Lord is not your righteousness? Do you think that Christ will spare you? No, he that formed you will have no mercy on you. If you are not of Christ, Christ himself shall pronounce you damned. And can you bear to think of being damned by Christ? Can you bear to hear Jesus say to you, "Depart from me, ye cursed, into everlasting fire, prepared for the devil and his angels." Do you think you can live in everlasting burnings? Is your flesh brass, and your bones iron? What if they were? Hell fire, that fire prepared for the devil and his angels, will heat them through and through. And can you bear to depart from Christ? O that heart piercing thought! Ask those holy souls, who are at any time bewailing an absent God, though but a few days or hours; ask them what it is to lose a sight and presence of Christ. See how they seek him sorrowing, and go mourning after him all the day long! And if it is so dreadful to lose the sensible presence of Christ only for a day, what must it be to be banished from him to all eternity?

JULY 8

Earnest Address (part 1)

Do not labor for the food that perishes, but for the food that endures to eternal life, which the Son of Man will give to you.
JOHN 6:27

First I address young people: many of you are well adorned as to your bodies, but are your souls naked? Which of you can say, "The LORD is my righteousness?" Which of you was ever dressed in this robe of invaluable price, without which you are no better than whited sepulchers in the sight of God? Do not forget your chief and only ornament. Seek for the Lord to be your righteousness, or burning will soon be upon you, instead of beauty! And to you of middle age, you busy merchants, you cumbered Marthas, who, with all your achievements have not yet gotten the Lord to be your righteousness, what profit will there be of all your labor under the sun if you do not secure this pearl of invaluable price? This one thing is so absolutely needful, that it alone will remain when all other things shall be taken from you. Therefore, labor no longer so anxiously for the meat which perishes, but seek from now on for the Lord to be your righteousness, a righteousness that will entitle you to life everlasting. And to the grey-headed sinners, I could weep over you, if you know not that the Lord is your righteousness! Haste then, aged sinners, and seek an interest in redeeming love! Alas, you have one foot already in the grave, your glass is just run out, your sun is just going down, and it will set and leave you in an eternal darkness, unless the Lord is your righteousness! O flee for your lives! Do not be afraid. All things are possible with God. If you come, though it is at the eleventh hour, Christ will in no wise cast you out.

JULY 9

Earnest Address (part 2)

But seek ye first the kingdom of God, and his righteousness; and all these things shall be added unto you.

MATTHEW 6:33

To the elderly again I say, seek for the Lord to be your righteousness, and beseech him to let you know how it is that a man may be born again when he is old! But I must not forget the lambs of the flock. To feed them was one of my Lord's last commands. I know that he will be angry with me if I do not tell them that the Lord may be their righteousness, and that of such is the kingdom of heaven (Matt. 19:14). Come then, ye little children, come to Christ; the Lord Jesus Christ shall be your righteousness. Do not think that you are too young to be converted. Perhaps many of you may be nine or ten years old, and yet you cannot say that the Lord is your righteousness. Many have said this, though they were younger than you. Come, then, while you are young. Perhaps you may not live to be old. Do not stay for other people. If your fathers and mothers will not come to Christ, then you must come without them. Let children lead them, and show them how the Lord may be their righteousness. Our Lord Jesus loved little children. You are his lambs; he bids me feed you. I pray that God will make you willing to take the Lord for your righteousness.

JULY 10

Light of the Son

Seventy weeks are decreed about your people and your holy city, to finish the transgression, to put an end to sin, and to atone for iniquity, to bring in everlasting righteousness, to seal both vision and prophet, and to anoint a most holy place.

DANIEL 9:24

The angels addressed the poor shepherds with the words, "Behold, I bring you glad tidings of great joy." If we have ears to hear, eyes to see, and if our hearts have experienced the grace of God, these tidings cause us to cry out with the Virgin Mary, "My soul doth magnify the LORD, and my spirit doth rejoice in God my Savior." It has been properly observed by some that it is one mark of God's divine goodness to his creatures that he is pleased to let light come in gradually upon the natural world. If the sun, from midnight darkness, was immediately to shine forth in its full meridian blaze, its great splendor would be apt to dazzle our eyes, and strike us blind again. But God is pleased to make light come gradually in, and by that means we are prepared to receive it. And as God is pleased to deal with the natural, so he has dealt with the spiritual world. Jesus did not appear in his full glory all at once, but as the sun rises gradually, so did the Lord Jesus, the Sun of righteousness, rise gradually upon men, with healing under his wings. Hence it was that our first parents had nothing to fix their faith upon, but that first promise, "The seed of the woman shall bruise the serpent's head." In future ages, at sundry times, and after divers manners, God was pleased to speak to our fathers by the prophets, before he spoke to us in these last days by his Son (Heb. 1:1-2), and it would seem that the prophets that were most dear to God had more peculiar and extraordinary revelations vouchsafed to them concerning Jesus Christ.

JULY 11

Confession and Supplication

But Jacob said, "I will not let you go unless you bless me."
GENESIS 32:26

We are told of the words of Daniel: "I set my face unto the Lord God, to seek by prayer and supplications, with fasting, and sackcloth, and ashes." It is beautifully expressed: "he set his face," as though he were resolved never to let his eye go off God until God was pleased to give him an answer. He was resolved, Jacob-like, to wrestle with the Lord until God would be pleased to give him the desired blessing. We are told that "he prayed unto the LORD, and made confession," not only of his own sins, but the sins of his people. Every word of it speaks of his exceeding concern for the public good. Daniel 9:20 says, "While I was speaking and praying, confessing my sin and the sin of my people Israel, and presenting my pleas before the LORD my God … the man Gabriel, whom I had seen in the vision at the first, came to me in swift flight at the time of the evening sacrifice." "While I was speaking at prayer" implies that God suffers us to lay all our complaints before him. He suffers us to talk with him as a man talks with his friend. We are never in a better frame to receive answers from above, than when we are humbling ourselves before the Lord. He was also confessing the sins of his people, and for those who perhaps seldom prayed for themselves. The angel is here represented as flying swiftly to show us how willing those blessed spirits are to bring good news to men. We are taught by our Lord to pray that God's will may be done by us "on earth, as it is done in heaven," that we may imitate a little of the alacrity and vigor which angels employ when they are sent on errands for God.

JULY 12

Inward Holiness

And therefore it was imputed to [Abraham] for righteousness. Now it was not written for his sake alone, that he was imputed to him; But for us also, to whom it shall be imputed, if we believe on him that raised up Jesus our Lord from the dead;

ROMANS 4:22-24 KJV

If I were to ask an enemy of the doctrine of free grace what we are to understand by the word righteousness, he may answer me, "It signifies what we commonly call moral honesty, or doing justice between man and man." Indeed, in various passages of Scripture, the word righteousness bears that meaning. I suppose we are to understand it in this way when we are told that Paul, preaching before Felix, "reasoned of temperance, of righteousness, and of a judgment to come." Felix had been a very unrighteous and unjust man, and therefore to convince him of his wickedness, alarm his conscience, and tell him to seek help in Jesus, Paul preached not only of temperance (for Felix had been a very intemperate man), but also of righteousness, of the necessity of doing justice, because he had been an unjust man. He also put before him the coming judgment in order to make him fly to Jesus Christ for deliverance. Righteousness also signifies inward holiness, wrought in us by God's blessed Spirit. It is the righteousness of Jesus Christ imputed to poor sinners when they believe in him. By the word "righteousness" we understand all that Christ has done and suffered in his active and passive obedience.

JULY 13

Covenantal Condescension

And the Lord God commanded the man, saying, "You may surely eat of every tree of the garden, but of the tree of the knowledge of good and evil you shall not eat, for in the day that you eat of it you shall surely die."

GENESIS 2:16

Here is the case between God and man. At first God made man upright. Moses' description of the origin and nature of man is short, but never was so full a description given. "In the image of God made he man," says Moses, being inspired by the Spirit of God. God said, and it was done; God commanded, and the world arose before him. With his words, "Let there be light," instantaneously light appeared. But when the lovely and blessed creature, man, was to be made, God called a council and said, "Let us make man after our own image." Without doubt, this image is to be understood with respect to man's soul; for as God is no bodily substance, man could not be made after his image in that way. So in this condition God made man. Adam stood as our representative. Adam and Eve had but one name originally: "God made man, and called their name Adam." God left Adam to his own free will; he was pleased to enter into a covenant with him, which indeed is an amazing instance of God's condescension. God might have ordered man to do so and so, and not made him any promise of a reward, but the great Creator was pleased to promise him that if he performed an unsinning obedience, if he abstained from eating a particular tree, that he and his posterity should live forever. But if he broke that command, in the day that he ate thereof, he and all his posterity were to die. Our Creator has descended with amazing kindness to the human race.

JULY 14

Stepping into the Sinners' Place

Their Redeemer is strong; the L*ORD of hosts is his name. He will surely plead their cause,*

JEREMIAH 50:34

God could have sent all of us to hell. John Calvin represents God's attributes as struggling one with another: Justice saying to God, "Is the law broken? Condemn the offender, and send him to hell." The mercy of God, his darling attribute, cries out, "Spare him, spare him." The wisdom of God contrives a way that justice might be satisfied, and yet mercy is still triumphant. How was that? The Lord Jesus, the dear Redeemer, interposes! He saw God wielding his flaming sword, and his hand taking hold of vengeance; the Lord Jesus Christ saw the sword ready to be sheathed in the blood of the offender, when no eye could pity, no angel could rescue. Just as the knife was to be put to the throat of the offender, the Son of God says, "Father, spare the sinner; let him not die. Father, Father, O hold thy hand; withdraw thy sword, for I come to do thy will. Man has broken thy law, and violated thy covenant. I do not deny that man deserves to be punished forever. But Father, what Adam could not do, if you will prepare me a body, I, in the fullness of time will go, and die for him. He has broken thy law, but I will go and keep it, that thy law may he honored. I will give a perfect, un-sinning obedience to all thy commandments, and so that you may justify ungodly creatures, I will not only go down and obey thy law, but I will go down and bleed; I will go down and die. Here I am; I will step in between thee and sinners, and be glad to have thy sword sheathed in my heart's blood for them."

JULY 15

Everlasting Love

And I will establish my covenant between me and you and your offspring after you throughout their generations for an everlasting covenant, to be God to you and to your offspring after you.

GENESIS 17:7

Our great God intended Christ's righteousness to extend to mankind even from eternity. All of you know that old love is the best love. When we have an old acquaintance, a friend that has loved us for many years, that love is indeed sweet. Though we may love new friends, yet when an old friend and a new friend meet together, we may say that the old is better. Now, dear child of God, this should endear God to us, to think that from all the ages of eternity, God had thoughts of you; God intended the Lord Jesus Christ to save your souls and mine. Hence it is that God, to endear Jeremiah to him, tells him, "I have loved thee with an everlasting love." When the Lord Jesus calls his elect people up to heaven, he says, "Come, you blessed of my Father." What follows? "Receive the kingdom prepared for you." For how long? "From the foundation of the world." All that we receive in time, all the streams that come to our souls, are the many streams flowing from that inexhaustible fountain of God's electing, sovereign, distinguishing and everlasting love. Therefore the righteousness of Jesus Christ may properly be called an everlasting righteousness, because God intended it from everlasting.

JULY 16

One Name under Heaven

Everyone to whom much was given, of him much will be required, and from him to whom they entrusted much, they will demand the more.

Luke 12:48

In one sense, Christianity is as old as creation. The righteousness of Jesus Christ may be called an everlasting righteousness because all the saints that have been saved, or that ever will be saved, are all saved by his righteousness. Many people are inquisitive to know what will become of the heathens that have never heard of Jesus Christ. I would say to such people, as the Lord Jesus Christ did to another curious inquirer, "What is that to thee? Follow thou me." Why should you and I trouble ourselves about the heathens? Are we not heathens? Why should we lose our time inquiring about what will become of the heathen, and not rather inquire what will become of our own souls? We may be sure that God will deal with heathens according to their light; if he has given them no revelation, then they will not be judged by a revelation. If they have not had a law, then they will be judged without law. But as for the Jews and Gentiles who have the gospel revealed to them, we may be sure that none were ever saved, or will be saved, except by the righteousness of Christ. It was through faith in him that Abel was saved. It was through the sacrifice of Jesus Christ that Abraham and all the prophets of old were accepted. There is no other name given under heaven, whereby we can be saved, but that of Christ.

JULY 17

Shaking off Corruption

And the rain fell, and the floods came, and the winds blew and beat on that house, but it did not fall, because it had been founded on the rock.

MATTHEW 7:25

Some people say that a person may be in Christ today, and go to the devil tomorrow. But, blessed be God, you have not learned Christ to be so! No, my dear friends, thanks be to God for that divine text, "There is now no condemnation to them that are in Christ Jesus." Though God's people may fall, and though many are full of doubts and fears, yet no wicked devil, nor your own depraved heart, shall be able to separate you from the love of God. God has fixed his heart upon you, and, having loved his own, he loves them unto the end. Jesus will never cease loving you until he has loved and brought you to heaven. Then he will rejoice and say, "Behold me, O my Father, and the dear children that you have given me. I have bought them with my blood, I have won them with my sword, and I now will wear them as jewels of my crown." Those whom God justifies, he also glorifies. Because Christ lives, we shall live also. Though I trust I have felt the grace of Christ, yet I find that I have as much need to come to Christ every day for fresh strength, as if I had never believed before. If I were to depend upon my own faithfulness, and not the faithfulness of the Son of God, I am sure I would soon desert Christ. But he is faithful who has promised! Our salvation depends not upon our free will, but upon God's free grace! Let the storms blow as long and high as they please, but they never shall be able to take him off the foundation. Though they may shake him, they will only shake off his corruption.

JULY 18

Grace of Heart

I have been crucified with Christ. It is no longer I who live, but Christ who lives in me. And the life I now live in the flesh I live by faith in the Son of God, who loved me and gave himself for me.

GALATIANS 2:20

The Lord Jesus Christ wrought righteousness for sinners upon the cross. Some antinomians, for lack of a proper distinction, run into a grievous error, telling us that because God intended to justify by the righteousness of Jesus Christ, therefore man is justified from all eternity. This is absurd, for a person cannot be justified until he actually exists. Therefore, though man is justified in God's mind from all eternity, yet it was not actually brought about until the Christ pronounced the blessed words, "It is finished." A new and living way for poor sinners was to be opened to the Holy of Holies by the blood of Christ. May this truth be wrought by his blessed Spirit into poor believers' hearts. All that Christ has done in his active and passive obedience will do us no good unless the Spirit of God brings it into our souls. As one expresses it, "An unapplied Christ is no Christ at all." To hear of Christ dying for sinners will only increase your condemnation, unless we have ground to say, by a work of grace wrought in our hearts, that the Lord Jesus has brought this home to us. Hence it is that the apostle when speaking of Christ says, "who loved me, and gave himself for me." O that dear, that great, that little, but important word "me." Happy are they who can apply the apostle's language to their own hearts, and say, "Blessed be God, who has wrought his righteousness by his blessed Spirit in my soul!"

JULY 19

Condescending Love

In whom we have boldness and access with confidence through our faith in him.

EPHESIANS 3:12

Consider the condescension and love of the Christ in submitting to be born of a virgin, especially as he knew that he was to be despised, scoffed at, and at last to die a painful, shameful, and ignominious death, being treated as though he were the off-scouring of all mankind. The consideration of these things should make us to admire the love of the Lord Jesus Christ, who was so willing to offer himself as a ransom for the sins of his people, that when the fullness of time was come, Christ came, made of a woman, made under the law, according to the eternal counsel of the Father. He did not come in glory or splendor, as him who brought all salvation with him. No, he was born in a stable and laid in a manger; oxen were his companions. Our Lord Jesus Christ stooped in amazing love to such low and poor things for our sakes. What love is this, that the Son of God would come into our world in so lowly a condition, to deliver us from the sin and misery in which we were involved by the fall of our first parents! The Lord Jesus Christ came to take our natures upon him and to die a shameful, painful, and accursed death for our sakes. He died for our sins to bring us to God. He cleansed us from the guilt of sin by his blood, he satisfied for our imperfections, and now, my friends, we have bold access unto him.

JULY 20

Remembering Christ's Birth

For this purpose I was born and for this purpose I have come into the world – to bear witness to the truth.

JOHN 18:37

Consider how far we have fallen from God, how vile and depraved our natures were, and how incapable we are to restore that image of God to our souls, which we lost in our first parents. When we think that the Lord Jesus Christ came to restore us to that favor with God that we had lost, so that we might find kindness and mercy in his sight, surely this calls for some return of thanks to our dear Redeemer for this love and kindness to our souls. How just it would have been for him to leave us in that deplorable and guilty state! It was free love that brought the Lord Jesus Christ into the world. What, shall we not remember the birth of our Jesus? Shall we celebrate the birth of our temporal king, and shall that of the King of kings be quite forgotten? Shall that which should be in chief remembrance be forgotten? God forbid! No, my dear friends, let us celebrate with joy in our hearts; let the birth of a Redeemer, who redeemed us from sin, wrath, death, and hell, be always remembered! May we sing forth all his love and glory, as long as life shall last here, and through an endless eternity in the world above! May we chant forth the wonders of redeeming love and the riches of free grace amid angels and archangels, cherubim and seraphim, without intermission, forever and ever! Let us consider our duty for the glory of God to celebrate the birth of our Lord Jesus Christ, an event that should be eternally remembered.

JULY 21

Accounting for Time

Making the best use of the time, because the days are evil.
EPHESIANS 5:16

This is a season for which there is no more allowance for wasting your precious time with unlawful entertainments, than any other. People are apt to flatter themselves that they are free and at liberty to spend whole evenings now with any diversion whatsoever, to pass away, as they call it, a tedious evening. They can do anything to pass away time, which is hastening as fast as a thought. Time is always upon the wing; it is no sooner present but it is now past, and it is no sooner come but it is gone. Do we have so much to do, and so little time to do it in, and yet we complain of time lying heavy upon our hands? Do we not have the devil and the beast to get out of our souls? Are not our natures to be changed, our corruptions to be subdued, our wills to be brought over to God, our hard hearts to be softened, all old things to be done away, and all things to become new in our souls? Is there not all this to be done? And yet we have too much time upon our hands! It is well that instead of having too much time, it be not found that we have too little, when we come to die. Then we shall wish, my friends, that we had made a better account of our time, and that we had improved it for the glory of God and the welfare of our immortal souls.

JULY 22

Moderation in All Things

Let your moderation be known unto all men. The LORD is at hand.

PHILIPPIANS 4:5

This is a time when many people are prone to indulge themselves in all manner of luxuries. Iniquity now abounds, and nothing can scarcely be seen but things of the greatest extravagance imaginable, not only for the necessities of the body, but to pamper it in lust, to feed its vices, to make us go on in sin, and to be a means for gratifying our carnal appetite. This wickedness is a means to make us forget the Lord of glory. It only makes us fit to do such drudgery as the devil shall set us about. These things only prepare us to run wherever the devil sends. This, instead of denying ourselves, is indulging ourselves; it is not, nor cannot be called, a celebration of the birth of our Lord Jesus Christ, when we are making ourselves worse than the beasts that perish. I am not speaking against eating and drinking of the good things of life, but against the eating and drinking of them to excess, because they thus disqualify us for the service of God. And to our fellow creatures they make us unsociable, and may occasion us to be guilty of saying and acting those things which we should be ashamed to think of, if we had only eaten or drunk with moderation. Whatever we partake of must be done to the honor and glory of God.

JULY 23

Setting a Watch

Watch and pray that you may not enter into temptation. The spirit indeed is willing, but the flesh is weak.

MARK 14:38

My dear friends, let me beseech you to set a watch over yourselves; be careful that you do not run into that company which may tempt you to evil. For would a man run himself into danger on purpose? Would a man enter himself into that company, where, before he goes, he knows he shall be exposed to great temptations? Do not think that you will be able to stand in such a situation. Therefore, if you have any reason to think that the company you are going into will be a temptation, I beseech you by the mercies of God in Jesus Christ that you would not run into it. I beseech you to examine your hearts with this question. How can you say, "Lead us not into temptation," when you are resolved to lead yourselves into it by running into the occasions of sins? You are commanded by Scripture to keep from the appearance of evil, and do you do that by running into the place and company where it is likely to be committed? No, this is so far from avoiding and shunning it, that it is a plain proof to the contrary. Take to heart the words of the psalmist in Psalm 119:101: "I hold back my feet from every evil way, in order to keep your word."

JULY 24

Redeeming the Time

For all that is in the world – the desires of the flesh and the desires of the eyes and pride in possessions – is not from the Father but is from the world.

1 JOHN 2:16

Alas! Many people, instead of devoting their time to the Lord, run into sin with their greediness, and devote their time to the devil and their own lusts. There are many who thus misspend their time and even neglect their earthly callings for a time to follow their earthly, sensual, and devilish pleasures. And the important matter is not whether other men cry out against you, for there can be Pharisees who mis-judge your conduct with a clouded man-centered view. Those living in hypocrisy can also deceive their fellow man as to the state of their heart. Those who are involved with the lusts and pleasures of the world may be good companions in the world's account but never so in the Lord Jesus Christ's. You cannot serve God and mammon; you must either lose your lusts, your pleasures, and your delights, or you cannot expect to find favor with God. For indeed, the ways that so many follow at this time are exceedingly sinful. Those who thus misspend their precious time, to the neglect of their families, are destroying themselves with their witness. O pray for grace to use our time wisely, to God's glory! "Redeeming the time, because the days are evil" (Eph. 5:16, KJV).

JULY 25

A New Yoke

Only let your manner of life be worthy of the gospel of Christ, so that whether I come and see you or am absent, I may hear of you that you are standing firm in one spirit, with one mind striving side by side for the faith of the gospel,

PHILIPPIANS 1:27

What can we do to employ our time to a more noble purpose, than to read of what our dear Redeemer has done and suffered; to read that the King of kings and Lord of lords came from his throne and took upon him the form of the lowliest of his servants? Surely when we read of the sufferings of our Savior, it should excite us to prayer that we might have an interest in the Lord Jesus Christ. We should pray that the blood, which he spilled upon Calvary, might make atonement for our sins, and that we might be made holy. May we be enabled to put off the old man with his deeds, and put on the new man, even the Lord Jesus Christ; that we may throw away the heavy yoke of sin, and put on the yoke of the Lord Jesus Christ. Indeed, my friends, these things call for earnest prayer that you may have an interest in this Redeemer. Pray that you may put on his righteousness, so that you may not come before him in your filthy rags or be found not having on the wedding garment.

JULY 26

Time Well Spent

I tell you, on the day of judgment people will give account for every careless word they speak,

MATTHEW 12:36

O do not, I beseech you, trust unto yourselves for justification, for you cannot be justified by the works of the law. I entreat that your time may be well spent, and if you are in company, let your time be spent in that conversation which profits. Let it not be about your dressing, your plays, your profits, or your worldly concerns, but let it be the wonders of redeeming love. O tell each other what great things the Lord has done for your souls. Declare unto one another how you were delivered from the hands of your common enemy, Satan, and how the Lord has brought your feet from out of the clay, and has set them upon the Rock of ages, the Lord Jesus Christ. In him, my friends, there is no slipping. In other conversation, by often repeating, you become fully acquainted with it, but of Christ there is always something new to raise your thoughts. You can never lack matter when the love of the Lord Jesus Christ is the subject. Let Jesus then be the subject, my friends, of all your conversation. Let your time be spent focused on him. O this is an endeavor, which, if you belong to Jesus, will last you to all eternity. Let others enjoy their gaming hours; you, my friends, let your time be spent in reading, praying, and religious conversation which will stand the trial best at the last day! Which do you think will bring most comfort and peace, in a dying hour? O live and spend your time now, as you will wish to have done when you come to die.

JULY 27

Provide for the Poor

Whoever oppresses the poor to increase his own wealth, or gives to the rich, will only come to poverty.

PROVERBS 22:16

Instead of running into an excess of wealth, let that money which you might expend to pamper your own bodies, be given to feed the poor. I am sure that you cannot act more agreeably for the glory of God than in relieving his poor distressed servants. Therefore, if any of you have poor friends or acquaintances who are in distress, I beseech you to assist them, and not only those of your acquaintance, but the poor in general. O my dear friends, by doing these things you will look forward to a better account one day, than all that you have expended to please the lust of the flesh, the lust of the eye, or the pride of life. Consider that Christ was always willing to relieve the distressed, and it is his command that we do so also. Will you not obey your King and Savior, the Lord Jesus Christ? Do not, my dear friends, be forgetful of the poor of this world. Consider that if providence has smiled upon you and blessed you with an abundance of the things of this life, God calls for some returns of genuine gratitude from you. Live with moderation as to your own possessions and a kind regard to the poor of this world. In doing so you will glorify your Savior.

JULY 28

Do not be Idle

Do not labor for the food that perishes, but for the food that endures to eternal life, which the Son of Man will give to you.
JOHN 6:27

God allows no one to be idle. In all ages of time, business has been commended. Therefore do not think that any season will excuse us in our callings. We are not, my friends, to labor for the things of this life inordinately, but we are to labor for them with all moderation. We are not to neglect our callings; no, we are to regard those places and stations of life, which God in his providence has thought convenient for us. Therefore, when you neglect your business to the hurt of your families, whatever pretence you thereby make for doing so, you are guilty of sin. You are not acting according to the doctrine of the gospel, but are breaking the commands of the Lord Jesus Christ, both according to his word, and to his own practice. During certain times of year, people are apt to take a little more liberty than usual, and if that time off from our vocations is not prejudicial to ourselves or our families, and is spent in the service of God and the good of immortal souls, then I do not think it sinful. But if there is too much reason to fear that the time is being spent upon our own lusts, then it is exceeding sinful, it is against our own souls, and it is against the good of our families. We then dishonor our dear Redeemer in the greatest degree.

JULY 29

Loving the Savior

So that Christ may dwell in your hearts through faith – that you, being rooted and grounded in love, may have strength to comprehend with all the saints what is the breadth and length and height and depth, and to know the love of Christ that surpasses knowledge,

EPHESIANS 3:17-18

Consider how you spend your time, whether it proceeds from a true love to your Redeemer, or whether there is not a worldly pleasure or advantage involved. If there is, our end is not right, but if it proceeds entirely from love to him who died and gave himself for us, then our time will be spent, not in the polite pleasures of life, but according to the doctrines and commands of the blessed Jesus. Our conversation will be in heaven. O think of the love of the Lord Jesus Christ. Jesus came into the world to save us from death and redeem us from the worst of slavery, from that of sin and the devil. Shall we spend no part of our time in conversing about our dear Savior? Shall we spend our time in those things that are offensive to him? Shall we not rather do all we can to promote his glory, and act according to his commands? O my dear brethren, be found in the ways of God. Strive to love, fear, honor and obey him, more than you have ever done yet. Let not the devil engross your time, and your dear Savior, who came into the world on your account, have so little. O be not so ungrateful to him who has been so kind to you. What could the Lord Jesus Christ have done for you more than he has? Do not abuse his mercy but let your time be spent in thinking and talking of his love.

JULY 30

Christ's Temptation

Then was Jesus led up of the Spirit into the wilderness to be tempted of the devil.

MATTHEW 4:1

We read that following Christ's forty-day fast, he was "afterwards an hungered," exceedingly so, no doubt. And now the important fight begins. For then the tempter – emphatically so called, because he first tempted our first parents to sin, and has ever since been unwearied in tempting their descendants – then the tempter, who in an invisible manner had been attacking our blessed Lord all the whole forty days, when he saw him hungering, and in such distressing circumstances, came to him, it would seem, in a visible shape, and probably transformed into the appearance of an angel of light. And what did he tempt him to? Nothing less than to doubt his being as the Son of God. "If thou be the Son of God, command that these stone be made bread." What! After the glorious Jesus had been proven to be God's Son, and repeatedly so in such a glorious manner? Yes, Satan knew and believed full well that he was, but he wanted to make our Lord to doubt of it. And why? Because he was in such a melancholy situation. But the holy Jesus saw through the disguised enmity of his antagonist, and scorning to distrust his righteous Father, answers him with a text of Scripture: "Man shall not live by bread alone, but by every word that proceedeth out of the mouth of God" (Matt. 4:4, KJV). What an amazing example our Savior is for us!

JULY 31

The Devil's Show

Then the devil took him by the holy city and set him on the pinnacle of the temple.

MATTHEW 4:5

Satan bids Christ to cast himself down, assuring him that God had promised in his word to order his angels to take care of him. But our Lord answers that it is written, "You shall not tempt the LORD your God." He says this that we should not distrust the goodness of God on the one hand or presume his protection on the other. So too he would not command the stones to become bread, needlessly and distrustfully to set up to provide for himself; neither would he presume upon God's power by casting himself down, though placed in a dangerous situation. Thus, our great Michael comes off conqueror in the second assault. And does the serpent feel his head bruised enough? Not at all; on the contrary, being more and more enraged at such unusual opposition and want of success, the devil takes him to an exceeding high place and shows him all the kingdoms of the world and the glory of them ... He showed our Savior crowns, but never told him those crowns were gilded with thorns; or, as Matthew Henry, my favorite commentator, says, "He showed him as in a landscape or airy representation in a cloud, such as that great deceiver could easily frame and put together, the glorious and splendid appearance of princes, their robes and retinue, their equipage and life-guards; the pomps of thrones and courts, and stately palaces; the sumptuous buildings in cities; the gardens and fields about the country seats, with the various instances of their wealth, pleasure, and gaiety; so as might be most likely to strike the fancy and excite the admiration and affection. Such was this show." Our Savior knew the devil's tactic very well, and let him go to the full length of his trickery that his victory over him might be the more illustrious.

AUGUST 1

Weak Converts

God may perhaps grant them repentance leading to a knowledge of the truth.

2 TIMOTHY 2:25

Now the gospel signifies good news and glad tidings: "Behold I bring you," said the angel, "glad tidings of great joy." Mean and contemptible as the office of a preacher may be thought now, the angels were glad of the commission to preach this gospel. Thomas Goodwin, that learned pious soul, says in his familiar way that God has but one Son and made a minister of him. And I add, he made an itinerant minister of him too. Some say that you must not preach the law. But you cannot preach the gospel without preaching the law; for you shall find, by and by, we are to preach something that the people must be saved by: it is impossible to tell them how they are to be saved, unless we tell them what they are to be saved from. The way the Spirit of God takes, is like that we take in preparing the ground. Do you think any farmers would have a crop of corn next year unless they plough now? You may as well expect a crop of corn on unploughed ground, as a crop of grace, until the soul is convinced of its being undone without a Savior … They serve Christ as the young man served the Jews that laid hold of him, who, when he found he was to be a prisoner for following Christ, left his garments; and so some people leave their profession. That makes me so cautious now, which I was not thirty years ago, of dubbing people converts so soon. I love now to wait a little, and see if people bring forth fruit; for there are so many blossoms which March winds you know blow away, that I cannot believe they are converts till I see fruit brought forth.

AUGUST 2

Conquests

Therefore let us leave the elementary doctrine of Christ and go on to maturity, not laying a foundation of repentance from dead works and of faith toward God.

HEBREWS 6:1

God's people shall be saved from the power of sin. Do not you remember that when Joshua was going on with his conquests, that there were some kings in a cave; and when he returned, he ordered them to bring the kings out for God's people to tread upon them. When I read that passage, I used to think these kings were like our corruptions hid in the cave of our hearts, and the stone of unbelief rolled to keep them in; but when we receive Christ by faith, and have pardon in him, our great Joshua takes away the stone, and says, "Bring out these kings, these corruptions, that have reigned over my people, and by faith let them tread on the necks of them." Our great Master says, "These signs shall follow them that believe in my name; they shall cast out devils, they shall speak with new tongues, they shall take up serpents, and if they drink any deadly thing it shall not hurt them." These were things peculiar, in one sense, to the apostles; but in the power of faith, and as brought home to every believer, he casts out devilish lusts; and if they had drunk any deadly thing, as God knows we have, they may do by them as Paul did by the viper, through the power of faith cast them off, and by this means prove that Christ is God. This is, my dear hearers, a present salvation. The wickedest wretch in the world will cry, "I hope to be saved," though they have no notion of being saved but after their death.

AUGUST 3

A Faint Uncertain Light

But the path of the righteous is like the light of dawn, which shines brighter and brighter until full day.

PROVERBS 4:18

Sometimes, instead of the sun there is only moonlight, which shows the difference a believer feels in his soul, both in relation to grace and comfort. Both sun and moon give light, but O how far superior is the one to the other: the moon gives a very faint, uncertain light, waxes and wanes, and at best is almost nothing when compared with the light, and the blessed reviving heat of the sun. Hence, my brethren, this world sometimes is a world of mourners. It is said, "that the days of our mourning shall be ended;" for if the text refer to the future state, as no doubt it does, it means that the days of believers here below are very often mournful, trying, and afflicting, though they end in joy, as our Lord intimates in opening his gospel sermon almost with these very words, "Blessed are those who mourn, for they shall be comforted" (Matt. 5:4). Some, perhaps, may think it is an odd kind of blessing: and though worldly people are fond of the fifth chapter of Matthew, and wonder that Methodists and gospel ministers do not preach oftener on that chapter, I am apt to believe, when you come to preach and open that word, they will not like that chapter any more than any other, because they are for a joyful Christ, and not for any mourning at all. Do you know God in Christ? Let me tell you, the more you are acquainted with him, the more your souls will be kept in a mourning state.

AUGUST 4

Genuine Birth

Blessed be the God and Father of our Lord Jesus Christ! According to his great mercy, he has called us to be born again to a living hope through the resurrection of Jesus Christ from the dead.

1 PETER 1:3

I have heard of a person who was in company once with fourteen ministers of the gospel, some of whom were eminent servants of Christ, and yet not one of them could tell the time God first manifested himself to their soul. Zaccheus's was a very quick conversion, perhaps not a quarter of an hour's conviction: this I mention that we may not condemn one another. The Lord works with each of us differently and in different seasons. We do not love the pope, because we love to be popes ourselves, and set up our own experience as a standard to others. Those that had such a conversion as the jailer, or the Jews; O, say you, we do not like to hear you talk of shaking over hell, we love to hear of conversion by the love of God and of being drawn to him for his great love; while others that were so shaken, as Robert Bolton and other eminent men were, may say, you are not Christians, because you had not the like terrible experience. You may as well say to your neighbor, you have not had a child, for you were not in labor all night. The question is, whether a real child be born, not how long was the preceding pain, but whether it were productive of a new birth, and whether Christ has been formed in your hearts. It is the birth that proves the reality of the thing.

AUGUST 5

As our Fate Turns

Whoever believes and is baptized will be saved, but whoever does not believe will be condemned.

MARK 16:16

O what an awful word is that in the latter clause of the text "whoever does not believe will be condemned." Pause for moment: I will give you time to think a little. If you would have Christ as good as his word of promise, remember he will be as good as his word of threatening. You hear the necessity of preaching the gospel because upon believing or non-believing, our salvation or damnation will turn. What, will you laugh at the minister that cries out, Lord, help you to come, come, come; do you think that we have nothing else to say, and are at a loss for words, when we cry come, come, come, to fill up our sermons? No, it is part of our commission … my fellow sinners we are come to tell you that our Master has a two-edged sword, as well as a golden scepter. If you will not come under the sound of the word, and do not feel the converting power of it, you must feel the confounding weight of it. I repeat it again to you … the very word is terrible, and God grant that you may never know how terrible it is. You are condemned already; whoever does not believe is so, why? Because he has not believed on the name of the Son of God. It is not his being a whoremonger or adulterer that will damn him, but his unbelief is the damning sin; for this he will be condemned; for ever banished from the presence of the ever-blessed God: and how will you rave, how will you tear, and how will you wring your hands when you see your relations, your friends, those whom you despised, and were glad they were dead out of your way, seeing them in Abraham's bosom and yourselves in torment!

AUGUST 6

More Blessed to Give

In all things I have shown you that by working hard in this way we must help the weak and remember the words of the Lord Jesus, how he himself said, "It is more blessed to give than to receive."

ACTS 20:35

I do not, for my part, wish people joy when they get money; only take care it does not get into and put your eyes out; if your money increase, let your zeal for good works increase. Perhaps some stranger will say, I thought you were against good works. I tell you the truth, I am against good works being put in the room of Christ as the ground of our acceptance. But we look upon it, if we have a right faith, our faith will work by love. Ever since I was a boy, I remember to have heard a story of a poor indigent beggar, who asked a clergyman to give him his alms, which being refused, he said, "Will you please, sir, to give me your blessing?" So he says, "God bless you." "O," replied the beggar, "you would not give me that, if it were worth any thing." There are many who will talk very friendly to you but if they suppose you are come for any thing, they will run away as from a pickpocket; whereas, if our souls prospered, we should count it more blessed to give than to receive; we should be free and generous with those gifts God has given us. When we rise from our beds, this should be our question to ourselves, "What can I do for God today? What can I do for the poor? Have I two, or five, or ten talents? God help me to do for the poor as much as if I knew I were die today."

AUGUST 7

Sleep of Death

So then let us not sleep, as others do, but let us keep awake and be sober.

1 THESSALONIANS 5:6

As for you who are quite negligent about the prosperity of your souls, who only mind your bodies, who are more afraid of a pimple in your faces, than of the rottenness of your hearts … You had better take care what you say, for fear God should take you at your word. I knew some tradesmen and farmers, and one had got a wife perhaps with a fortune too, who prayed they might be excused. They never came to the supper, and God sent them to hell for it too; this may be your case. I was told today of a young woman, that was very well on Sunday when she left her friends, when she came home was racked with pain, had an inflammation in her bowels, and is now a breathless corpse. Another that I heard of, a Christless preacher, that always minded his body, when he was near death he said to his wife, "I see hell opened for me, I see the damned tormented, I see such a one in hell, that I debauched; in the midst of his agony he said, I am coming to thee, I must be damned, God will damn my soul," and died. Take care of jesting with God; there is room enough in hell, and if you neglect the prosperity of your souls, what will become of you? What will you give for a grain of hope, when God requires your souls?"

AUGUST 8

Love Pangs

On my bed by night I sought him whom my soul loves; I sought him, but found him not.

SONG OF SOLOMON 3:1

I mention one thing more, which is, that you must be converted or be damned, and that is plain English, but not plainer than my Master made use of: "whosoever does not believe shall be condemned." I do not think I spoke that loud enough for you to hear; our Lord said, "whosoever does not believe shall be damned." This is the language of our Lord. It is said of one of the primitive preachers that he used to speak the word "damned" so that it struck all those who heard. We are afraid of speaking this word for fear of offending others; at the same time they despise the minister for not being honest to his Master. Some have said, and still stand to it, that hell is only a temporary punishment. Who told them this – a temporary punishment? This is nothing but a guilty conscience – O, go to Bedlam! Ask a child of God what he feels when his Lord is absent. Ask the spouse what she felt when she cried, "Have you seen him whom my soul loves?" Ask a child of God when he is using his plaintive language: "Why do you stand far off, O Lord" and he will tell you that it is a hell to his soul to be but one moment without the presence of his beloved. And if his absence for a quarter of an hour can scarce be borne by a child of God, what must that soul undergo that is commanded to depart from him for ever? And yet these very words were said to those that thought they bid fair for heaven; to these Jesus says, "I know you not."

AUGUST 9

Desiring God

You cannot serve God and money.

MATTHEW 6:24

Do you think there can be any argument against turning directly to God? Is there anyone here who will but consider, for a moment, whether there is truth in what I say? Or, perhaps, you say, "I believe men ought to be converted but I do not care to be converted yet." Is this not acting like a cardinal when told he was elected pope, and desired to come that night and have the honor of pope conferred on him, but because it was late in the night, said, "It is not a work of darkness; I will wait for the morning," before which they elected another people and he lost his triple crown. You may think of putting off repentance until the morning, but before the morning you may be damned. Why will you not be converted now? If you were in prison, and a person would take you out, you would choose to be let out tonight before morning that you might sleep the better; why will you not do that for your soul, you would for your body? "Well, I would be converted, but I shall be laughed at;" suppose you were to have it promised you should have a ten thousand pound lottery ticket but you must be laughed at all your lifetime. There is none but would say, "Give me the ten thousand pounds and call me Methodist as long as I live;" so, if you loved God and your souls you would say, "Give me God and call me what you will." … let the world see that you are not ashamed of God's badge; let the devil and his agents preach to you; they can proclaim their sin like Sodom; they are not ashamed of going to balls and assemblies, to parties of pleasure, and subscribing to horse-races. Is the gospel the glory of the land, and are you ashamed of the gospel?

AUGUST 10

Awake, Poor Sinners

If anyone thirsts, let him come to me and drink.

JOHN 7:37

Do not be angry with me if I knock at your doors and cry, "Poor sinners, awake!" May God help you to take care that you do not sleep in an unconverted state tonight. The court is just sitting, the executioner stands ready, and before tomorrow, Jesus may say of some of you, "Bind them hand and foot." The prisoners tomorrow will have their hands tied behind them, their thumb-strings must be put on, and their fetters knocked off; they must be tied fast to the cart, the cap put over their faces, and the dreadful signal given: if you were their relations, would not you weep? Do not be angry, then, with a poor minister for weeping over them that will not weep for themselves. If you laugh at me, I know Jesus smiles. I cannot force a cry when I will; the Lord Jesus Christ be praised, "I am free from the blood of you all." If you are damned for want of conversion, remember you are not damned for want of warning. Thousands that have no gospel preached to them, may say, "Lord, we never heard what conversion is," but you are gospel proof; and if there is any deeper place in hell than another, God will order a gospel despising Methodist to be put in there. You will have dreadful torments; indeed, to whom so much is given, much will be required. How dreadful to have minister after minister, preacher after preacher, say, "Lord God, I preached but they would not hear." Think of this you who profess religion, and may God make you possessors of the same.

AUGUST 11

Ascribe to God the Praise

You who fear the L*ORD, praise him!*

PSALM 22:23

How empty was our former Boast,
Our Foolishness of Pride,
When in ourselves we put our Trust,
And on our Works rely'd!

Strong in the Freedom of our Will,
Firm in our Nature's Pow'rs,
We thought to gain the heav'nly Hill,
And seize the Crown as ours.

Our good Desires, our Hearts sincere,
Our best Endeavors stood,
T' atone for our Transgression here,
In Place of Jesu's Blood.

Alas for us: we knew not then
His Blood and Righteousness,
Thro' which alone the Sons of Men
Are sav'd by richest Grace.

But now, O gracious God, your Love,
Has taught us better Things;
Our All is giv'n us from above,
From you Salvation springs.

AUGUST 12

God's Sun Dial

In the same way, let your light shine before others, so that they may see your good works and give glory to your Father who is in heaven.

Matthew 5:16

My dear brothers, from our first coming into the world until our passing out of it, all the Lord's children have found, some more and others less, that they have had dreadful as well as blessed times, and that all has been overruled to bring them nearer to God. But I believe, I am sure, that if it were put to their choice, true believers would rather know that their souls were well with God than to have immense sums of money left to them. And it is supposed that we may not only know it ourselves, and so be assured of our eternal state, but that others also may know it, that their profiting may appear to all. O, may all that converse with us see it in us; we may frequently sit under the gospel but if we do not take a great deal of care, however orthodox we are, we shall fall into gross error and be content with how we were some thirty years ago … there is not a single Christian who is acquainted with Jesus Christ but wishes his soul prospered more than his body. The great question is how we shall know whether our soul prospers? ... we may know by marks … if the marks upon the soul of a believer are like a sun-dial, they are marks to prove that we are upon the right foundation. If the sun does not shine on the sun-dial, there is no knowing what time it is; but let it shine, and instantaneously you know the time of the day; this is not known when it is cloudy; and who dare to say but that a child of God for want of the Sun of righteousness shining upon his heart, may write bitter things against himself?

AUGUST 13

Dying Witnesses

I will seek him whom my soul loves.

Song of Solomon 3:2

There was once a blessed, dear saint, who was for twenty-five days burned up with a fever, enough to scorch any creature up. Yet she was one filled with love and power divine and was able to say, "If I were not supported, the agony of my body would make me impatient;" yet she never said a murmuring word but in the midst of all cried out to those who could hear her, "God is love! O my joys! O the comforts that I feel!" And in her last moments, she cried out, "I am a-coming, dear Lord, I am a coming," and so sweetly she slept in Jesus. If this is enthusiasm, may God give us a good share of it when we come to die! These are dying and yet living witnesses that God is love. She was in raptures when her minister went to see her; she desired me to tell you that God is love … her body is to be put to bed at noon but her soul is crying, "O the joys! The joys of being saved by a blessed Emmanuel!" Now will anyone dare to deny this evidence? Do you see worldly people work themselves up into that frame when they die? Visit them when they are near death and you will see them in the vapors. They are so afraid of dying that the doctor will not suffer others to come near to them, no, not common clergymen, for fear they should dampen their spirits … but they that are born from above, that are made new creatures in Christ, feel something that smiles upon them in death.

AUGUST 14

Prayer's Marrow

Give attention to the sound of my cry, my King and my God, for to you do I pray.

Psalm 5:2

I do not know anything more variously expressed in the Scriptures than believing. Why? Because it is the marrow of the gospel. Without faith we cannot be justified, either in our persons or our performances. Therefore, the Holy Ghost has variously expressed it to let us see the importance of the point. Scripture expresses it by coming, trusting, receiving, and relying under a felt conviction that we are lost, undone, and condemned without him. For as a good old Puritan observes, Christ is beholden to none of us for our hearts. We should never come to Jesus until we feel that we cannot live without him. We are like the woman with the issue of blood; she spent a great deal of money on physicians; if she had just a few cents more she never would have come to Christ. But having spent all, and hearing that Jesus was to come her way, she felt a sense of her need and impotence. Having experienced the insufficiency of all other means, her circumstances moved her to come to Christ, saying in her heart, "If I could but touch the hem of his garment, I should be made whole; Jesus, the Son of David, would have mercy on me." She did not ask for a prayer book, but spoke from her heart, and her few words, uttered from a sense of misery and weakness, were more rhetoric, more music in the ears of God, than any extemporaneous prayer uttered by a gifted man who admires himself for his own talent.

AUGUST 15

Dreadful Visitation

The earth shall be utterly empty and utterly plundered; for the Lord has spoken this word.

Isaiah 24:3

You have often met with affliction, my dear hearers, and I believe you may persuade yourselves that affliction is at hand, which makes such deep impressions when sent and blessed by heaven as to thaw your very hearts. Faith, like some glasses to view objects near us, sets them in so strong a light that we cannot help being affected with the weight of the impression. Hence the prophets, when under a divine impulse, foresaw things at a distance and spoke and wrote of them as though they were actually present. They sang of judgment and mercy in such strong and persuasive strains as to convince the reality of their existence. Isaiah, who had a courtly education, seems to excel in this kind of speaking; a person of good natural, as well as acquired abilities, which being tempered by the Holy Ghost, made him a kind of an angel of an orator, of a writer, and a prophet … He wrote of the dreadful calamities coming on the land and so strong was his persuasion that he writes as though he saw the things taking place. "Behold, the Lord will empty the earth and make it desolate, and he will twist its surface and scatter its inhabitants" (Isa. 24:1). How much is expressed in a few words … So you see that the visitation would be universal; that it should fall on all sorts of people.

AUGUST 16

Beloved of the Lord

But you, beloved, building yourselves up in your most holy faith and praying in the Holy Spirit.

JUDE 20

We are beloved of the Lord if we are brought to abhor and renounce that which stands between the Lord and us; I mean, our cursed self-righteousness. Can I prove that I have renounced my own duties, that I am sick of my duties as well as my sins? None but the beloved of the Lord see this. An enemy to the Lord may have this in his head, but it is only a friend of the Lord that has this in his heart. A talkative professor can speak of it; you may teach, perhaps, a parrot to pray, but it is odd to talk like a parrot and experience like a Christian. Now, if I have renounced my own righteousness, and been helped to trust to Christ's, to believe in the Son of God, let Satan say what he will, I am sure I am the beloved of the Lord, for none but those that are beloved by him with an everlasting love, are brought to believe in him. I may know I am beloved of the Lord, from what? Why, experiencing his love shed abroad in my heart by the Holy Spirit. Jonathan loved David as his own soul. Most of you know what love is, in a carnal sense; and if there be a union of souls between creature and creature, surely there must be a union of souls between the Creator and the creature beloved of God; it cannot be otherwise for this love will have its effects.

AUGUST 17

Love in our Hearts

May the Lord *direct your hearts to the love of God and to the steadfastness of Christ.*

2 Thessalonians 3:5

I am beloved of the Lord, if, having his love in my heart, I show it by loving those he has loved. Some people may say, "I love you, but I do not love those about you, your friends;" you are not bound to love all alike but it may teach you to be civil to that person's beloved. As soon as ever we hear of a Christian, as soon as ever we hear of a believer, as soon as ever we hear of a sinner turning to God, we should rejoice and be like the angels in heaven who rejoice over one sinner's repentance. Some people may say, "I love dearly to hear of a person's being converted by such a minister; I love dearly to hear of persons converted by a dissenter, I love dearly to hear of persons converted by a churchman, but I do not like people should be converted by this and that person." I believe there are a great many people whose hearts are thus narrow, but this mixture is not of God. And I pray God they may know it by experience; that they may know they are beloved of God, then they will rejoice when other people are brought to believe on him, whoever is made the instrument. Grace and mercy are with all those who love the Lord Jesus in sincerity. What would have become of poor Paul if he had only loved his own followers: the Romans he never saw till he was taken there a prisoner, but he loved all the rest of the apostles, wrote letters to all sorts, not to their particular parties or churches, but to all those who truly loved the Lord Jesus. If we love in this manner we may be assured that we are the beloved of the Lord, for none but the Lord could beget such love in us.

AUGUST 18

Dwelling in Safety

The beloved of the Lord dwells in safety. The High God surrounds him all day long, and dwells between his shoulders.
DEUTERONOMY 33:12

What is to be done to those that are beloved of the Lord? Here we are told that they shall dwell in safety. Observe the expression that the prophet uses: "they shall dwell in love." Will God indeed dwell on earth? Yes, God dwells in our earthly hearts, made heavenly by the grace of God. Did any ever hear such an expression from the mouth of God: "I will be your God; I am your shield and exceeding great reward?" He does not say an angel shall go. If God had only said that we should be kept by angels, I am certain our wicked hearts would despair because they would deceive all the angels in heaven. But God says that he will be our keeper. Our God shall dwell on high and give us bread and water. We are kept by his mighty power, through faith, to everlasting salvation. We shall dwell between his shoulders. The government of the church, the world, and all, are upon our Redeemer's shoulders and the Lord's everlasting arms are under his people. We shall dwell in safety, and very often we are the safest when we think we are most in danger. Those who are lovers of the Lord Jesus shall dwell safely with God on earth and eternally with him in heaven. Oh, may God bless this foolishness of preaching to some of God's poor, and, perhaps, doubting beloved ones … If you can wrap yourselves in God, let the world hate you; God's children are the greatest on earth.

AUGUST 19

Guarding Hearts

He who sits in the heavens laughs; the L*ORD holds them in derision.*

PSALM 2:4

When Pontius Pilate and the Jews conspire to destroy the cause of God, the Lord not only has them in derision but over-rules even their malice and violence to promote that very cause they attempted to destroy; so that it is a very wrong maxim, and argues great ignorance in us, to imagine that God never brings about his designs by the means and instrumentality of wicked men. This is the Papists' objection against the Reformation: great pains have been taken to blacken the reformers, and to make it believed that a reformation could not be good, that was begun by people of bad character, and a king of an immoral life. But so far is this from eclipsing, that it illustrates the wisdom and goodness of divine Providence, in obliging the wicked to do what they never designed, and over-ruling their counsels for the fulfilling God's holy, wise, and sovereign decree. This observation naturally arises from the words that were spoken by, as far as I can judge, one of the vilest men upon the earth. You doubtless know his name, Balaam, who, though florid in his expressions, and high in profession of intercourse with God and puts on a fine face of religion, was but a rotten-hearted hypocrite, for he divined for money, made a trade of religion; and so loved the wages of unrighteousness, as to have wished to curse even those whom God had blessed … Achilles, the Grecian hero, is said to be capable of being wounded only in the heel, but bad priests, ministers, and people, have a great deal more dangerous part to be wounded in, that is, the palm of the hand – if you can keep that secure from being wounded with gold, never fear; the devil cannot have his end.

AUGUST 20

God's Inner Working

The law of the LORD is perfect, reviving the soul; the testimony of the Lord is sure, making wise the simple.

PSALM 19:7

If we look round the world and survey the works of creation, "the heavens declare the glory of God, and the sky above proclaims his handiwork" (Ps. 19:1). If we look further down upon these bodies of ours, if we consider the curious form of them, we may cry, "What has God made?" – surely I am fearfully and wonderfully made! When we consider that we are made up of the four elements; when we consider to what casualties we are exposed, how wonderfully these bodies have been kept up when thousands have dropped into the grave before us … we shall never go to heaven unless God works powerfully on our souls. Supposing you and I now were to forget all created beings, supposing we were to forget our neighbors tonight, and to hear only for ourselves, as the shades of the evening are coming on, and as we are going shortly to rest, may be to rise no more in this lower world. What if we should steal a little time from our shop, a little time from our worldly business, as we know not but we may be called to judgment tomorrow, and ask and say, "O my soul, what has God wrought in your heart?" I am glad to hear you are so inquisitive. Observe, what God has indeed wrought – for whatever is done in us is all done by God; it is all done by an almighty power and is the effect of infinite wisdom. Supposing then you and I are new creatures, has God, O my soul, wrought in you a deep, penitent, and humbling sense of your transgressions against his holy law?

AUGUST 21

Storms

In this you rejoice, though now for a little while, if necessary, you have been grieved by various trials.

1 PETER 1:6

How shall we know whether our faith is good or not? We often pray, "Lord, give us Abraham's faith," but never pray, "give us Abraham's trial" at the same time. I was once in Scotland, at a great man's house, where several rich people were, who knew Jesus. God, having blessed my labors at a former visit, I was desired by the noblemen to pray; and I remember, I prayed that the Lord would give us great faith and patience – "O," said Satan, as strong as if he had spoke to me, "do not pray for that, for you shall have great trials." "O," said I, "if that is the case, I will turn the devil's prayer against himself;" and so I prayed, "O Lord, give us great grace, and never mind what trials." Often, when we are under temptations, God takes us at our words. Some experience great blessings when they are on the mountaintops, and pray for faith and patience, but never think of coming down and feeling the storm again. But fire, my brethren, not only burns and purges, but you know it separates one thing from another, and is made use of in chemistry and mechanical businesses. What could we do without fire? It tries metal, to purge it. God knows that we are often purged more in one hour by a good sound trial than by a thousand manifestations of his love. It is a fine thing to come purified, to come pardoned, out of the furnace of affliction; it is intended to purge us.

AUGUST 22

Knowing Ourselves

Do not be deceived.

1 CORINTHIANS 15:33

Come then, O suffering saints, to you the word of this salvation is sent. I do not know who of you are the followers of the Lamb; may the Spirit of the living God point them out. May every one be enabled to say, "I am one of his!" O, says one, I have been watching and very attentive tonight, but you have not mentioned my burnings; what do you think of my burning lusts? What do you think of my burning corruptions? What do you think of my burning pride? O, perhaps some of you will say, thank God, I have no pride at all; like the Bishop of Cambray, as mentioned by Isaac Watts, who said, he had received many sins from his father Adam, but, thank God, he had no pride – Alas! We are all as proud as the devil. What do you think of the passion that burns not only themselves but also all around them? What do you think of enmity? What do you think of jealousy, is not this something that burns the bush? And there are some people that pride themselves they have not got so much of the beast about them, they never got drunk, scorn to commit murder, and at the same time are as full of enmity, envy, malice, and pride, as the devil. May God help such persons to see their own condition. Happy is it that Christ can dwell in the bush, when we, ourselves, cannot dwell there … we can take that from other people what we cannot bear from our own flesh and blood. If God did not bear with us more than we bear with one another, we should all have been destroyed every day.

AUGUST 23

Wandering Sheep

My Father, who has given them to me, is greater than all, and no one is able to snatch them out of the Father's hand.

JOHN 10:29

If you belong to Jesus Christ, he is speaking of you when he says, "I know my sheep." What does he mean when he says, "I know them"? He knows their number, he knows their names, he knows every one for whom he died; and if there were to be one missing for whom Christ died, God the Father would send him down again from heaven to fetch him. "My Father, who has given them to me is greater than all, and no one is able to snatch them out of the Father's hand" (John 10:29). Indeed, of all those whom the Father has given to Christ, he has lost none. Christ knows his sheep; he not only knows their number but the words speak of the peculiar knowledge and notice he takes of them. He takes as much care of them as if there were but that one single sheep in the world. To the hypocrite, Christ says, "I do not know you," but he knows his saints; he is acquainted with all their sorrows, trials, and temptations; he bottles up all their tears, knows their domestic trials, inward corruptions, wanderings, and he takes care to fetch them back again. There was a saying of a great preacher, "God has a great dog to fetch his sheep back." Do you not know that when the sheep wander, the shepherd sends his dog after them, to fetch them back again? So, too, when Christ's sheep wander, he lets the devil go after them and suffers him to bark at them, who, instead of driving them farther off, is made a means to bring them back to Christ's fold.

AUGUST 24

Natural Mirrors

For if anyone is a hearer of the word and not a doer, he is like a man who looks intently at his natural face in the mirror.
JAMES 1:23

To walk with God implies that the Spirit of God removes the power of the natural heart. Perhaps it may seem hard to some, but our own experience daily proves what the Scriptures in many places assert, that the carnal mind, the mind of the unconverted man, and even the mind of the regenerate, so far as any part of him remains unrenewed, is enmity against God himself. Indeed, one may well wonder that any creature, especially that lovely creature man, made after his Maker's own image, should ever have any enmity, much less a prevailing enmity, against that very God in whom he lives, moves, and has his being. But so it is. Our first parents contracted it when they fell from God by eating the forbidden fruit … and this same enmity rules and prevails in every man that is naturally engendered of the offspring of Adam … He that cannot set his seal to this knows nothing yet, in a saving manner, of the Holy Scriptures, or of the power of God. And all that do know this, will readily acknowledge, that before a person can be said to walk with God, the prevailing power of this heart-enmity must be destroyed: for persons do not walk and keep company together, who entertain an irreconcilable enmity and hatred against one another … It is destroyed in every soul that is truly born of God, and gradually more and more weakened as the believer grows in grace, and the Spirit of God gains a greater and greater ascendancy in the heart.

AUGUST 25

Cast Down

Why are you cast down, O my soul, and why are you in turmoil within me? Hope in God; for I shall again praise him, my salvation.

PSALM 42:5

What are persons cast down for? What are some of you disquieted within you for? I have reason to believe that there are many of you that have arrows of conviction stuck fast in your souls … if this be the case, that God is thus at work, let the devil roar, and we will go on in the name of the Lord. And what are you cast down for? Some poor soul will say, with a sense of sin, the guilt of it, the enmity of it, the very aggravated circumstances that attend it, appear and set themselves as in battle-array before me. Once I thought I had no sin, at least I thought that sin was not so exceeding sinful, but I now find it such a burden, I could almost say with Cain, "it is greater than I can bear." And, perhaps, some of you are so cast down, as in your haste to say, as Colonel Gardiner, that great man of God, who said when under conviction, "I believe God cannot be just, unless he damn my wicked soul." Is this your case? Are you wicked, are you so cast down, so disquieted, that you cannot rest night or day? Shall I send you away without any comfort? Shall I send you away from here as the legal preachers do? … no, no, that is the law; but the gospel comes and says, "Turn your face to God." Do not think that God is dealing with you as an absolute God, as a God outside of Christ. Remember what Luther said, "I would have nothing to do with an absolute God; as such, he is a consuming fire." Trust God in Christ, and throw yourself upon the Son of God.

AUGUST 26

The Devil's Work

Submit yourselves therefore to God. Resist the devil, and he will flee from you.

JAMES 4:7

You say you are cast down because you are weary of temptation. You feel that not only has God departed from you but also an evil spirit has moved upon you, to torment you. You are haunted with evil thoughts and are a terror to yourself. Come, then, hear what David says in his psalms: "As the heart pants after the water-brooks, so pants my soul after you, O God." What do you say of that? If you have a mind to see the beauty of this verse, then surely you will read James Hervery's Theron and Aspasio, which will live on in print when its current despisers are long dead. Those who are accustomed to disparage him will one day be obliged to own that he was one of the greatest luminaries that we ever had, and one that has laid down the doctrines of the gospel in a manner to charm and allure the great and noble souls of our time. Well, anyway, you say unbelief dogs you, and where will you go? Well, still trust in God, he will come to you and shine his countenance upon you; he will command his loving-kindness to shine in your hearts, and his song shall be over you all through the night. Though it be night-time, there is still some moon, blessed be God, or some stars; and if there is a fog that you cannot see so clearly, God can still quiet his people in the dark and make his enemies to flee. Do not fear him, God will comfort you and punish the devil for tempting you.

AUGUST 27

Loving as Christ Loved

If you really fulfill the royal law according to Scripture, "You shall love your neighbor as yourself," you are doing well.

JAMES 2:8

John had the honor of leaning on Christ's bosom and of being called, "the disciple whom Jesus loved." He was also called a son of thunder and was so suddenly turned into a son of lightning that he would have called down fire from heaven to consume his Master's enemies. Consequently, though he was of a naturally fiery temper, yet the change in his heart was so remarkable, that if a judgment may be formed by his writings, he seems as full of love, if not fuller, than any of his fellow apostles. In fact, he has been called the apostle of love; "For this is the love of God, that we keep his commandments" (1 John 5:3a). He learned pity and benevolence of the Father of mercies: and to show how Christian friendship is to be cultivated, he not only wrote letters to churches in general, even to those he never saw in the flesh, but private letters to particular saints, friends to whom he was attached, and wealthy rich friends, whom God had, by his Spirit, raised up to be helpers of the distressed. Happy would it be for us, if we could all learn that simplicity of heart, which is displayed in these particular words. Happy if we could learn this one rule, never to write a letter without something of Jesus Christ in it; for, as Matthew Henry observes, if we are to answer for idle words, much more for idle letters; and if God has given us our pens, especially if he has given us "the pen of a ready writer," it will be happy if we can improve our literary correspondence for his glory and one another's good.

AUGUST 28

Burning Bush

Count it all joy, my brothers, when you meet trials of various kinds.

JAMES 1:2

Whatever your trials are, let this be your prayer, "Lord, though the bush is burning, let it not be consumed." I think that is too low, let it be thus: "Lord, when the bush is burning, let me not burn lower as the fire does, but let me burn higher and higher. I thank you, my God, for trouble; I thank you, my God, for putting me into these afflictions one after another. I thought I could sing a requiem to myself, that I should have a little rest, but trouble came from that very quarter where I might reasonably expect the greatest comfort. I thank you for knocking my hands off from the creature; Lord, I believe, help my unbelief;" and thus you will go on blessing God to all eternity. By and by the bush shall be translated to the paradise of God; no burning bush in heaven, except the fire of love, wonder, and gratitude; no trials there, troubles are limited to this earth; above, our enemies cannot reach us. Perhaps some of you here wonder at the marvel of a bush that burns and is not consumed; do not wonder so; it is the work of God. Though burning, the bush was not consumed; neither shall the believer be consumed in the fire of trial. But woe to you, unbeliever, who undergo trials and are so burned in them; turn you to God and repent; convert and repent before the eternal fires of hell consume you and you are no more.

AUGUST 29

Great Pardons

Who is a God like you, pardoning iniquity and passing over transgression for the remnant of his inheritance? He does not retain his anger forever, because he delights in steadfast love.
MICAH 7:18

If any of you are awakened and convinced, the Lord grant that you may never rest until you know for certain that you belong to the Lord. Perhaps you wonder if God can love you, a drunkard, a Sabbath-breaker, a whoremonger, an adulterer, an unclean wretch of a soul? Tell me, what was Paul? What was the jailer? What were the three thousand who were converted all at once? What was their case? No, what about Adam, the first sinner? And what of Adam and Eve both? They all received the mercy of God and Eve is called "the mother of all living" because she is the mother of all believers. Come then at a venture, throw yourselves upon Christ and do not say, "Pardon my iniquities because they are small," but "Lord, pardon my iniquities because they are great." … Though man may not forgive you, yet God the Father will; and though the law is called a fiery law, yet there is, blessed be God, a new and living way. Oh, sinners! Oh, sinners! May God help you to venture and strive, though you have none of the marks of grace, to come to worship and cast yourself on his crown. That you would know you are the beloved of God, dwell in safety on earth, and after death be conveyed to dwell with and love to all eternity, may God grant for Christ's sake.

AUGUST 30

Days of Grace

And the LORD said, I have surely seen the affliction of my people which are in Egypt, and have heard their cry by reason of their taskmasters; for I know their sorrows.

EXODUS 3:7 KJV

Blessed be God that there are days of grace. Oh, that this day may prove to be an accepted time. Oh, that today might be the day of salvation. "Oh! Angel of the everlasting covenant, come down; you blessed, dear comforter, have mercy, mercy, mercy upon the unconverted, upon our unconverted friends, upon the unconverted part of this auditory. All you have to do is speak, and it shall be done. Command, O Lord, and it shall come to pass." Turn the burning bushes of the devil into burning bushes of the Son of God. Who knows but God may hear our prayer, who knows but God may hear this cry, "I have seen, I have seen the afflictions of my people; the cry of the children of Israel is come up to me, and I am come down to deliver them." God grant this may be his word to you under all your trouble; God grant he may be your comforter. The Lord awaken you that are dead in sin, and though on the precipice of hell, God keep you from tumbling in: and you that are God's burning bushes, God help you to stand to keep this coat of arms, to say when you go home, Blessed be God, "the bush is burning, but not consumed."

AUGUST 31

God's Arrows

For your arrows have sunk into me, and your hand has come down on me.

Psalm 38:2

What has God wrought in you? Has he even given this conviction to you, not a little fight now and then, or a qualm of you conscience? The devil and natural conscience may do this, but when it is wrought in your heart by the Spirit of God, it goes to the bottom, the arrow sticks fast, and a poor soul sometimes endeavors to pray, endeavors to pull it out, all but in vain. Has God wrought this in your soul? Now, when God works this change in the soul, the devil is always busy in tempting the poor convicted sinner to despond, if not despair. Ignorant formalists, who are some of the worst people under heaven, when a person is under conviction, think the devil is got into them, whereas the devil is in themselves; for the devil hoodwinks people, and he endeavors to persuade them that there is no harm done to God by sinning against him. It is God who wounds the soul, and it is he that heals it. Has God wrought in you not only a deep and humbling sense of the outward acts of sin, but a humbling sense of the inward corruptions of your heart? Has he led you beyond the streams, through the powerful operations of his Spirit, to the fountainhead? When he has done so, then are we Christians indeed; and this cannot be the work of the devil, which never did, nor do I know whether he can, show a person the inward corruptions of his heart; it must be the Spirit of God.

SEPTEMBER 1

Apples of False Gold

God doth know that in the day ye eat thereof, then shall your eyes be opened, and ye shall be as gods, knowing good and evil.

GENESIS 3:5 KJV

What child of God can expect to escape slander when God himself was thus slandered even in paradise? Surely the understanding of Eve must have been, in some measure, blinded, or she would not have suffered the tempter to speak such perverse things. In what odious colors is God here represented! "For God knows that when you eat of it your eyes will be opened, and you will be like God, knowing good and evil;" that is, equal with God. So that the grand temptation was that they should be hereafter under no control, equal, if not superior, to God that made them, knowing good and evil. Eve could not tell what Satan meant by this; but, to be sure, she understood it of some great privilege, which they were to enjoy. And thus Satan now points out a way that seems right to sinners, but does not tell them the end of that way is death. To give strength and force to this temptation, in all probability, Satan, or the serpent, at this time plucked an apple from the tree and ate it before Eve; by which Eve might be induced to think, that the sagacity and power of speech, which the serpent had above the other beasts, must be owing, in a great measure, to his eating that fruit; and, therefore, if he received so much improvement, she might also expect a like benefit from it. All this, I think, is clear; for, otherwise, I do not see with what propriety it could be said, "When the woman saw that it was good for food." How could she know it was good for food, unless she had seen the serpent feed upon it?

SEPTEMBER 2

God for Us

And we know that for those who love God all things work together for good, for those who are called according to his purpose.

ROMANS 8:28

Since Christ is praying for us, whom should then we fear? And since he has promised to make us more than conquerors, of whom should we be afraid? No, though a house of devils are set in array against us, let us not be afraid; though there should rise up the hottest persecution against us, yet let us put our trust in God. What though Satan, and the rest of his apostate spirits, are powerful, when compared with us; yet, if put in competition with the Almighty, they are as weak as the meanest worms. God has them all reserved in chains of darkness unto the judgment of the great day. So far as he permits them, they shall go, but no farther; and where he pleases, there shall their proud malicious designs be stayed. We read in the gospel, that though a legion of them possessed one man, yet they could not destroy him; nor could they so much as enter into a swine, without first having leave given them from above. It is true, we often find they foil us, when they assault us; but let us be strong, and very courageous; for, though they bruise our heels, we shall, at length, bruise their heads. Yet a little while, and he that shall come, will come; and then we shall see all our spiritual enemies put under our feet. What if they do come out against us, like so many great Goliaths; yet, if we can go forth, as the stripling David, in the name and strength of the Lord of hosts, we may say, "O Satan, where is your power? O fallen spirits, where is your victory?"

SEPTEMBER 3

Above all Things

No, in all these things we are more than conquerors through him who loved us.

ROMANS 8:37

"Finally, be strong in the LORD and in the strength of his might. Put on the whole armor of God, that you may be able to stand against the schemes of the devil" (Eph. 6:10). Let us, therefore, consider this text and now conclude: let us be strong and very courageous, and let us put on the whole armor of God that we may be able to stand against the fiery darts of the wicked one. Let us renounce ourselves, and the world, and then we shall take away the armor in which he trusts, and he will find nothing in us for his temptations to work upon. We shall then prevent his malicious designs; and being willing to suffer ourselves, shall need less sufferings to be sent us from above. Let us have our loins girt about with truth; and for a helmet, the hope of salvation; "praying at all times in the Spirit, with all prayer and supplication" (Eph. 6:18). Above all things, let us take the sword of the Spirit, which is the Word of God and the shield of faith, looking always to Jesus, the author and finisher of our faith, who for the joy that was set before him, endured the cross, despising the shame, and is now sat down at the right hand of God. To which happy place, may God of his infinite mercy translate us all, through our Lord Jesus Christ. To whom, with the Father, and the Holy Ghost, three persons and one eternal God, be all honor and glory, now and for evermore.

SEPTEMBER 4

Thorns and Roses

The way of a sluggard is like a hedge of thorns, but the path of the upright is a level highway.

PROVERBS 15:19

You see, my dearly beloved brothers, that our way through the wilderness of this world to the heavenly Canaan is beset with thorns, and that there are sons of Anak to be grappled with, before you can possess the rose, the Promised Land. But let not these, like so many false spies, discourage you from going up to fight the Lord's battles, but say with Caleb and Joshua, "No, we will go up, for we are able to conquer them." Jesus Christ, that great captain of our salvation, has in our stead, and as our representative, baffled the grand enemy of mankind, and we have nothing to do, but manfully to fight under his banner, and to go on from conquering to conquer. Our glory does not consist in being exempted from, but in enduring temptations. "Blessed is the man who endures temptation;" and again, "Count it all joy," when you fall into various temptations. And in that perfect form our blessed Lord has prescribed to us, we are taught to pray, not so much to be delivered from all temptation, as from the evil of it. While we are on this side of eternity, it is necessary that temptations come; and, no doubt, "Satan has desired to have all of us, to sift us as wheat." Who should we fear? For he that is for us, is by far more powerful, than all that are against us. Jesus Christ, our great High Priest, is exalted to the right hand of God and sits there to make intercession for us, that our faith fail not.

SEPTEMBER 5

Over-Much Righteousness

Be not righteous over much; neither make thyself over wise: why shouldest thou destroy thyself?

ECCLESIASTES 7:16 KJV

Righteousness over-much? Is there any danger of that? Is it even possible? Can we be too good? If we give any credit to the express word of God, we can neither be too good nor too righteous. The command given by God to Abraham is very strong: "Walk before me, and be blameless." The same he again lays upon all Israel: "You shall be perfect and without blemish before the LORD your God." Noah is said to have been blameless before the Lord his God (Gen. 6:9). And lest any should think to excuse themselves from this obligation, by saying, it ceased when the old law was abolished, our blessed Savior ratified and explained it: "Be perfect, even as your Father in heaven is perfect." So that until our perfection surpasses that of our heavenly Father, we can never be too good nor righteous over-much; and as it is impossible we should ever surpass, or even come up to him in the perfection of goodness and righteousness, it follows in course that we never can be good or righteous in excess. "You shall be blameless before the LORD your God" (Deut. 18:13) … in our text it is plain that the royal Preacher was speaking in the person of a vain worldling when he said, "Be not righteous over much," whereby he meant to exhort the truly righteous not to be dismayed, terrified, or disturbed from their constant pursuit of greater and greater perfection of righteousness, until they rest in Christ; notwithstanding the derision, fleshly persuasion, ill-treatment and persecution of worldly men.

SEPTEMBER 6

Godly Persecution

Persecuted, but not forsaken; struck down, but not destroyed.
2 CORINTHIANS 4:9

What shall I say to those who persecute their neighbors for living godly in Christ Jesus? Howl and weep for the miseries that shall come upon you; for a little while the Lord permits you to ride over the heads of his people; but, by and by, death will arrest you, judgment will find you, and Jesus Christ shall put a question to you, which will strike you dumb, "why persecuted you me?" You may plead your laws and your canons, and pretend what you do is out of zeal for God; but God shall discover the cursed hypocrisy and serpentine enmity of your hearts, and give you over to the tormentors. It is well, if in this life God does not send some mark upon you. He pleaded the cause of Naboth when innocently condemned for blaspheming God and the king; and our Lord sent forth his armies, and destroyed the city of those who killed the prophets, and stoned them that were sent unto them. If you have a mind therefore to fill up the measure of your iniquities, go on, persecute and despise the disciples of the Lord. Know, therefore, that God shall bring you to judgment for all your actions. No, those you now persecute shall be your judges and sit on the right-hand of the Majesty on high while you are dragged by infernal spirits into the lake that burns with fire and brimstone and the smoke of our torment shall be ascending up forever and ever.

SEPTEMBER 7

Our Great Adversary

Be sober-minded; be watchful. Your adversary the devil prowls around like a roaring lion, seeking someone to devour.
1 PETER 5:8

The word "Satan," in its original meaning, refers to an adversary; and in its general acceptation, is made use of to point out to us the chief of the devils, who, for striving to be as God, was cast down from heaven, and is now permitted with the rest of his spiritual wickedness in high places to walk up and down and seek someone to devour. We hear of him immediately after the creation, when in the shape of a serpent, he lay in wait to deceive our first parents. He is called "Satan," in the book of Job, where we are told, that "when the sons of God came to present themselves before the Lord, Satan also came amongst them." As the Scripture also speaks in the Chronicles; "and Satan moved David to number the people." In the New Testament he goes under different denominations; sometimes he is called the evil One, because he is evil in himself, and tempts us to evil. Sometimes he is called, "the Prince of the power of the air;" and, "the spirit that now rules in the children of disobedience," because he resides chiefly in the air, and through the whole world; all who are not born of God, are said to lie in him. He is an enemy to God and goodness; he is a hater of all truth. Why else did he slander God in paradise? Why did he tell Eve, "You shall not surely die?" And why did he promise to give all the kingdoms of the world, and the glories of them, to Jesus Christ, if he would fall down and worship him?

SEPTEMBER 8

Barrenness of Soul

The wilderness and the dry land shall be glad; the desert shall rejoice and blossom.

ISAIAH 35:1

When persons are first awakened to the divine life, because grace is weak and the sinful nature still strong, God is sometimes pleased to grant them extraordinary illuminations of the Spirit; but when they are grown to maturity, then he frequently seems to leave them to themselves; and not only so, but permits a horrible deadness and dread to overwhelm them; at which times Satan will not be wanted to vex and tempt them to impatience, to the great discomfort of their souls. But do not be afraid, for this is no more than your blessed Redeemer, that spotless Lamb of God, has undergone before you; yes, witness his bitter agony in the garden when his soul was exceeding sorrowful, even unto death. See when he sweat great drops of blood, falling to the ground; see when the sense of the divinity was drawn from him, and Satan, in all probability, was permitted to set all his terrors before him unfettered. Rejoice, my brothers, when you fall into like circumstances, knowing that you are partakers of the sufferings of Christ. Consider, that it is necessary such inward trials should come, to wean us from the immoderate love of sensible devotion, and teach us to follow Christ, not merely for his loaves, but out of a principle of love and obedience. In patience, therefore, possess your souls, and be not terrified by Satan's suggestions. Still persevere in seeking Jesus in the use of means, though it be sorrowing; and though through barrenness of soul, you may go mourning all the day long … for God will be made known to you again.

SEPTEMBER 9

Distractions

Submit yourselves therefore to God. Resist the devil, and he will flee from you.

JAMES 4:7

Have not some of you, when you have been lifting up holy hands in prayer, been pestered with such a crowd of the most horrid insinuations, that you have been often tempted to rise off from your knees, and been made to believe your prayers were an abomination to the Lord? ... or when, with the rest of your Christian brothers, you have crowded round the holy table, and taken the sacred symbols of Christ's most blessed body and blood into your hands, instead of remembering the death of your Savior, have you not employed in driving out evil thoughts, as Abraham was in driving away the birds, that came to devour his sacrifice; and thereby have been terrified, lest you have eaten and drunk your own damnation? But do not marvel at this, as though some strange thing happened unto you; for this has been the common lot of all God's children … Do not think that God is angry with you for these distracting, though ever so blasphemous thoughts; no, he knows it is not you, but Satan working in you; and therefore, notwithstanding he may be displeased with, and certainly will punish him; yet he will both pity and reward you. And though it be difficult to make persons in your circumstances to believe so; yet I doubt not but you are more acceptable to God when performing your holy duties in the midst of such involuntary distractions than when you are wrapped up by devotion into the third heavens; for you are then suffering, as well as doing the will of God at the same time … Be not driven from the use of any ordinance whatever, on account of those abominable suggestions; for then you let Satan get his desired advantage over you.

SEPTEMBER 10

Eternal Glories

May all who seek you rejoice and be glad in you! May those who love your salvation say evermore, "God is great!"
PSALM 70:4

When you suffer for truth's sake, rejoice for your reward shall be in heaven. For to you it is given not only to believe, but also to suffer, and perhaps remarkably too, for the sake of Jesus! This is a mark of your discipleship, an evidence that you live godly in Christ Jesus. Fear not, therefore, and do not be discouraged … Jesus, your Lord, your life, comes and his reward is with him. Though all men forsake you, yet he will not; no, the Spirit of Christ and of glory shall rest upon you. In patience possess your souls. Sanctify the Lord God in your hearts. Be in nothing terrified by your adversaries: on their part Christ is evil spoken of; on your part he is glorified. Be not ashamed of your glory, since others can glory in their shame. Think it not strange concerning the fiery trial wherewith you are or may be tried. The Devil rages, knowing that he has but a short time to reign. He or his emissaries have no more power than what is given them from above: God sets them their bounds, which they cannot pass; and the very hairs of your head are all numbered. Fear not; no one shall set upon you to hurt you, without your heavenly Father's knowledge … The Lord shall reveal himself to you, as to the man that was born blind. Jesus Christ shall take you up to eternal glories. If they carry you to prison, and load you with chains, so that the iron enter into your souls, even there shall Christ send an angel from heaven to strengthen you, and enable you, with Paul and Silas, to sing his praises through the night.

SEPTEMBER 11

Satan's Devices

So likewise, whosoever he be of you that forsaketh not all that he hath, he cannot be my disciple.

Luke 14:33 KJV

Satan may tempt us with our carnal friends and relatives. This is one of the most common and one of the most artful devices he makes use of to draw young converts away from God. For when he cannot prevail over them by himself, he will do what he can to influence others who are close to the newborn Christian. So he tempted Eve, that she might in turn tempt Adam. So he stirred up Job's wife to bid him to curse God and die. Thus he made use of Peter's tongue, to persuade our blessed Lord to spare himself from the sacrifice that saved the world and thereby decline those sufferings that alone could preserve us from suffering the vengeance of eternal fire. And thus, in these last days, he often stirs up our most powerful friends and dearest intimates, to dissuade us from going in that narrow way which alone leads us to eternal life. But our blessed Lord has furnished us with a sufficient answer to all such suggestions. "Get behind me, adversaries, all who hinder me in the path of truth," for otherwise they will be an offense to you; for they do not savor the things of God but the things of men. Whoever, therefore, among you are resolved to serve the Lord, prepare your souls for many such temptations as these, and forsake all to follow Christ.

SEPTEMBER 12

Be Aware

Put on the whole armor of God, that you may be able to stand against the schemes of the devil.

Ephesians 6:11

When a person has for some little time tasted the good word of life and felt the powers of the world to come, he is often highly transported with that sudden change he finds in himself. But then Satan comes at such a time to puff him up with a high conceit of his own experiences as if he were some great person. He will tempt him to think ill of his brothers, as though he were better or holier than they. Take heed, therefore, and beware of this most evil device of our spiritual adversary; for as honor is before humility, so a haughty spirit goes before a fall, and God is obliged when under such circumstances to send us some humbling visitation (or permit us to fall) as he did Peter into some grievous sin, that he might learn not to be so high minded. To put a stop to all these suggestions to pride, let us remember that Christ was the one who chose us, we did not choose him; we have nothing but what we have received. Indeed, the free grace of God alone has made the difference between us and others; and were God to leave us to ourselves, and to the deceitfulness of our own hearts for but one moment, we would be utterly undone and as wicked and weak as others. "God resists the proud but gives grace to the humble."

SEPTEMBER 13

It is Written

Then Jesus was led up by the Spirit into the wilderness to be tempted by the devil.

MATTHEW 4:1

Thus, in all his temptations of the Holy Jesus, Satan chiefly aimed to make him question whether he was the Son of God. "If you are the Son of God," do so and so. With many such desponding thoughts, no doubt, he filled the heart of Saint Paul when he continued three days neither eating nor drinking water; and therefore he speaks by experience, when he says, in the words of the text, "We are not ignorant of his devices," that he would endeavor to drive the incestuous person to despair. But let not any of you be influenced by him, to despair of finding mercy. For it is not the greatness or number of our crimes, but impenitence and unbelief, that will prove our ruin: No, were our sins more in number than the hairs of our head, or of a deeper dye than the brightest scarlet; yet the merits of the death of Jesus Christ are infinitely greater, and faith in his blood shall make them white as snow. Answer always, therefore, his despairing suggestions, as our Lord did, with an "It is written." Tell him, you know that your Redeemer lives forever to make intercession for you; that the Lord has received from him double for all your crimes: And though you have sinned much, that is no reason why you should despair, but only why you should love much, having had so much forgiven.

SEPTEMBER 14

We are Justified

So that being justified by his grace we might become heirs according to the hope of eternal life.

TITUS 3:7

"But you are justified," says the apostle; which is as though he had said that you have had your sins forgiven and are looked upon by God as though you never had offended him at all. For this is the meaning of the word "justified," in almost all the passages of Holy Scripture where this word is mentioned. Thus, when this same apostle writes to the Romans, he tells them, "whom God called, those he also justified." And that this word "justified," implies a blotting out of all our transgressions, is manifest from what follows, "them he also glorified," which could not be if a justified person was not looked upon by God, as though he never had offended him at all. And again, speaking of Abraham's faith, he tells them, that, "Abraham believed God, and it was counted to him as righteousness" (Rom. 4:3). Abraham believed; that is, he believed in the one who clears the guilty and ungodly man; for it is a law term and alludes to a judge acquitting an accused criminal of the thing he is charged with. So, the psalmist says, "Blessed is the man to whom the Lord does not impute sin." From all which proofs, and many others that might be urged, it is evident that by being justified we are to understand being so acquitted in the sight of God as to be looked upon as though we never had offended him at all. And in this sense we are to understand that article, which we profess to believe in our creed; that is, "I believe in the forgiveness of sins."

SEPTEMBER 15

Fear and Trembling

Abraham said, "God will provide for himself the lamb for a burnt offering, my son." So they went both of them together.
GENESIS 22:8

Some think that Abraham by faith saw the Lord Jesus afar off, and here spoke prophetically of that Lamb of God already slain in decree, and hereafter to be actually offered up for sinners. This was a lamb of God's providing indeed to satisfy his own justice, and to render him just in justifying the ungodly. What is all our fire and wood, the best preparations and performances we can make or present, unless God had provided himself this Lamb for a burnt-offering? He could not away with them. The words will well bear this interpretation. But, whatever Abraham might intend, I cannot but think he here made an application, and acquainted his son, of God's dealing with his soul; and at length, with tears in his eyes, and the utmost affection in his heart, cried out, "You are to be the lamb, my son; God has commanded me to provide you for a burnt-offering, and to offer thee upon the mountain which we are now ascending" … when we are told, that Abraham bound Isaac, we do not hear of his complaining, or endeavoring to escape, which he might have done, being (as some think) near thirty years of age, and, it is plain, capable of carrying wood enough for a burnt-offering. But he was partaker of the like precious faith with his aged father, and therefore is as willing to be offered, as Abraham is to offer him … O that unbelievers would learn of faithful Abraham, and believe whatever is revealed from God, though they cannot fully comprehend it … We have sufficient testimony that God has spoken to us by his Son, why should we not also believe, though many things in the New Testament are above our reason?

SEPTEMBER 16

How to hear Sermons

He who has an ear, let him hear what the Spirit says to the churches.

REVELATION 2:7A

If an earthly king was to issue out a royal proclamation, on performing or not performing the conditions therein contained, the life or death of his subjects entirely depended, how solicitous would they be to hear what those conditions were? And shall not we pay the same respect to the King of kings, and Lord of lords, and lend an attentive ear to his ministers, when they are declaring, in his name, how our pardon, peace, and happiness may be secured? When God descended on Mount Sinai in terrible majesty, to give unto his people the law, how attentive were they to his servant Moses? And if they were so earnest to hear the thunderings or threatenings of the law, shall not we be as solicitous to hear from the ministers of Christ, the glad tidings of the gospel? Whilst Christ was himself on earth, it is said, that the people hung upon him to hear the gracious words that proceeded out of his mouth. And if we looked on ministers as we ought as the sent of Jesus Christ, we should hang upon them to hear their words also. Besides, the sacred truths that gospel ministers deliver are not dry insipid lectures on moral philosophy, intended only to amuse us for a while; but the great mysteries of godliness, which, therefore, we are bound studiously to liken to, left through our negligence we should either not understand them, nor by any other means let them slip.

SEPTEMBER 17

To the Ends of Earth

Go therefore and make disciples of all nations.

MATTHEW 28:19A

I believe that everyone ought to take all opportunities to hear sermons. That there have always been particular persons set apart by God to instruct and exhort his people to practice … Jude tells us that "Enoch, the seventh from Adam, prophesied (or preached) concerning the LORD's coming with ten thousand of his saints to judgment." And Noah, who lived not long after, is styled by St. Peter, "a preacher of righteousness." And though in all the intermediate space between the flood and giving of the law, we hear but of few preachers, yet we may reasonably conclude, that God never left himself without witness, but at sundry times, and after diverse manners, spoke to our fathers by the patriarchs and prophets. But however it was before, we are assured that after the delivery of the law, God constantly separated to himself a certain order of men to preach to, as well as pray for his people; and commanded them to inquire their duty at the priests mouths. And though the Jews were frequently led into captivity, and for their sins scattered abroad on the face of the earth, yet he never utterly forsook his church, but still kept up a remnant of prophets and preachers, as Ezekiel, Jeremiah, Daniel, and others, to reprove, instruct, and call them to repentance. Thus was it under the law. Nor has the church been worse, but infinitely better provided for under the gospel. For when Jesus Christ, that great High Priest, had through the eternal Spirit offered himself, as a full, perfect, sufficient sacrifice and satisfaction for the sins of the whole world, and after his resurrection had all power committed to him, both in heaven and earth, he gave commission to his Apostles, and in them to all succeeding ministers, to go and preach the gospel to every creature.

SEPTEMBER 18

Godly Homes

And the people said to Joshua, "The LORD our God we will serve, and his voice we will obey."

JOSHUA 24:24

Visit our churches and you may perhaps see something of the form of godliness still among us. But even that is scarcely to be met within private houses. So that were the blessed angels to come, as in the patriarchal age, and observe our spiritual economy at home, would they not be tempted to say as Abraham to Abimilech, "Surely, the fear of God is not in this place" (Gen. 20:11). How such a general neglect of family religion first began to overspread the Christian world, is difficult to determine. As for the primitive Christians, I am positive it was not so with them. No, they had not so learned Christ, as falsely to imagine religion was to be confined solely to their assemblies for public worship; but, on the contrary, behaved with such piety and exemplary holiness in their private families that Saint Paul often styles their house a church … if we consider that every governor of a family ought to look upon himself as obliged to act in three capacities as a prophet, to instruct; as a priest, to pray for and with; as a king, to govern, direct, and provide for them. It is true indeed, the latter of these, their kingly office, they are not so frequently deficient in but as for the two former, their priestly and prophetic office, like Gallio, they care for no such things … every house is as it were a little parish, every governor (as was before observed) a priest, every family a flock; and if any of them perish through the governor's neglect, their blood will God require at their hands.

SEPTEMBER 19

A Living Sacrifice

I appeal to you therefore, brothers, by the mercies of God, to present your bodies as a living sacrifice, holy and acceptable to God, which is your spiritual worship.

ROMANS 12:1

The death of Jesus Christ has turned our whole lives into one continued sacrifice; and whether we eat or drink, whether we pray to God, or do anything to man, it must all be done out of a love for, and knowledge of him who died and rose again, to render all, even our most ordinary deeds, acceptable in the sight of God. If we live by this principle, if Christ be the Alpha and Omega of all our actions, then our least are acceptable sacrifices; but if this principle be wanting, our most pompous services avail nothing: we are but spiritual idolater; we sacrifice to our own net; we make an idol of ourselves, by making ourselves, and not Christ, the end of our actions: and, therefore, such actions are so far from being accepted by God, that, according to the language of one of the Articles of our Church, "We doubt not but they have the nature of sin, because they spring not from an experimental faith in, and knowledge of Jesus Christ." Were we not fallen creatures, we might then act, perhaps, from other principles; but since we are fallen from God in Adam, and are restored again only by the obedience and death of Jesus Christ, the face of things I entirely changed, and all we think, speak, or do, is only accepted in and through him.

SEPTEMBER 20

God's Fools

For the foolishness of God is wiser than men, and the weakness of God is stronger than men.

1 Corinthians 1:25

Some, indeed, may please themselves in knowing the world while others boast themselves in the knowledge of a multitude of languages; but could we speak with the tongues of men and angels, or did we know the number of the stars, and could call them all by their names, yet, without experimental knowledge of Jesus Christ, and him crucified, it would profit us nothing. The former, indeed, may procure us a little honor, which comes from man; but the latter only can render us acceptable in the sight of God. If we are ignorant of Christ, God will be to us a consuming fire. Christ is the way, the truth, and the life; no one comes to the Father except through him. He is the Lamb slain from the foundation of the world and no one was ever received into glory but by an experimental application of his merits to their hearts. We might as well think to rebuild the tower of Babel, or reach heaven with our hands, as to imagine we could enter therein by any other door, than that of the knowledge of Jesus Christ. Other knowledge may make you wise in your own eyes, and puff you up; but this alone edifies and makes wise unto salvation. As the meanest Christian, if he knows but this, though he knows nothing else, will be accepted; so the greatest master in Israel, the most letter-learned teacher, without this, will be rejected. His philosophy is mere nonsense, his wisdom mere foolishness in the sight of God.

SEPTEMBER 21

The Almost Christian

Almost thou persuadest me to be a Christian.

ACTS 26:28 KJV

An almost Christian, if we consider him in respect to his duty to God, is one that halts between two opinions; he wavers between Christ and the world; he would reconcile God and Mammon, light and darkness, Christ and Belial. It is true, he has an inclination to religion, but then he is very cautious that he does not go too far in it, his false heart crying out to spare himself. He prays indeed that God's will would be done on earth, as it is in heaven, but still he is very partial in his obedience and fondly hopes that God will not be extreme to mark everything he has done amiss, even though an inspired apostle has told him that he who offends in one point is guilty of all. But, chiefly, the Almost Christian is one that depends on outward ordinances and on that account considers himself righteous and despises others. He is a stranger to the divine life as any person whatsoever. He is fond of the form of religion but despises its power, that is, godliness in the heart. He goes on year after year, attending the means of grace but then like Pharaoh's lean cow he is never the better but rather the worse for them. If you consider him in respect to his neighbor, he is one that is strictly just to all; but then this does not proceed from any love of God or regard to man, but only through a principle of self-love: because he knows dishonesty will spoil his reputation, and consequently hinder his thriving in the world.

SEPTEMBER 22

Worldly Fools

Indeed, I count everything as loss because of the surpassing worth of knowing Christ Jesus my Lord. For his sake I have suffered the loss of all things and count them as rubbish, in order that I may gain Christ.

PHILIPPIANS 3:8

There is perhaps no greater example of the worthlessness of learning than the great Saint Paul, a great scholar in all what the world calls fine learning. He was bred up at the feet of Gamaliel, and profited in the knowledge of books, as well as in the Jewish religion, above many of his equals, as appears by the language, rhetoric, and spirit of his writings; and yet, when he came to know what it was to be a Christian, he counted all things as loss that he might win Christ and be found in him, not having a righteousness of his own but that which comes through faith … he was absolutely determined not to know anything, or to make nothing his study, but what taught him to know Jesus Christ, and him crucified. Hence then, appears the folly of those who spend their whole lives in heaping up other knowledge; and, instead of searching the Scriptures, which testify of Jesus Christ, and are alone able to make them wise unto salvation, disquiet themselves in a pursuit after the knowledge of such things, as when known, concern them no more, than to know that a bird dropped a feather upon one of the Pyrenean mountains … hence it is they appear mere fools in the things of God; so that when you come to converse with them about the great work of redemption wrought out for us by Jesus Christ, and of his being a propitiation for our sins, a fulfiller of the covenant of works, and a principle of new life to our souls, they are quite ignorant of the whole matter; and prove, to a demonstration, that, with all their learning, they know nothing yet and are mere infants in learning.

SEPTEMBER 23

Tell us so

How long will you keep us in suspense? If you are the Christ, tell us plainly.

JOHN 10:24

Our Lord always made the best of every opportunity; and we are told, "he walked in the temple in Solomon's porch." One would have thought the scribes and Pharisees would have put him in one of their stalls, and have complimented him with desiring him to preach, but no, they let him walk in Solomon's porch. Some think he walked by himself, nobody choosing to keep company with him. I think I can see him walking and looking at the temple, and foreseeing within himself how soon it would be destroyed; he walked pensive, to see the dreadful calamities that would come upon the land, for not knowing the day of its visitation; and it was to let the world see he was not afraid to appear in public: he walked, as much as to say, "Have any of you anything to say to me?" and he put himself in their way, that if they had any things to ask him, he was ready to resolve them; and to show them, that though they had treated him so ill, yet he was ready to preach salvation to them. "So the Jews gathered around him and said to him, 'How long will you keep us in suspense? If you are the Christ, tell us plainly'" (John 10:24). They came round about him when they saw him walking in Solomon's porch; now, say they, we will have him, now we will attack him … they wanted him to tell them so they could impeach him to the governor.

SEPTEMBER 24

Christ's Sheep

Truly, truly, I say to you, I am the door of the sheep. If anyone enters by me, he will be saved and will go in and out and find pasture.

JOHN 10:7, 9

The devil always wants to make it believed that God's people, who are the most loyal people in the world, are rebels to the government under which they live; "If you are the Christ, tell us plainly." Our Lord does not let them wait long for an answer; honesty can soon speak: "I told you, and ye believed not; the works that I do in my Father's name, they bear witness of me." Had our Lord said, "I am the Messiah," they would have taken him up; he knew that, and therefore he joined the wisdom of the serpent with the innocence of the dove. He appealed to his works and doctrine, and they would not believe from them that he was the Messiah, he would not argue with them further. "But," he adds, "you believe not because you are not my sheep." Their unbelief was the greatest grief of heart to Christ. Christ's sheep hear his voice; they tried to puzzle him, to confuse him with their conduct, but they are mistaken; they do not believe because they do not belong to Christ. The great Solomon Stoddard once preached on these words from our text, "But you believe not, because you are not my sheep" – a strange text to preach upon to awaken sinners in the congregation, but God blessed it mightily so that two hundred souls were awakened by that sermon. May God grant such success to attend the labors of all his faithful ministers.

SEPTEMBER 25

Receiving the Spirit

Have ye received the Holy Ghost since ye believed?

ACTS 19:2 KJV

Since one great work of the Holy Spirit is to convince us of sin, and to set us upon seeking pardon and renewing grace, through the all-sufficient merits of a crucified Redeemer, whosoever has felt the power of the world to come, awakening him from his spiritual lethargy, cannot but be always crying out, "Lord, what would you have me to do?" Or, in the language of the importunate blind Bartimeus, "Jesus, Son of David, have mercy on me." The blessed Jesus, as he received the Holy Spirit without measure, so he evidenced it by nothing more than his frequent addresses at the throne of grace. Accordingly, we read that he was often alone on the mountain praying; that he rose a great while before day to pray: no, that he spent whole nights in prayer. And whosoever is made partaker of the same Spirit which the holy Jesus, will be of the same mind, and delight in nothing so much, as to "draw nigh unto God," and lift up holy hands and hearts in frequent and devout prayer. It must be confessed, indeed, that this spirit of supplication is often as it were sensibly lost, and decays, for some time, even in those who have actually received the Holy Sprit. Through spiritual dryness and barrenness of soul, they find in themselves a listlessness and backwardness to this duty of prayer; but then they esteem it as their cross, and still persevere in seeking Jesus, though it be sorrowing: and their hearts, notwithstanding, are fixed upon God, though they cannot exert their affections so strongly as usual, on account of that spiritual deadness, which God, for wise reasons, has suffered to benumb their souls.

SEPTEMBER 26

Turning from Sin

We know that whosoever is born of God sinneth not; but he that is begotten of God keepeth himself, and that wicked one toucheth him not.

1 JOHN 5:18

The expression "does not sin" does not imply the impossibility of a Christian's sinning: for we are told that no one is without sin, and that if anyone does sin, we have an advocate with the Father, Jesus Christ the righteous (1 John 2:1). Rather, this phrase means that a man who is really born again of God does not willfully commit sin or live in a habitual practice of it. For how shall he that is dead to sin, as every converted person is, live any longer therein? It is true, a man that is born again of God, may, through surprise, or the violence of a temptation, fall into acts of sin – just witness the adultery of David, and Peter's denial of his Master. But then, like them, he quickly rises again, goes out from the world, and weeps bitterly; he washes the guilt of sin away by the tears of sincere repentance, joined with faith in the blood of Jesus Christ. Then he takes double heed to his ways for the future, and perfects holiness in the fear of God … whereas the unconverted sinner is quite dead in trespasses and sins. Or, if he does abstain from gross acts of it, through worldly selfish motives, yet, there is some right eye he will not pluck out; some right hand which he will not cut off; some specious Agag that he will not sacrifice for God; and thereby he is convinced that he is but a mere Saul: and consequently, whatever pretensions he may make to the contrary, he has not yet received the Holy Spirit.

SEPTEMBER 27

Godly Living

So whether you eat or drink, or whatever you do, do all to the glory of God.

1 CORINTHIANS 10:31

The spiritual man is not so taken up with the affairs of another life, as to neglect the business of this one. No, a truly spiritual man dares not stand any day idle; but then he takes care, though he labors for the meat that perishes first to secure that which endures to everlasting life. Or, if God has exalted him above his brothers, yet, like Moses, Joseph, and Daniel, he, notwithstanding, looks upon himself as a stranger and pilgrim upon earth; he is homeward bound, having received a principle of new life; he walks by faith and not by sight; and his hopes being full of immortality, he can look on all things here below as vanity and vexation of spirit. In short, though he is in, yet he is not of the world; and as he was made for the enjoyment of God, so nothing but God can satisfy his soul. The ever-blessed Jesus was a perfect instance of overcoming the world. For though he went about continually doing good, and always lived as in a press and throng; yet, wherever he was, his conversation tended heavenwards. In like manner, he that is joined to the Lord in one spirit will so order his thoughts, words, and actions, that he will evidence to all that his conversation is in heaven. On the contrary, an unconverted man being of the earth, is earthy; and having no spiritual eye to discern spiritual things, he is always seeking for happiness in this life, where it never was, will, or can be found.

SEPTEMBER 28

Christian Charity

Beloved, let us love one another, for love is from God, and whoever loves has been born of God and knows God.

1 JOHN 4:7

By this love we are not to understand a softness and tenderness of mere nature, or a love founded on worldly motives, as any natural person may have, but a love of our brethren, proceeding from love towards God. In other words, loving all peoples in general because of their relation to God; and loving good men in particular, for the grace we see in them, and because they love our Lord Jesus in sincerity. This is Christian charity, and that new commandment which Christ gave to his disciples. New, not in its object, but in the motive and example whereon it is founded, even Jesus Christ. This is that love which the primitive Christians were so renowned for, that it became a proverb, "See how these Christians love one another." And without this love, though we should give all our goods to feed the poor, and our bodies to be burnt, it would profit us nothing. Further, this love is not confined to any particular set of men, but is impartial and catholic: it is a love that embraces God's image wherever it beholds it, and that delights in nothing so much as to see Christ's kingdom come. This is the love wherewith Jesus Christ loved mankind: He loved all, even the worst of men, as appears by his weeping over the obstinately perverse; but wherever he saw even the least appearance of the divine likeness, that soul he loved in particular.

SEPTEMBER 29

To our Utmost

Charity never faileth.

1 CORINTHIANS 13:8 KJV

Nothing is more valuable and commendable, and yet, not one duty is less practiced, than that of charity. We often pretend concern and pity for the misery and distress of our fellow-creatures, but yet we seldom commiserate their condition so much as to relieve them according to our abilities; but unless we assist them with what they may stand in need of, for the body as well as for the soul, all our wishes are no more than words of no value or regard, and are not to be esteemed or regarded. For when we hear of any deplorable circumstance in which our fellow-creatures are involved, be they friends or enemies, it is our duty, as Christians, to assist them to the utmost of our power … Paul had been showing that spiritual gifts were divers; that God had disposed of one blessing to one, and another to another; and though there was a diversity of blessings, God did not bestow them to one person, but gave to one a blessing which he denied to another, and gave a blessing, or a gift to the other which might make him as eminent in one way, as the other's gift made him so in another. Though there are these divers spiritual gifts, they are all given for some wise end, even to profit withal, and to that end they are thus diversely bestowed. We are not, on the one hand, to hide those gifts which God has given us: neither are we, on the other, to be so lavish of them, as to spend them upon our lusts and pleasures, to satisfy our sensual appetites, but they are to be used for the glory of God, and the good of immortal souls.

SEPTEMBER 30

We Preach Christ

But we preach Christ crucified, a stumbling block to Jews and folly to Gentiles, but to those who are called, both Jews and Greeks, Christ the power of God and the wisdom of God.

1 Corinthians 1:23-24

But why did Saul preach Christ? He did so because he had felt the power of Christ on his own soul. And here is the reason why Christ is so seldom preached, and his divinity so slightly insisted on in our churches: because the generality of those that pretend to preach him have never felt a saving work of conversion upon their own souls. How can they preach, unless they are first taught of and then sent by God? Saul did not preach Christ before he knew him; no more should anyone else. An unconverted minister, though he could speak with the tongues of men and angels, will be but as a sounding brass and tinkling cymbal to those whose senses are exercised to discern spiritual things. Ministers who are unconverted may talk and marvel of Christ, and prove from books that he is the Son of God; but they cannot preach with the demonstration of the Spirit and with power, unless they preach from experience, and have had a proof of his divinity, by a work of grace wrought upon their own souls. God forgive those who lay hands on an unconverted man (i.e. ordain him), knowing that he is such. I would not do it for a thousand worlds … Lord Jesus, keep your own faithful servants pure and let them not be partakers of other men's sins.

OCTOBER 1

Hating Christ

The LORD is not slow to fulfill his promise as some count slowness, but is patient toward you, not wishing that any should perish, but that all should reach repentance.

2 PETER 3:9

Repentance is the carnal and corrupt disposition of men being changed into a renewed and sanctified disposition. A man that has truly repented is truly regenerated. It is a different word for one and the same thing; the motley mixture of the beast and devil is gone; there is, as it were, a new creation wrought in your hearts. If your repentance is true, you are renewed throughout, both in soul and body; your understandings are enlightened with the knowledge of God and of the Lord Jesus Christ; and your wills, which were stubborn, obstinate, and hated all good, are obedient and conformable to the will of God. Indeed, our deists tell us, that man now has a free will to do good, to love God, and to repent when he will; but indeed, there is no free will in any of you but to sin; your free will leads you so far that you would, if possible, pull God from his throne … Thus, by that repentance, the whole soul will be changed, you will have new inclinations, new desires, and new habits. You may see how vile we are by nature, that it requires so great a change to be made upon us, to recover us from this state of sin, and therefore the consideration of our dreadful state should make us earnest with God to change our condition, and that change, true repentance implies; therefore, my brothers, consider how hateful your ways are to God while you continue in sin; how abominable you are unto him, while you run into evil: you cannot be said to be Christians while you are hating Christ and his people.

OCTOBER 2

Better Things

Therefore, my brothers, whom I love and long for, my joy and crown, stand firm thus in the LORD, my beloved.

PHILIPPIANS 4:1

I hope better things of you, my brothers, than to be false in your profession of the truth. Go to God in prayer and be earnest with him, that by his Spirit he would convince you of your miserable condition by nature, and make you truly sensible thereof. Be humbled; be humbled, I beg you, for your sins! Having spent so many years in sinning, what can you do less than be concerned to spend some hours in mourning and sorrowing for the same, and be humbled before God? Look back into your lives, call to mind your sins, as many as possibly you can, the sins of your youth, as well as of your riper years; see how you have departed from a gracious Father, and wandered in the way of wickedness, in which you have lost yourselves, the favor of God, the comforts of his Spirit, and the peace of your own consciences; then go and beg pardon of the Lord through the blood of the Lamb, for the evil you have committed, and for the good you have omitted. Consider, likewise, the heinousness of your sins; see what very aggravating circumstances thy sins are attended with, how you have abused the patience of God, which should have led you to repentance. When you find your heart hard, beg God to soften it, cry mightily to him and he will take away your stony heart and give you a heart of flesh. Resolve to leave all your sinful lusts and pleasures; renounce, forsake, and abhor, your old sinful course of life, and serve God in holiness and righteousness all the remaining part of life.

OCTOBER 3

This Sensual World

I have seen everything that is done under the sun, and behold, all is vanity and a striving after wind.

ECCLESIASTES 1:14

O the folly and madness of this sensual world … Consider, therefore, while you are going on in a course of sin and unrighteousness to think of the consequence that will attend your misspending of your precious time; your souls are worth being concerned about. For if you can enjoy all the pleasures and diversions of life, at death you must leave them; it will put an end to all your worldly concerns. Will it not be deplorable to have your good things here, all your earthly, sensual, devilish pleasures, which you have been so much taken up with, all over? The thought for how trifling a concern you have lost eternal welfare will gnaw your very soul and pain you. All your wealth and grandeur will stand as nothing; you cannot carry anything into the other world to which you are going; the sensual life you have spent in this sensual world will then be a constant hell to you … Now you enjoy the means of grace, as the preaching of his word, prayer, and sacraments; and God has sent his ministers out into the fields and highways, to invite, to woo you to come in; but they are tiresome to you because you would rather have your sensual pleasures: before long, my brothers, they will be over and you will be no more troubled with them. Soon you would wish to give ten thousand worlds for but one moment of their time, to hear the sweet words of forgiving grace, but alas, it will be too late; you will cry for a drop of that precious blood which you now trample under your feet. O, change now; hear the gospel and be converted all you ends of the earth!

OCTOBER 4

Nothing more Certain

And I heard the altar saying, "Yes, LORD God the Almighty, true and just are your judgments!"

REVELATION 16:7

There is nothing more certain than that we are to appear before the judgment-seat of Christ, to be rewarded according to the deeds done in the body, whether they have been good or evil. However so hard this saying may seem at first, it is a truth eternally written in our hearts. Bad as the world is, blessed be God, there are great numbers among us, who either through the restraints of religious education or from self-love and reputation, abstain from some of the viler sins in society, and look with detestation upon those who indulge in them. But then because of an over-eager pursuit after the things of sense and time, their souls become numb and fall into a spiritual slumber, and by degrees become dead to God and the things of true religion; they are deaf to all the precious invitations of the gospel and act as the most abandoned prodigals. It is remarkable, therefore, that our Savior, knowing the wickedness of the heart, would still come and preach his gospel, that he would come and tabernacle among us, become one of us, and die for us. "And the master said to the servant, 'Go out to the highways and hedges and compel people to come in, that my house may be filled. For I tell you, none of those men who were invited shall taste my banquet'" (Luke 14:23).

OCTOBER 5

Into the Wilderness

Your fathers ate the manna in the wilderness, and they died.
JOHN 6:49

Dearly beloved, today you are invited to take a walk into the wilderness, to behold, sympathize with, and get instruction and comfort from a Savior who was tempted. In the conflict, he proves himself to be God's beloved Son, and the Father gives evidence that he was pleased in and with him. Consider how our great Michael fought with and overcame the dragon … Jesus had been publically baptized and was thus inaugurated to his mediatorial office by the opening of the heavens and the Spirit of God descending on him as a dove. God spoke of his Son: "This is my beloved Son, with whom I am well pleased" (Matt. 3:17). Then, when he came from the solemn ordinance of baptism he was about to show himself openly to Israel, being full of the Holy Spirit, even then he was led as a champion into the field of the enemy to engage and conquer. He was led into a lonesome, wide, and howling wilderness; probably, says Matthew Henry, into the great wilderness of Sinai. He was thus there forty days and forty nights as Moses and Elijah were before him; all these fasts were miraculous and therefore though we are taught that fasting is a Christian duty, yet we are not to imitate them in this extremity; rather, we are to fast under the normal operations of the Spirit; to fast for so long, for us, is no doubt superstitious, presumptuous, and sinful. During these forty days, our Lord felt no hunger; his converse with heaven was his meat and drink; but afterwards he was hungry and that is when the tempter came to him.

OCTOBER 6

The Godly Poor

For the love of money is the root of all kinds of evils. It is through this craving that some have wandered away from the faith and pierced themselves with many pangs.

1 TIMOTHY 6:10

Did the tempter come to Christ when he saw that he was hungry? Then let those of you who are reduced to a low estate learn that an hour of poverty is an hour of temptation, not only to murmur and doubt your own sonship and the divine favor, but also to advance yourself through unlawful means. "If you are the Son of God, command these stones into bread." Remember the prayer of Agur who begged for moderation "lest I be poor and steal and profane the name of my God" (Prov. 30:9). Learn, therefore, you godly poor to be upon your guard and remember that poverty and temptations are no marks of your being cast off by God; for your Lord was hungry, he was tempted to doubt his sonship on account of this. Learn not to distrust the Lord but to see him as your Father who is in heaven. Angels came and ministered to Jesus, and he who is Lord of the angels will send some kind of messenger or other to relieve your wants. Your extremity will be Christ's opportunity. Make your wants known to him, for he cares for you … and those of you who are rich in this world, watch and pray unless you fall into Satan's temptations. Those who are exalted above your fellow man, as on the pinnacle of the temple, take heed lest by spiritual pride, vanity, or any other sin that entangles you cast yourselves down. Oh, that it may be said of us as the papists used to say of Luther: "That German beast does not love gold."

OCTOBER 7

Worthy of the Gospel

Only let your manner of life be worthy of the gospel of Christ.
PHILIPPIANS 1:27A

It is the apostle Peter's advice to the married persons of his time that they should walk as becomes the gospel of Christ, that those who were without might be won to embrace the Christian religion by seeing and observing their pious conversation coupled with fear. What the apostle presses on married persons we find elsewhere enjoined on each member of the church. We are commanded by the Lord to let our light shine before men, and so to glorify our Father who is in heaven. Paul tells us to redeem the time; that is, to embrace every opportunity to do others good. But, alas, those who do not live such Christian lives and who yet profess the truth are so far from gaining converts to Christ. For how can it be expected that infidels should honor our God when Christians themselves despise him? Or that any should embrace our religion when professors make so light of one of its strictest commands? No, to our grief and shame be it spoken; it is by these impieties that our religion has become a by-word among the heathen; that the sacred authority of Jesus and his doctrine is despised, and God's name blasphemed among the Gentiles. These cannot but be sad stumbling blocks and offences in the way of our godly living. We may say of them as our Lord did of Judas: "It would have been better for that man if he had not been born" (Matt. 26:24); or, "I tell you that it will be more tolerable on the Day of Judgment for the land of Sodom than for you" (Matt. 11:24).

OCTOBER 8

One Thing Needful

But Martha was distracted with much serving. And she went up to him and said, "Lord, do you not care that my sister has left me to serve alone? Tell her then to help me."

LUKE 10:40

It was the amiable character of our blessed Redeemer that he went about doing good; this great motive, which animated all his actions, brought him to the house of his friend Lazarus at Bethany, and directed his behavior there. Though it was the season of recess from public labor, our Lord brought the sentiments and the pious cares of a preacher of righteousness into the parlor of a friend. There his doctrine dropped as the rain and distilled as the dew on the happy little circle that were then surrounding him. Mary, the sister of Lazarus, with great delight made one amongst them; she seated herself at the feet of Jesus in the posture of an humble disciple; and we have a great deal of reason to believe, that Martha, his other sister, would gladly have been with her there; but domestic cares pressed hard upon her, and she burdened with much serving, being perhaps too solicitous to prepare a sumptuous entertainment for her heavenly Master, and the train that attended him. Happy are they, who, in a crowd of busyness, do not lose something of the spirituality of their minds, and of the composure and sweetness of their tempers. This good woman comes to our Lord with too impatient a complaint, insinuating some little reflection, not only on Mary but on him too. "Lord, do you not care that my sister has left me to serve alone? Tell her to help me." Our Lord, willing to take all opportunities of suggesting useful thoughts, answers her in these words: "Martha, Martha, you are anxious and troubled about many things, but only one thing is needful."

OCTOBER 9

Resolve for Christ

Do not lie to one another, seeing that you have put off the old self with its practices.

COLOSSIANS 3:9

You who have been swearers and cursers, you, who have been harlots and drunkards, you, who have been thieves and robbers, you, who have hitherto followed the sinful pleasures and diversions of life, let me beseech you, by the mercies of God, that you would no longer continue therein but that you would forsake your evil ways, and turn to the Lord, for he waits to be gracious to you; he is ready, he is willing, to pardon you of all your sins; but do not expect Christ to pardon you of sin, when you run into it, and will not abstain from complying with the temptations; but, if you will be persuaded to abstain from evil and choose the good, to return to the Lord and repent of your wickedness, he has promised he will abundantly pardon you … and will love you freely. Resolve now this day to have done with your sins forever; let your old ways and you be separated; you must resolve against it, for there can be no true repentance without a resolution to forsake it. Resolve for Christ, resolve against the devil and his works, and go on fighting the Lord's battles against the devil and his emissaries; attack him in the strongest holds he has, fight him as men, as Christians, and you will soon find him to be a coward; resist him, and he will fly from you. Resolve, through grace, to do this, and your repentance is half done: but then take care that you do not ground your resolutions on your own strength, but in the strength of the Lord Jesus; he is the way, he is the truth, and he is the life; without his assistance you can do nothing, but through his grace strengthening you, you will be enabled to do all things.

OCTOBER 10

Gross Folly

For not all have faith.

2 THESSALONIANS 3:2

For you have either repented or you have not; you are believers in Christ or you are unbelievers. If you have never truly repented of your sins and never have forsaken your lusts, do not be offended if I speak so plainly to you; for it is in love, love to your souls, that constrains me to speak so plainly to you. I shall lay before you your great danger and the misery to which you are exposed while you remain unrepentant. And oh, that this may be a means of making you flee to Christ for pardon and forgiveness. While your sins are not repented of you are in danger of death and if you should die, you would perish forever. There is no hope of any who live and die in their sins, but that they will dwell with devils and damned spirits to all eternity. And how do we know we shall live much longer? We are not sure of seeing our own habitations this night in safety. Why then would you be at ease and pleasure while your sins are not pardoned? As sure as the word of God is true, if you die in this condition, you will be shut out of all hope and mercy for endless ages and shall pass into eternal misery. So what are all your pleasures worth? They last for a moment and have only a short continuance; it is gross folly to choose the transitory over the eternal.

OCTOBER 11

The Great Work of God

Do not be anxious about anything, but in everything by prayer and supplication with thanksgiving let your requests be made known to God.

PHILIPPIANS 4:6

It is the care of the soul, as opposed to the cares of the body, to which our Lord gently admonished Martha. The care of the soul implies a readiness to hear the words of Christ, to seat ourselves with Mary at his feet, and to receive both the law and the gospel from his mouth. It supposes that we learn from this divine teacher the worth of our souls, their danger and their remedy, and that we become above all things solicitous about their eternal salvation. Thus heartily repenting of all our sins and cordially believing the everlasting gospel, we receive the Lord Jesus for righteousness and life, resting our souls on the value of his atonement and the efficacy of his grace. It imports the sincere dedicating of ourselves to the service of God and a faithful adherence to it, notwithstanding all oppositions rising from our inward corruptions and outward temptations, and a resolute perseverance in the way of gospel dependence until we receive the end of our faith in our complete salvation. Thus, this "one thing needful" represents various things in Scripture: sometimes it is called "regeneration," or "the new creature;" other times "his love and keeping his commandments;" still other times, "faith" or "receiving Christ and believing in him," which is often represented as the "great work of God" (John 6:29), the great thing which God in his glorious gospel requires, as well as by his Spirit produces in us.

OCTOBER 12

Sorrow and Grief

How long must I take counsel in my soul and have sorrow in my heart all the day?

PSALM 13:2

Our sorrow and grief for sin must not spring merely from a fear of wrath. For if we have no other ground but that it proceeds from self-love, and not from any love for God. And if love for God is not the chief motive in your repentance, your repentance is in vain and not to be esteemed true. Many, in our days, think their crying to God is repentance, and that God will forgive them as such; but indeed, they are mistaken; it is not the drawing near to God with our lips, while our hearts are far from him, which he regards. Repentance does not come by fits and starts; no, it is one continued act of our lives; for as we daily commit sin, so we need a daily repentance before God to obtain forgiveness for those sins we commit. It is not your confessing yourselves to be sinners, it is not knowing your condition to be sad and deplorable, so long as you continue in your sins; your care and endeavors should be, to get the heart thoroughly affected therewith, that you may feel yourselves to be lost and undone creatures. Christ came to save such as are lost; and if you are enabled to groan under the weight and burden of your sins, then Christ will ease you and give you rest. And until you are thus sensible of your misery and lost condition, you are a servant to sin and to your lusts, under the bondage and command of Satan, doing his drudgery: you are under the curse of God and liable to judgment. Consider how dreadful your state will be at death, and after the Day of Judgment, when you will be exposed to such miseries which the ear has not heard, neither can the heart conceive, and that to all eternity, if you die impenitent.

OCTOBER 13

Glorious Mansions

Have you an arm like God, and can you thunder with a voice like his?

JOB 40:9

What communication can there be between a sinless God and a creature full of sin, between a pure God and an impure creature? If you were to be admitted to heaven, with your present tempers, in your impenitent condition, heaven itself would be a hell to you; the songs of the angels would be as enthusiasm and would be intolerable for your tastes, if you remain unconverted; therefore, you must have these tempers changed, you must be holy as God is. He must be your God here, and you must be his people, or you will never dwell together to all eternity. If you hate the ways of God and cannot spend an hour in his service, how will you think to be easy to all eternity, in singing praises to him that sits upon the throne, and to the Lamb forever. This is to be the employment, my brothers, of all those who are admitted into this glorious place, where neither sin nor sinner is admitted, where no scoffer ever can come, without repentance from his evil ways, a turning unto God and a cleaving unto him. This must be done before any can be admitted into the glorious mansions of God, which are prepared for all that love Jesus. Therefore, repent of your sins; O my dear brethren, it makes my blood run cold, in thinking that any of you should not be admitted into the glorious mansions above … fly to him for relief … and you shall live and reign, you shall love and live, and live and love with this Jesus to all eternity.

OCTOBER 14

True Physic

No temptation has overtaken you that is not common to man. God is faithful, and he will not let you be tempted beyond your ability, but with the temptation will also provide the way of escape, that you may be able to endure it.

1 CORINTHIANS 10:13

Did our Lord, by prayer, fasting, and temptation, prepare himself for his public ministry? Surely, then, all those who press to be inwardly moved by the Holy Spirit to take upon the office and administration of the church should prepare in the same manner. For though the knowledge of books and men are good in their places, yet without a knowledge of Satan's devices, a minister will be only like a physician who undertakes to prescribe to a sick people without knowing what medicines to administer. It is to be feared that certain ministers have sent many heaven-laden and afflicted souls to surgeons for bloodletting instead of directing them to the blood of Christ to cleanse their hearts and consciences; hence, conviction of sin is looked upon as delirium and violent temptations are censured as madness. Hence it is that truly sorrowful souls have been directed to plays, novels, romances, and marry company to divert them from being too spiritual. Blind guides lead them! Surely, they deserve no better a title than murderers of souls … do not go to them; instead, if you would be useful in binding up the broken-hearted, prepare yourselves for great and many temptations. For Luther said: "prayer and meditation, reading and temptation, make a minister."

OCTOBER 15

Turning the Veil

And I saw the dead, great and small, standing before the throne, and the books were opened. Then another book was opened, which is the book of life. And the dead were judged by what was written in the books, according to what they had done.

REVELATION 20:12

What if we could add the testimony of the dead? What if God were to turn aside the veil between us and the invisible world and permit the most careless sinner to converse for a few moments with the inhabitants of the other side? If you were to ask a happy spirit, which trod the thorniest road to paradise or passed through the fieriest trial, "Was it worth your while to labor so much and to endure so much for what you now possess?" Surely, if the blessed in heaven were capable of answering such, we would be overwhelmed with the glories they now posses. On the other hand, if you could inquire of one tormented in the flames below, if you could ask him, whether his former employments were an equivalent and worthy of the sufferings and despair he now owns, what answer do you suppose he would give? Perhaps an answer of so much horror and rage as you would not be able to so long endure. And if he could not answer, surely there would be such profound language in that silence, a language in the darkness, flames, and groans of that infernal prison, which would speak to your very soul what the word of God has to clearly testified to you of the state of the damned.

OCTOBER 16

Happiness Lost (1)

From the days of John the Baptist until now the kingdom of heaven has suffered violence, and the violent take it by force.
Matthew 11:12

Care of the soul is needful because without this your happiness will be forever lost. A crown of everlasting glory is not surely such a trifle as to be thrown away on a person who is so careless and who will not in good earnest pursue it. God does not ordinarily deal this way, even with the bounties of his common providence, which are comparatively of little value. As to these, the hand of the diligent makes rich and he would be thoroughly distracted rather than prudent who should expect to get an immense estate merely by wishing for it or without some resolute plan and pursuance of a proper course or action to obtain it. That we may not foolishly dream of obtaining heaven in the midst of indolence and sloth; we are expressly told in the word of God that the kingdom of heaven suffers violence, and the violent take it by force, and therefore are we extorted to strive with the greatest intensity and eagerness of mind to enter through the strait gate because many who wish to enter it will not be able to (Luke 13:24). No, when our Lord makes the most gracious promises to the humble petitioner, he does it in such a manner as to exclude the hopes of those who are careless and indifferent. Ask and it shall be give to you; seek and you shall find; knock and the door shall be opened.

OCTOBER 17

Happiness Lost (2)

From the days of John the Baptist until now the kingdom of heaven has suffered violence, and the violent take it by force.
MATTHEW 11:12

Surely, if I could say no more as to the fatal consequences of your neglect than this, that your eternal happiness will be lost if you so neglect your souls as not to be careful in season and out. I would say enough to impress every mind who hears these words to consider what eternity means and so to reflect on the utmost necessity of attending to the duties of true religion. To fall into a state of everlasting forgetfulness might indeed appear as a refuge to a mind filled with the apprehension of eternal misery, but oh, how dreadful a refuge it is! Surely it is such a refuge as a vast precipice (from which a man falling would be dashed to pieces in a moment) might appear to a person pursued by the officers of justice that he might be brought out to a painful and lingering execution. If an extravagant youth would have reason to look around with anguish, on some fair and ample paternal inheritance, which he had sold or forfeited merely for the riot of a few days, how much more melancholy would it be for a rational mind to think that its eternal happiness is lost for any earthly consideration whatever? What tormenting thoughts! To reflect back on one's life and wish that you might have attended to the most important things in light of eternity; you might have been great and happy beyond expression, not merely for a little span of ten thousand thousand ages, but for ever. A line reaching even to the remotest star would not have been able to contain the number of ages, nor would millions of years have been sufficient to write them down.

OCTOBER 18

Denying Self

The eye is the lamp of the body. So, if your eye is healthy, your whole body will be full of light.

MATTHEW 6:22

Self-denial is the grand secret of our holy religion. It is this, my brothers, which distinguishes the true Christian from the mere moralist and formal professor; and without which, none of our actions are acceptable in God's sight. For if your eye be single, says our blessed Lord, if you aim simply to please God without any regard to your own will, your whole body (or all your actions) will be full of light, agreeable to the gospel, which is called "light." But if your eye be evil; that is, if your intention be diverted to any other way, your whole body (and all your actions) will be full of darkness, sinful and unprofitable; indeed, we must not only do the will of God but do it because it is his will. Since we pray for God's will to be done, we must do so cheerfully and out of this principle: because God wills it; and if we would live as we pray, we must go and do likewise. But further, we must renounce our wills in doing, so we must renounce them in preferring the will of God. Whatever befalls us, we must say, with good old Eli, "It is the LORD; let him do what seems good to him;" or with one who is infinitely greater than Eli, "father, not my will but yours be done." O Jesus, your will was innocent, and yet you renounced it; o, teach us, even us, Savior, to submit our wills to yours, in all the evils which shall be brought upon us; and in every good thing teach us to give thanks since it is your blessed will concerning us!

OCTOBER 19

At Wisdom's Gate

Come to me, all who labor and are heavy laden, and I will give you rest.

MATTHEW 11:28

Let me speak a word to you who have not yet known the love of Christ in your souls, but are still waiting for his appearance. Let me speak to you a word of invitation: wait still on the Lord and do not forsake him, though he may not answer your petitions at once or twice seeking unto him; hold on, do not leave seeking him, and you shall have an answer of peace. Remember the poor man who was lame and had lain at the pool of Bethesda for thirty-eight years for relief, yet at last he found that it was worth waiting for and he obtained his desire, he was healed and could walk again. If you are but zealous for the Lord and seek after Jesus, if your zeal is according to godliness and you pray to him with his Spirit, you shall certainly have an answer of peace and shall find it is good to seek unto the Lord; you will be adopted into his family and by his Spirit be enabled to cry, "Abba, Father." O, then, do not leave but be continually waiting at wisdom's gate, and you shall find all her ways to be ways of pleasantness and all her paths peace; then, you shall find that it is worth waiting on the Lord Jesus when you shall have his Spirit within you; all the power of men or devils cannot make you forsake the ways of the Lord Jesus Christ. If you do but once taste of his pardoning love, it will be so delightful to you that you will cry for more and more; you will be full but not satisfied; you will hunger and thirst for more of Jesus, and all your thirsting will turn into joy for everlasting and endless ages.

OCTOBER 20

The Christian's Breath

Brothers, pray for us. Greet all the brothers with a holy kiss.
1 THESSALONIANS 5:25-26

If we inquire why there is so little love to be found among Christians these days, we soon find that the very characteristic, by which everyone should know that we are the disciples of the holy Jesus, is almost banished out of the Christian world; indeed, we shall find it, in a great measure, owing to a neglect or superficial performance of that excellent part of prayer, intercession, or imploring the divine grace and mercy on behalf of others. Some forget this duty of praying for others because they seldom remember to pray for themselves; and even those who are constant in praying to their Father who is in heaven are often so selfish in their addresses to the throne of grace that they do not enlarge their petitions for the welfare of their fellow Christians as they ought. Thereby they fall short of attaining that Christian charity, that unfeigned love to their brothers, which their sacred profession obliges them to aspire after, and without which, though they should bestow all their goods to feed the poor, and even give their bodies to be burned, yet it would profit them nothing. We must remember that it is every Christian's duty to pray for others as well as for himself … prayer is a duty founded on natural religion; the very heathens never neglected it, though many Christian heathens among us do. It is so essential to Christianity that you might expect to find a living man without breath as a true Christian without the spirit of prayer and supplication.

OCTOBER 21

For our Salvation

For we did not follow cleverly devised myths when we made known to you the power and coming of our Lord Jesus Christ, but we were eyewitnesses of his majesty.

2 PETER 1:16

The power of Christ's resurrection avails believers nothing unless they experience its power in raising their dead souls to life. For Christ's chief end in rising from the dead was to enter heaven as our representative and to send down the Holy Spirit to apply that redemption he had finished on the cross to our hearts by working an entire change in them. Without this, Christ would have died in vain. For it would have done us no service to have his outward righteousness imputed to us unless we had an inward inherent righteousness wrought in us. Because, being altogether conceived and born in sin, and consequently unfit to hold communion with an infinitely pure and holy God, we cannot possibly be made meet to see or enjoy him until a thorough renovation has passed upon our hearts. Without this, we leave out the Holy Spirit in the great work of our redemption. But as we were made by the joint concurrence and consultation of the blessed Trinity; and as we were baptized in their name, so must all of them concur in our salvation: as God the Father made us, and the Son of God redeemed us, so must the Holy Spirit seal and sanctify us, or otherwise we have believed in vain and our faith is as nothing. This, then, is what the apostle Paul means by "the power of Christ's resurrection" and this is what we are to experientially know, that Christ rose for our salvation.

OCTOBER 22

God's Goodness

In your goodness, O God, you provided for the needy.
PSALM 68:10

The Lord supplies his People's Need
Jehovah is his Name;
In Pastures Green he makes them feed
Beside the living Stream.

He bring their wand'ring Spirits back,
When they forsake his Ways,
And leads them for his Mercy's sake,
In Paths of Truth and Grace

When they walk thro' the Shades of Death,
His Presence is their Stay;
A Word of his supporting Breath
Drives all their Tears away.

His Hand in Sight of all their Foes
Does still their Table spread;
Their Cup with Blessings overflows,
His Oil anoints their Head.

The sure Provisions of Our God,
Attend us all our Days:
O may his House be our Abode,
And all our Work his Praise!

OCTOBER 23

Miracle at Cana

In the beginning was the Word, and the Word was with God, and the Word was God … This the first of his signs, Jesus did at Cana in Galilee, and manifested his glory. And his disciples believed in him.

JOHN 1:1; 2:11

Saint John had in view, when he wrote his gospel, to prove the divinity of Jesus Christ, the very word who was not only from everlasting with God but who was really God blessed forever, against those arch-heretics Ebion and Cerinthus, whose pernicious principles too many follow in these last days. For this purpose, you make take notice, that John, more than any other evangelist, is more particular in relating our Lord's divine discourses as he is the glorious miracles which he wrought, in turning water into wine, not by a power derived from another, like Moses or the other prophets, but from a power inherent in himself. The words of our text have reference to that notable miracle which Christ performed, his first miracle on earth, and thereby gave proof of his eternal power and godhead. "This, the first of his signs, Jesus did at Cana in Galilee, and manifested his glory. And his disciples believed in him." The miracle here spoken of, turning water into wine at a marriage feast, reveals many things; we may observe that if our Lord were present at a marriage, then, to deny marriage to any order of men, as the papists do, is certainly a doctrine of devils. Rather, marriage is honorable for all … I am persuaded that the devil cannot lay a greater snare for young Christians than to tempt them equally to yoke themselves with unbelievers, as all who are not born again of God.

OCTOBER 24

Lovers of God

If anyone comes to me and does not hate his own father and mother and wife and children and brothers and sisters, yes, even his own life, he cannot be my disciple.

LUKE 14:26

We must deny ourselves not only in our understandings and wills but also in our affections. More specifically, we must deny ourselves the pleasurable indulgence and self-enjoyment of riches. "If any man will come after me, he must forsake all and follow me." And again, to show the utter inconsistency of love for worldly things with the love of the Father, Jesus tells us, "Unless a man forsake all that he hath, he cannot be my disciple" (Luke 14:33, KJV). Now, these texts are not to be taken in a literal sense, as though they obliged rich persons to go and sell all that they have and give to the poor (for that would make them unable to help the poor in the future), but, however, they certainly imply that we are to sit loose to, sell and forsake all in affection, and be willing to part with everything when God shall require it of us. We must use the world as though we had it not, and as though we were in the world but never part of it. Therefore, we must see ourselves as stewards and not proprietors of the manifold gifts of God. We must provide for our households and ourselves what is necessary and expend the rest, not in indulgences and ornaments, but in clothing, feeding, and relieving the naked, hungry, and distressed disciples of Jesus Christ. We must not be lovers of pleasure more than we are lovers of God.

OCTOBER 25

A Divine Magnet

Is it not written, "My house shall be called a house of prayer before all the nations?"

MARK 11:17A

Our text implies that the hearts of all true believers are the seats of prayer. For this end were we built and adorned with such furniture ... Let no one say that such daily prayer is impracticable or at least practicable for only a few and for those who are not hurried in the common affairs of life. For this practice of daily prayer is the common duty and privilege of all true Christians. We are enjoined to pray without ceasing and to rejoice in the Lord always; these are necessary duties for all who bear the name of Christ. And though it must be owned that it is hard for persons to do who are immersed in the world, to serve the Lord without distraction, yet we are bound to do it; we must confess that the lamp of devotion, even in the best of saints, sometimes burns too dimly, yet those who are the temple of the living God must find prayer to be their very element ... indeed, those who love the Lord will find praying as easy as corrupt men do swearing ... brothers, the love of God is in all. When once we are possessed of this, as we certainly must be if we are temples of the living God, mediation, prayer, praise, and other spiritual exercises become habitual and delightful. When once touched with this divine magnet, forever after our souls feel the divine attraction and continually turn to its center, God.

OCTOBER 26

Like a Scroll

If you will not wake up, I will come like a thief, and you will not know at what hour I will come against you.

REVELATION 3:3B

We are all brought into the world in a dreadful disordered condition. For as the root is, so must the branches be. So we are told that Adam gave birth to a son in his own likeness or with the same corrupt nature which he had himself after he had eaten the forbidden fruit. And experience as well as Scripture proves that we are also born in sin and corruption, and therefore incapable while in such a state to hold communion with God. For as light cannot have communion with darkness, so God can have no communion with such polluted sons of Belial. Here, then, appears the end and design of why Christ was manifest in the flesh; that is, to put an end to our inward corruption and to restore us to that primitive dignity in which we were first created. So Christ shed his own precious blood to satisfy his Father's justice for our sins; thereby he procured for us the Holy Spirit, who should once more re-stamp the divine image upon our hearts and make us capable of living with and enjoying the blessed God. This was the great end of our Lord's coming into the world; no, this is the only end why the world is now being kept in being. For as soon as the numbers of the elect come in, the heavens shall be wrapped up like a scroll, the elements shall burn with fervent heat, and the earth, and all therein, shall melt.

OCTOBER 27

With a Child's Heart

Truly, I say to you, unless you turn and become like children, you will never enter the kingdom of heaven.

Matthew 18:3

Search the Scriptures with a humble child-like disposition. For whosoever does not read them with this temper shall in no ways enter into the knowledge of the things contained in them. For God hides the sense of them from those that are wise and prudent in their own eyes, and reveals them only to babes in Christ. For babes are those who think they know nothing yet as they ought to know; who hunger and thirst after righteousness, and humbly desire to be fed with the sincere milk of the word that they may grow thereby. Fancy yourselves, therefore, when you are searching the Scriptures, especially when you are reading the New Testament, to be with Mary sitting at the feet of the holy Jesus, and be as willing to learn what God shall teach you, as Samuel was, when he said, "Lord, speak, for your servant listens." Oh that the unbelievers would pull down every high thought and imagination that exalts itself against the revealed will of God! O that they, as newborn babes, would desire to be fed with the pure milk of the word! Then we should have them no longer scoffing at divine revelation, nor would they read the Bible any more with the same intent the Philistines brought out Samson, to make sport at it; but they would see the divine image and superscription written upon every line. They would hear God speaking unto their souls by it, and, consequently, be built up in the knowledge and fear of him, who is the Author thereof.

OCTOBER 28

The Great Feast

Again he sent other servants, saying, "Tell those who are invited, See, I have prepared my dinner, my oxen and my fat calves have been slaughtered, and everything is ready. Come to the wedding feast."

MATTHEW 22:4

God the Father is ready; God the Son is ready; God the Holy Spirit is ready; the blessed angels above are ready, and the blessed saints below are ready to welcome you to the gospel feast. There is a perfect and everlasting righteousness that is now available to you by Jesus Christ. God, now, upon honorable terms can freely acquit the guilty; God can now be just and yet still justify the ungodly; for he has made Christ to be sin for us; he who knew no sin, that we might be made perfect and righteous in him. The fatted calf has been slain, and Christ, our Passover, has been sacrificed for us. Come, therefore, all you who are sinners and feed upon him in your hearts by faith, with thanksgiving. For Jesus' sake, do not make excuses; do not let a piece of ground, five yoke of oxen, or even a spouse, keep you from this great supper. These you may enjoy as the gifts of God, and make use of them to your Mediator's glory, and yet still be present for the gospel feast. True and undefiled religion does not take away but greatly enhances the comforts of life. Our Lord did not pray that we should be taken out of the world but that we should be delivered from the evil of it. There is room at the cross; there is room in his heavenly mansions.

OCTOBER 29

Worth Enough

Glorious things of you are spoken, O city of God.

PSALM 87:3

Do not say that your sins are too many and too great to expect to find mercy. No, be they ever so many, be they ever so great, but the blood of the Lord Jesus will cleanse you from all. God's grace, my brothers, is free, rich, and sovereign. Manasseh was a great sinner, and yet he was pardoned; Zaccheus was gone far from God and went out to see Christ, with no other view but to satisfy his curiosity; and yet Jesus met him, and brought salvation to his house. Manasseh was an idolater and murderer, yet he received mercy; the other was an oppressor and extortionist who had gotten riches by fraud and deceit, and by grinding the faces of the poor; so did Matthew, too, and yet they all found mercy. Have you been blasphemers and persecutors of the saints and servants of God? So was Saint Paul, yet he received mercy. Have you been common harlots, filthy and unclean persons? So was Mary Magdalene, and yet she received mercy. Have you been a thief? The thief on the cross found mercy. I despair of none of you, however vile you have been; I say, I despair of none of you, especially when God has had mercy on such a wretch as I am. Remember the poor Publican, how he found favor with God when the proud, self-conceited Pharisee, who, puffed up with his own self-righteousness, was rejected. If you will go to Jesus, as the poor Publican did, under a sense of your own unworthiness, you shall find favor; there is worth enough in the blood of Jesus to pardon greater sinners than he has yet pardoned.

OCTOBER 30

Our Asylum

God is our refuge and strength, a very present help in trouble.
Psalm 46:1

Blessed be God, if we have an interest in Christ, God is our help, God is our asylum, our city of refuge, a place appointed by God himself, to which the pursued saints may flee by faith, and be safe. The wicked have no notion of this when they are in trouble. What is their refuge? Let a soul be under spiritual trouble and cry out, "What can I do to be saved?" Let him go to a carnal minister, an unconverted wretch, that knows nothing of this matter, and what shall he be told? "Oh, go and play some cards and divert yourself from your troubles." That is to say, "the devil must be your refuge." Worldly people have worldly refuges; and Cain would see as if he were in earnest when he said, "My punishment is greater than I can bear;" what does he do? He goes and diverts himself by building a city. The devil, my brothers, will give you leave to amuse yourselves; you may have your choice of diversions, only take care to be diverted from God, and the devil is sure to have you; but the believer has something better; faith sweeps away the refuge of lies and the believer turns to his God and says, "O my God, you are my asylum. I fly to you for rest and comforts, for peace and health;" "Trust in him at all times, O people; pour out your heart before him; God is a refuge for us" (Ps. 62:8).

OCTOBER 31

Glorious Things

Glorious things of you are spoken, O city of God … From of old no one had heard or perceived by the hear, no eye has seen a God besides you, who acts for those who wait for him.
PSALM 87:3; ISAIAH 64:4

I am afraid, my dear hearers, that even believers themselves, those who have tasted of the grace of God, do not reflect and meditate as they ought on the glorious and amazing happiness they are called to experience in this life by the Spirit of God. Rather, we content ourselves too much with our hopes and if we attain to a good hope, through grace, we are ready to think we have stepped up to the last step of the gospel ladder and have nothing more to do than to rest in that hope without ever attaining to an abiding and full assurance of faith. If we would examine the Scriptures and not choose to bring them down to us, but beg God to raise our hearts to them, we shall find that the believer is made partaker of the grace of life as well as an heir: the one is on earth, the other in heaven, and one is only a foretaste of the other. The blessed prophet Isaiah, speaking of the privileges of the children of God, says, "What no eye has seen, nor ear heard, nor the heart of man imagined, what God has prepared for those who love him." God grant that we may be of this happy number! Hence, like an evangelist, the prophet draws aside the veil, and, as one inspired by the Spirit of God, and filled with the rays of divine light, gives us a transporting view of the gospel state and the glory that the church militant enjoys below before its triumphant state above.

NOVEMBER 1

For a Sight of Him

Then Job answered the L*ORD and said: "I know that you can do all things … I heard of you by the hearing of the ear, but now my eye sees you."*

JOB 42:1, 5

Descend from Heav'n immortal Dove,
Stoop down and take us on your Wings,
And mount, and bear us far above
The Reach of these inferior Things.

O for a Sight, a pleasing Sight!
Of our Almighty Father's Throne!
There sits our Saviour, crown'd with Light,
Cloth'd in a Body like our own.

Adoring Saints around him stand,
And Thrones and Pow'rs before him fall,
The God shines gracious thro' the Man,
And sheds sweet Glories on them all.

When shall the Day, dear Lord, appear,
That we shall mount to dwell above,
And stand and bow among them there,
And view your Face, and sing your Love?

NOVEMBER 2

Religious Society

Let us consider how to stir up one another to love and good works.

HEBREWS 10:24

God has given us a harvest, and there has been many who gathered in; a winnowing time will come. His fan is already in his hand. Yet a little while and I am persuaded he will thoroughly purge his flour. The shepherds must first be smitten; and next, endeavors will be used to scatter the sheep. The religious societies Satan has undoubtedly desired to have, that he may sift them as wheat. My brothers, watch and pray one for another, that you may be enabled to stand in such an hour of temptation, and having done all, to stand. Do not be ashamed of that wherein you ought to glory. Religious society is of divine extraction. As God made man, so God said, "It is not good that man should be alone. I will make a help meet for him." Meet, as I take it, not merely for his body (man had few bodily wants in paradise) but chiefly and primarily for his better part; that is, his soul, that he might have one to converse with of his own species, bone of his bone, and flesh of his flesh. It is true, man is now a fallen, but yet he is a social creature: and as the end of his coming into this world was to prepare for a better; so without doubt the chief end of society in general, and of religious society in particular, is, that we may be great helps for each other in the great work of our salvation.

NOVEMBER 3

Moonlight

He made the moon to mark the seasons, the sun knows its time for setting.

PSALM 104:39

Sometimes instead of the sun there is only moonlight, which shows the difference a believer feels in his soul, both in relation to grace and comfort. Both sun and moon give light, but oh, how far superior is the one to the other. The moon gives only a very faint, uncertain light, waxes and wanes, and at best is almost nothing when compared with the light, and the blessed reviving heat of the sun. Hence, my brothers, this world sometimes is a world of mourners. It is said that our days of morning shall end, for in heaven we shall find peace, and here below believers are very often mournful, trying, and afflicting, though they end in joy as our Lord intimates in his opening his gospel with these words: "Blessed are they that mourn, for they shall be comforted." Some may think in odd kind of blessing, those who only preach a joyful Christ and are not for any mourning at all. Do you know God in Christ? Let me tell you this – the more you are acquainted with him, the more you will know mourning; scarce can a person be converted without knowing mourning before and after his repentance. Jesus said, "Can the wedding guests mourn as long as the bridegroom is with them? The days will come when the bridegroom is taken away from them, and then they will fast" (Matt. 9:15).

NOVEMBER 4

Honeycomb

And Enoch walked with God: and he was not, for God took him.

GENESIS 5:24 KJV

It is an honorable and pleasing thing to walk with God. The wisest of men has told us that wisdom's "ways are ways of pleasantness, and all her paths are peace" (Prov. 3:17). And I remember pious Matthew Henry, when was about to pass on to eternal life, said to his friend, "You have heard many men's dying words, and these are mine: 'A life spent in communion with God is the pleasantest life in the world.'" I am sure I can set to my seal that this is true. Indeed, I have been listed under Jesus' banner only for a few years; but I have enjoyed more solid pleasure in one moment's communion with my God than I should or could have enjoyed in the ways of sin, though I had continued to have gone on in them for thousands of years. And may I not appeal to all you that fear and walk with God, for the truth of this? Has not one day in the Lord's courts been better to you than a thousand? In keeping God's commandments, have you not found a present, and very great reward? Has not his word been sweeter to you than the honey or the honeycomb? O what have you felt, when, Jacob-like, you have been wrestling with your God? Has not Jesus often met you when meditating in the fields, and been made known to you over and over again in breaking of bread? Has not the Holy Ghost frequently shed the divine love abroad in your hearts abundantly, and filled you with joy unspeakable, even joy that is full of glory? I … freely acknowledge the yoke of Christ to be easy, and his burden light; or to use the words of one of our prayer books, "his service is perfect freedom."

NOVEMBER 5

Godly Sorrow

He will wipe away every tear from their eyes, and death shall be no more, neither shall there be mourning, nor crying, nor pain anymore, for the former things have passed away.

REVELATION 21:4

When a poor believer is acquainted with Jesus Christ, he mourns for having crucified the Son of God, and you will mourn for the same sin after conversion. Surely, you should mourn for the sins you committed before your conversion as you do for those afterwards. For David writes when an old man, "Remember not the sins of my youth or my transgressions; according to your steadfast love remember me, for the sake of your goodness, O LORD" (Ps. 25:7). And Paul mourned for his persecution of true Christians prior to his own conversion; and all this after he was caught up into the third heaven. See Mary rushing into the house, washing her Lord's feet with her tears and wiping them with her hair. Do not suppose that she was as fancily dressed as women are now; rather, she did not make such an ape of herself, but her hair was very fine, in an honest way, and she breaks the alabaster box of ointment … see her at the feet of her Savior, and Jesus Christ answers her and says she loves much because much had been forgiven. I ask you, dear Christians, if the sweetest times you ever knew were not those when you saw the crucified Savior; when you could say, "Lord, you forgive me; I feel it, know it, but I cannot forgive myself."

NOVEMBER 6

The Worst Light

My lyre is turned to mourning, and my pipe to the voice of those who weep.

JOB 30:31

A true believer will mourn over his corruptions ... I have often learned something from the difference of glasses. You look into the common glasses and see yourselves so fine, and admire your person, dress, and so on; but when you see yourself through a microscope, how many worms are discovered on your fine skin, enough to make you ashamed of the vermin and filth that is found there. So it is in faith, that glass would show you so much corruption cleaving to your every action that you would become sin-sick and mourn that you have known God for so long but are so little like him. What does Paul say? "Who shall deliver me from this body of death?" And yet, notwithstanding, he knows that there is no condemnation for those in Jesus Christ, and yet still cries out, "O, wretched man that I am!" I would have thought, O, rather how happy are you – formerly a persecutor and now a preacher, a man honored with the third heaven – but no, he saw himself as a wretched man; this was the habitual temper of his heart. Some people are humbled by fits and starts, but Paul felt his sins daily. Many things that we are not concerned about, Paul looked up them as such that made his heart ache because he thought he could not live near enough to God ... this reminds me of a good woman who was charmed with Thomas Manton and said to him, "O, sir, you have made such an excellent sermon today; I wish I had your heart." He answered, "Do you so, good woman? You had better not wish for it, for if you had it you would wish for your own again." Thus, the best men see themselves in the worst light.

NOVEMBER 7

Thousand Things

For everything there is a season … a time to weep, and a time to laugh; a time to mourn, and a time to dance.

ECCLESIASTES 3:1, 4

How many thousand things are there that make you mourn here below? Who can tell the tears that godly parents shed for their ungodly children? Do you not know, you young folks, what plague your own children may be to you someday? Therefore, hear your parents and listen to them when it is a time of grace … I once asked a godly widow, "Madam, how is your son?" She turned aside with tears, and said, "Sir, he is no son to me now." … It is a difficulty with some to know how to behave towards unconverted relations. If you do not go to them, they will say you are precise; if you do, and are faithful, they will soon show you they have enough of your company. This sends a godly person home mourning; and then there comes a thought, "Shall I speak to them any more, or let them go to the devil?" This is not like parting from your friends by death, but burying them alive. When dead, we know we must submit, but to part from friends, those we loved, and thought to have lived with till we came to heaven, is mournful indeed. Moreover, the poor state of the church makes many a minister and close-walker with God to weep over the desolations of the sanctuary, and to mourn for those that will not mourn for themselves. Thus our Lord wept over Jerusalem, "O Jerusalem, Jerusalem, how often would I have gathered your children, as a hen gathers her chickens."

NOVEMBER 8

Buried in Shadows

Consider and answer me, O LORD my God; light up my eyes, lest I sleep the sleep of death.

PSALM 13:3

Bury'd in Shadows of the Night,
We lie, till Christ restores the Light;
Wisdom descends to heal the Blind,
And chase the Darkness of the Mind.

Lost guilty Souls are drown'd in Tears,
'Till the atoning Blood appears;
Then they awake from deep Distress,
And sing the Lord our Righteousness.

Jesus beholds where Satan reigns,
Binding his Slaves in heavy Chains:
He sets the Pris'ners free, and breaks
The iron Bondage from our Necks.

Poor helpless Worms in you possess
Grace, Wisdom, Power, and Righteousness;
You are our mighty All, may we
Give our whole Selves, O Lord, to you!

NOVEMBER 9

Poor Souls

You serpents, you brood of vipers, how are you to escape being sentenced to hell?

MATTHEW 23:33

Bishop Usher's opinion was, and I heartily agree with it, that those who value themselves most because of their beauty and dress, and do not love God on earth, will be most deformed in hell, and their bodies suffer proportionally there. There is no dressing in hell, nothing but fire and brimstone there, and the wrath of God always waiting on you, O sinner, whoever you are, man or woman. There was a fine saying of James MacLaine, who was executed some years ago, when the cap was pulling over his eyes, "Must I never see the light of your sun any more? Lord Jesus Christ, you Son of Righteousness, arise with healing under your wings on my departing soul." May the Lord Jesus do that for all of us! When you are damned, the days of your mourning will be but at their beginning; there is no end of your mourning in hell. There is but one song, if it may be called so, in hell, that is, "How I am tormented in this flame!" Consider all this, you who forget God, and may he bless you with godly sorrow. Believers, pray for those who are hell-bound; some may wonder why you cry so; tell them you cry for them. Perhaps you will say as a wicked one did to a poor woman in Scotland when thousands were awakened there: seeing her weep, he said, "What do you weep for?" "For this people," she said. "Weep for yourself," he answered. "I do; but what is my soul compared to all these poor souls!"

NOVEMBER 10

There is a River

There is a river whose streams make glad the city of God, the holy habitation of the Most High.

PSALM 46:4

There is a river, a river in which believers swim, the streams whereof make their waiting hearts glad for joy … may God be your refuge and continue to be your refuge. You are in God's particular care and the proof that he has made you his peculiar care is seen in his love for you. O, go to the house of God, in the tabernacle, where God delights to dwell, and there you will meet with God and never leave until God would remove you from hence. Whatever trials await you, remember that God will care for you. Though you may have lost your husband, God will be to you as a better husband; may you find him better to you than ten thousand husbands. May he make up the awful chasm that death has made, and may the Lord be your refuge in time and your portion in eternity, and you will be forever blessed … May God grant that his church be filled with his presence and glory … May the Lord be your Master forever, that you may be the Lord's servants, however you are so disposed in this world. O, may God help us to sing the 46th Psalm, "God is our refuge and strength, a very present help in trouble. Therefore we will not fear though the earth gives way, though the mountains be moved into the heart of the sea, though its waters roar and foam, though the mounts tremble at its swelling" (Ps. 46:1). May the river of the living God make glad your hearts, and may you be with God to all eternity.

NOVEMBER 11

Evangelical Faith

We were buried therefore with him by baptism into death, in order that, just as Christ was raised from the dead by the glory of the Father, we too might walk in newness of life.

ROMANS 6:4

I believe, my dear hearers, that the longer you live the more you will find that the royal preacher spoke truth when he said, "There is nothing new under the sun." For as God is always the same so the world, the flesh, and the devil, will be always the same – frail, vile, inimical, and deceitful. New scenes will always surprise us not because they are really new but because they are new to us. Our lives are mostly taken up with viewing only the present appearance of things; we have neither time nor leisure to look back as we ought, or might, upon the events of providence, or the effects of the doctrines of grace. I do not say that my thoughts always run in religious channels, but I wish they did. The Bible contains the unchangeable truths of God, and I am not surprised by the present opposition to the teachings of the good old Puritans and the Dissenters on the "evangelical doctrine" of justification by faith alone. They would strive and endeavor to explode the doctrine as dangerous and destructive to holiness, which they would seem to strive after; but they know nothing of the doctrine according to godliness, nor of the apostle's teaching on evangelical faith, which evidences itself as genuine when it works; it is a working faith but it is not because of works that one is justified; for we are justified in Christ alone, apart from works. "What shall we say then? Are we to continue in sin that grace may abound?" – by no means! "How can we who died to sin still live in it?" (Rom. 6:1-2).

NOVEMBER 12

So many Splendid Sins

For by grace you have been saved through faith. And this is not your own doing; it is the gift of God.

EPHESIANS 2:8

What is there in our performances to recommend us to God? Our persons are in an unjustified state by nature, and we deserve to be damned ten thousand times over. And what must our performances be? We can do no good thing by nature. Indeed, "those who are in the flesh cannot please God" (Rom. 8:8). You may do things materially good but you cannot do a thing formally and rightly good; that is, you may do good to others (and rightly so), but you cannot do good to God; nature cannot act above itself. It is impossible for a man who is unconverted to act for the glory of God. He cannot do anything in faith and we are told that "whatever does not proceed from faith is sin" (Rom. 14:23). After we are renewed, yet we are renewed but in part. Indwelling sin continues in us and there is a mixture of corruption in all our duties. So, then, after we are converted if Jesus Christ were to accept us only according to our works, our works would damn us, for we cannot even pray as the moral law requires ... I can say that I cannot pray but that I sin; my repentance wants to be repented of, and my tears need to be washed in the precious blood of my dear Redeemer. Our best duties are as so many splendid sins. Before you can speak peace to your heart, you must not only be sick of your original and actual sin, but you must be made sick of your righteousness, of all your duties and performances ... if you never felt that you had no righteousness of your own, if you never felt the deficiency of your own righteousness, you cannot come to Jesus.

NOVEMBER 13

Burning Sun

Praise him, sun and moon, praise him, all you shining stars!
PSALM 148:3

I believe the minutest philosophers, and those who have the greatest skill in astronomy, cannot perceive there has been any abatement in the heat of the sun since God first commanded it to rule the day. Then surely, if my God can make a sun that for so many thousands of years shall irradiate, enlighten, and warm the world, without losing any of its light and heat, so does the Sun of righteousness, the Son of God, arise upon the children of God with healing under his wings; he raises, warms, nourishes, and comforts his people, and we have the gospel on the ends of the earth, as well as those who had the honor of conversing with him in the days of his flesh. I mention this in answer to all those who have wrote against the Methodists, and represented them as fanatics. There is no other way of talking against the divine influence, but by allowing it was so formerly, but that it is not so now – they say the primitive Christians had it but it is not to be so with us now as it was formerly. O, my brethren, what fools these great men are when they talk about things they know nothing of. Give them a polyglot [i.e. a Bible with many translations], give them a lexicon, give them a geographical text, or the chronological part of the Scripture, and they have something to say – but when they come to talk of the Spirit of God they see the word "Spirit," and they read the word "grace" but while they read it their hearts cry because their knowledge puffs them up.

NOVEMBER 14

Our Peace

Do two walk together, unless they have agreed to meet?
AMOS 3:3

Walking with God implies that a person is actually reconciled to God the Father, in and through the all-sufficient righteousness and atonement of his dear Son. "Do two walk together, unless they have agreed to meet?" (Amos 3:3). Jesus is our peace as well as our peacemaker. When we are justified by faith in Christ, then, but not until then, we have peace with God. Consequently we cannot be said until then to walk with him. Walking with a person is a sign and token that we are friends with that person, or at least, though we have been at variance, we are now reconciled and have become friends again. This is the great errand that gospel ministers are sent out upon. To us is committed the ministry of reconciliation: as ambassadors for God, we are to beseech sinners, in Christ's stead, to be reconciled unto God, and when they comply with the gracious invitation, and are by faith brought into a state of reconciliation with God, then, and not until then, may they be said to begin to walk with God … and walking with God consists especially in the fixed habitual bent of the will for God, in habitual dependence upon his power and promise, in habitual voluntary dedication of our all to his glory, in habitual eyeing of his precepts in all we do, and in habitual complacence in his pleasure in all we suffer.

NOVEMBER 15

Let us Weep

Humble yourselves before the LORD, and he will exalt you.
JAMES 4:10

Let us humble ourselves and let us be ashamed and abashed before God, and wonder that he has not struck us into hell when we have been complaining so much that the fire was too hot. Let us weep for our stubbornness. Happy are they who used to be put into the fire betimes! It is good for us to bear the yoke of our youth. Some years ago, when I was at the Orphan-house, they told me they were going to yoke two steers together, one sturdy and old, and the other a little one. As soon as they put on the yoke, he kicked once or twice and then bore it well. O, thought I, it is a good thing to be yoked by the Lord. Are any of you now in the furnace, are any of you troubled, or can any of you say that you have no trouble? A calm is sometimes the forerunner of a storm; thank God, you are not in the fire; surely you have been in the fire. There is the devil's fire, the fires of "the lust of the flesh, the lust of the eye, and the pride of life." God help you to come out of these fires, lest they damn your souls forever. You must be put either in the devil's fire or God's fire, and the devil's fires are hottest, because there is no God to support under the trouble they bring upon the soul. Oh, what a dreadful thing it is to be in the devil's fire, and to go out of the fire of the devil here to burn with the devil in hell hereafter!

NOVEMBER 16

Sacrifice of Love

Lead me in your truth and teach me, for you are the God of my salvation; for you I wait all the day long.

PSALM 25:5

Religion turns our whole life into one continued sacrifice of love for God. As a needle, when once touched by a lodestone, turns to a particular pole, so the heart that is touched by God's love turns to his God again. I shall have occasion to take notice of it, by and by, when I am aboard a ship; for as soon as I get on board, I generally place myself in one particular place under the compass that hangs over my head. I often look at it by night and by day; when I rise, the needle turns to one point, and when I go to bed, I find it turns to the same point; and often, while I have been looking at it, my heart has been turned to God, saying, "Lord Jesus, as that needle, touched by the lodestone, turns to one point, O may my heart, touched by the magnet of your love, turn to you!" A great many people think they never worship God but when at church; and a great many are very modest on the Lord's Day, though many begin to leave that off. I know of no place, upon the face of the earth, where the Sabbath is kept as it is at Boston. If a single person were to walk in Boston streets in time of worship, he would be taken up. It is not trusted to poor insignificant men, but the justices go out in time of worship and walk with a white wand – if they catch any person walking in the streets they put them under a black rod … When a soul is turned to God, every day is a Sabbath, every meal is a spiritual refreshment, and every sentence he speaks should be a sermon.

NOVEMBER 17

Grace for us

Grace to you and peace from God our Father and the LORD Jesus Christ.

1 CORINTHIANS 1:4

The word "grace" is a very complex word and takes in all that the blessed Spirit of God does for a poor sinner, from the moment he first draws his breath, and brings him to Jesus Christ, until he is pleased to call him by death. And as it is begun in grace, it will be swallowed up in an endless eternity of glory hereafter; this is called "the grace of our Lord Jesus Christ." Why so? It is because the Lord Jesus Christ purchases this gift for us. Moses gave the Law, but grace and truth came by Jesus Christ, the Son of God. If it were not for the purchase of a Mediator's blood, if it were not that Jesus Christ had bought us with a price, even with the price of his own blood, you and I should never have had, you and I could never have had, the grace of God manifested at all to our souls. The covenant of works being broken, our first parents stood convicted before God: they were criminals, though they did not care to own it; condemned before God, and in themselves, so that like their children they make excuses for their sin. Man by nature had but one neck, and, if God had pleased to have done it, he might justly have cut it off at one blow; but no sooner had man incurred the curse of the law, but behold a Mediator is provided, under the character of the seed of the woman, which should bruise the serpent's head: implying what the Redeemer was first to do without, and afterwards to do in the hearts of all his people. Well, therefore, are we taught in our church collects to end all our prayers with the words, "through Jesus our Lord."

NOVEMBER 18

Jesus Crucified

We know that Christ, being raised from the dead, will never die again; death no longer has dominion over him.

ROMANS 6:9

You that pass by, behold the Man,
The Man of Grief condemn'd for you,
The Lamb of God for Sinners slain,
Weeping to Calvary pursue.

His sacred Limbs they stretch, they tear,
With Nails they fasten to the Wood—
His sacred Limbs—expos'd and bare,
Or only cover'd with his Blood.

See there! his Temples crown'd with Thorns,
His bleeding Hands extended wide,
His streaming Feet transfixt and torn
The Fountain gushing from his Side.

Oh, you dear suff'ring Son of God,
How does your Heart to Sinners move!
Help us to catch your precious Blood,
Help us to taste your dying Love.

NOVEMBER 19

Early Grace

Let no one despise you for your youth, but set the believers an example in speech, in conduct, in love, in faith, in purity.

1 TIMOTHY 4:12

It would be endless to recount the sins and offences of my younger days. They are more in number than the hairs of my head. My heart would fail me at the remembrance of them was I not assured that my Redeemer lives ever to make intercession for me. However the young man in the gospel might boast how he had kept the commandments from his youth, with shame and confusion of face I confess that I have broken them all from my youth. Whatever foreseen fitness for salvation others may talk of and glory in, I disclaim any such thing. If I trace myself from my cradle to my manhood, I can see nothing in me but a fitness to be damned; I here speak the truth, and do not lie. If the Almighty had not prevented me by his grace, and wrought most powerfully upon my soul, quickening me by his free Spirit when dead in trespasses and sins, I had now either been sitting in darkness, and in the shadow of death, or condemned, as the due reward of my crimes, to be for ever lifting up my eyes in torments. But such was the free grace of God to me, that though corruption worked so strongly in my soul, and produced such early and bitter fruits, yet I can recollect very early movings of the blessed Spirit upon my heart, sufficient to satisfy me that God loved me with an everlasting love, and separated me even from my mother's womb, for the work to which he afterwards was pleased to call me.

NOVEMBER 20

Gospel Marrow

Of this gospel I was made a minister according to the gift of God's grace, which was given me by the working of his power.
EPHESIANS 3:7

You, dear sir, have charged me with the offence of reviving the old Calvinistic disputes concerning predestination. I suppose you mean, justification by faith, the imputed righteousness of Christ, man's utter inability to repent or do good works, which you say happily slept for so many years. But if this is my shame, I glory in it. For what is this but the reviving of the essential articles of the Church of England, which are undoubtedly Calvinistic, and which, by your own confession, have slept for so many years. This is too true. But however you may count this as happiness, yet, in my opinion, it is one of the greatest judgments that have befallen our nation. And if it had not been for the remnant of free grace, many of our church's articles would have happily slept for years more. These are the real sentiments of my heart. Can we really plead for a justification of works in the sight of God? Were the great apostle of the Gentiles now living, what anathemas would he pronounce against just Judaizing doctrines? Were Luther on earth, how would he thunder against such a charge! For he calls justification by faith alone the article upon which the church stands or falls. This is the great fundamental point in which we differ from the Church of Rome.

[From a letter to Thomas Church, dated May 22, 1744]

NOVEMBER 21

Our Baptismal Vows

Let us hold fast the confession of our hope without wavering, for he who promised is faithful.

HEBREWS 10:23

The apostle in his Epistle to the Hebrews exhorts them to hold fast the profession of their faith without wavering and soon after adds, as a most effectual means to so desirable an end, "Let us consider how to stir up one another to love and good works, not neglecting to meet together, as is the habit of some, but encouraging one another" (Heb. 10:24-25). As Christianity was not then the national religion, I suppose the assemblies here intended were not such as our public congregations but rather little private societies, or associations, or churches, as was the custom of the primitive Christians who, we are told, continued steadfastly in the apostle's doctrine, and in fellowship one with another. This was the apostle's exhortation to the Christians of those times; and I am fully persuaded there never were more occasions for renewing it than the age wherein we live. Nothing has more alarmed the enemies of the cross of Christ than the zeal that God has stirred up in the hearts of many to put in practice this apostolical injunction. Dance balls, plays, horse races, and such like unchristian and fatal entertainments are condoned and supported by public authority. Few have had courage to speak, preach, or write for the suppressing them so plainly and publicly as they ought; but, if the children of God meet together, as they are required by the word of God, to build up each other in their most holy faith, almost everyone's mouth is opened against them. No, with grief it must be spoken, even many of our masters in Israel, who ought to be patterns and promote every good word and work, are approving the sinful diversions of the age … which is contrary to their baptismal vows.

NOVEMBER 22

Watch Providence

But for me it is good to be near God; I have made the LORD *God my refuge, that I may tell of all your works.*

PSALM 73:28

All that we have to do is to pray and watch Providence … What makes me to think that this is a call from God is that it will be convenient for taking my degree and improving me in my studies. Whether it be or no, God only knows. "Father, into your hands I commend my spirit, for you have redeemed me, O Lord, you God of truth." I approve greatly of your reading Matthew Henry. God works by him here greatly and may the Lord prosper it in your hands. Never leave off watching, reading, praying, and striving, until you experimentally find Christ Jesus formed within you. In a particular manner, my dear friend, watch against all temptations to sloth. When you receive the sacrament, earnestly endeavor to be inwardly bettered by it the week following. Live every day as holily as you can. Be frequent in self-examination morning and evening. Pray earnestly from your heart. Wrestle with God, and beg him to hasten the new birth. Moreover be careful, diligent in your calling, labor hard with your own hands that you may have to give to him that needs. And labor not so much for the meat that perishes as to neglect pursuing that which endures to eternal life. "Therefore, brothers, since we have confidence to enter the holy places by the blood of Jesus, by the new and living way that he opened for us through the curtain …" (Heb. 10:19-20).

[From a letter dated April 2, 1736]

NOVEMBER 23

Faith by Love

But you, beloved, building yourselves up in your most holy faith and praying in the Holy Spirit.

JUDE 20

We must not expect to be saved, or in any way recommend ourselves to God, by any or all the works of righteousness which we have done, or shall, or can do. Jesus is our righteousness, our whole righteousness: imputed to us, instead of our own … Christ, by his sacrifice and perfect obedience, has every way fulfilled the law for us. God will not require to be paid twice. Christ bought our justification with a great price, even with his own blood. It comes to us freely, without any regard to works past, present, or to come. This is the constant language of Christ and his apostles … justified by or through faith, and not for faith; for faith is only a means or instrument whereby the whole righteousness of Jesus Christ is applied to the sinner's soul; and whosoever does thus believes in his heart, setting to his seal that God is true may be assured that his pardon is sealed in heaven, notwithstanding he has lived in an open breach of God's commandments all his life-time before … so, this faith will not be dead, idle or inactive. This is not a faith of the head or a bare assent to things credible (the devils believe and tremble) but it is a faith of the heart, a living principle of new life, infused into the soul by the Spirit of God, thus applying inwardly what Christ has won for us … these are proofs of our justification in God's sight; and as so many tokens of his gratitude and love for what God has done for our soul. This is what the apostle styles a "faith working by love."

NOVEMBER 24

Band of Brothers

Be sober-minded; be watchful. Your adversary the devil prowls around like a roaring lion, seeking someone to devour.
1 PETER 5:8

Why should not the children of God, notwithstanding their little differences, unite in one common interest against spiritual wickedness in high places? Oh, that all who call themselves Christians were thus minded! How should we see the kingdom of Christ come with power, and Satan like lightning fall from heaven! From the beginning, it has been his policy to divide Christians into sects and parties, hoping not only to weaken their interest but also to make them thereby believe that religion wholly consists in being of this or that particular communion. This subtlety of that old serpent has so prevailed that though we all profess to hold one Lord, one faith, one baptism, yet numbers look upon those who differ from them, and that only in externals, almost as creatures of another species, and forbid us with such even to eat. This was once the state of the Jewish, as it is now of the Christian church – but God showed his dislike of such a temper by convincing Peter in a miraculous manner that he was henceforward to call nothing common or unclean but freely to converse with all who feared him and worked righteousness … do not be disobedient to this heavenly vision; for our sakes was it written, "as many as the Lord our God shall call." The self-righteous, and perhaps some who are weak in faith, will censure and condemn your conduct (as the brothers did Peter) when they behold your free conversation in Christ with others of different communions: but Peter has furnished you with an answer, "If then God gave the same gift to them as he gave to us when we believed in the Lord Jesus Christ, who was I that I could stand in God's way?" (Acts 11:17). How dare we, then, make a difference when God has made none?

NOVEMBER 25

Union and Communion

Therefore, confess your sins to one another and pray for one another, that you may be healed.

JAMES 5:16A

Do not content yourselves with reading, singing and praying together; but set some time apart to confess your faults and communicate your experiences one to another. For want of this most of the old societies in London are sunk into a dead formality … They meet on a Sabbath evening, read a chapter, and sing a psalm, but seldom, if ever, acquaint each other with the operations of God's Spirit upon their souls; notwithstanding this was the great end and intention of those who first began these societies. Hence it is that they have only the form of godliness left amongst them, and continue utter strangers to the state of one another's hearts. How love or the power of religion can subsist in such a lukewarm and superficial way of proceeding is very hard to conceive. Do not let your coming together be thus in vain, but plainly and freely tell one another what God has done for your souls. To this end, meet with a few others once a week to tell each other what is in your hearts; that you may then also pray for and comfort each other, as need shall require. None but those that have experienced it can tell the unspeakable advantages of such a union and communion of souls. By this means, brotherly love will be excited and increased amongst you, and you will learn to watch over one another for good. This will teach you the better how to pray, and to give thanks for each other in your private retirement, and happily prevent and deliver you from many snares of the devil: for Satan loves that we should keep his temptations to ourselves, but cares not so much to mess with those whom he knows will tell his devices to other believers.

NOVEMBER 26

On Election

Listen, my beloved brothers, has not God chosen those who are poor in the world to be rich in faith, and heirs of the kingdom, which he has promised to those who love him?

JAMES 2:5

Dear Mr. Wesley,

How has the doctrine of election a tendency to overthrow the whole Christian revelation? It does not. Who ever thought, that God's declaration to Noah, that seedtime and harvest should never cease, could afford an argument for the neglect of ploughing or sowing? Or that the unchangeable purpose of God, that harvest should not fail, rendered the heat of the sun or the influence of the heavenly bodies unnecessary to produce it? No more does God's absolute purpose of saving his chosen preclude the necessity of the gospel revelation or the use of any of the means through which he has determined the decree shall take effect. Nor will the right understanding, or the reverent belief of God's decree, ever allow or suffer a Christian in any case to separate the means from the end, or the end from the means. And since we are taught by the revelation itself that this was intended and given by God as a means of bringing home his elect, we receive it with joy, prize it highly, use it in faith, and endeavor to spread it through all the world, in the full assurance, that wherever God sends it, sooner or later, it shall be savingly useful to all the elect within its call. How then, in holding this doctrine, do we join with modern unbelievers, in making the Christian revelation unnecessary? No, dear sir, you mistake. Infidels of all kinds are on your side of the question. Deists, Arians, Socinians, all criticize God's sovereignty and stand up for universal redemption.

[From a Letter to John Wesley in Answer to His Sermon on Free Grace]

NOVEMBER 27

Reason and Scripture

And they devoted themselves to the apostles' teaching and the fellowship, to the breaking of bread and the prayers.

ACTS 2:42

Christian devotion signifies a life given or devoted to God. Consequently, he and he alone is the devout man who lives no longer to his own will or after the way and spirit of the world but to the sole will of God; who considers God in everything; who makes all the parts of his common life, as well as his more immediate religious exercises, parts of piety, by doing every thing in the name of Jesus Christ and under such rules as are conducive to promote God's glory. Reason and Scripture plainly evince the truth of this … everything that lives, whether in heaven or earth, whether they be thrones or principalities, men or angels, are all bound by the laws of their creation to live wholly to the praise and glory God who is Father of them all. We acknowledge that God alone is to be the rule and measure of our prayers; that in them we are to look wholly to him, and act wholly for him; that we are only to pray in such a manner, and for such things, and with such ends as are suitable to his glory … we are to be equally pious in all other parts of our lives: for were it not our strict duty to live by reason, and to devote all the actions of our lives to God; were it not absolutely necessary, and our highest privilege to walk before him in wisdom and holiness, and all heavenly conversation, doing everything in his name, and for his glory, there would be no excellence and wisdom in the most heavenly prayers.

NOVEMBER 28

A Prayer when under Spiritual Desertion

The troubles of my heart are enlarged; bring me out of my distress.
PSALM 25:17

Ever blessed Redeemer, who was in all things tempted like as we are, except for sin. O you, lover of souls, who in the days of your flesh did offer up strong cries and tears and was heard in what you feared. O you restorer of mankind who was in such agony in the garden that you did sweat great drops of blood … O you Almighty High Priest, who, when through the eternal Spirit you were about to make your soul an offering for sin was deserted of your Father and did cry out in bitterness of soul, "My God, My God, why have you forsaken me?" O you, who now sit at the right hand of God the Father, continually to make intercession for us, look down, I beg you, upon me … for you have turned away for face, and lo, I am troubled. You have taken off my chariot-wheels, and I drive heavily; you have permitted a cloud to overshadow me, and a horrible darkness, fearfulness, and dread to overwhelm me, so that my spirit would utterly sink within me, did I not believe you would yet turn again and visit me. Father, if it is possible, remove this horrible darkness; but if my soul cannot be make perfect without it, your holy, your blessed will be done … Deal with me as seems good in your sight. Only let your grace be sufficient for me; and in the midst of my agonies send down, I beg you, an angel from heaven to strengthen me … grant that my faith fail not … my most loving Master and compassionate Redeemer … enable me to walk by faith, and not by sight, and to seek you in the use of all appointed means … Lord, I believe; help my unbelief … lift up the light of your countenance upon me; restore me to the joy of your salvation … for the sake of your dear son Jesus Christ.

NOVEMBER 29

Acts of Praise

Bless the L*ORD*, *O my soul, and all that is within me, bless his holy name!*

PSALM 103:1

Let us magnify that great God whom angels praise, whom dominions adore, whom powers fall down and tremble before; whose excellent glory cherubim and seraphim proclaim with loud incessant voices: let us bear a part in this heavenly song, and together with angels and archangels, and all the company of heaven, laud and magnify that glorious name; let us tune our voices with theirs, and though we cannot reach their pitch, yet will we exert the utmost of our skill and power to sing with them, "Holy, holy, holy, Lord God of hosts; heaven and earth are full of your glory"… For these are the happy spirits who offer a sacrifice of pure praise before the throne of God continually, who are ever wrapped in the contemplations of his perfections; and see them, not like us through a glass darkly, but near at hand, and face to face. What tongue can express, what thought conceive, the admirable beauty, the exact order, the numberless multitude of this heavenly host? The inexhaustible source of joy springing from the beatific vision; the fervent love which ministers delight without torment; the ever-growing desire, which rises with their satisfactions, and the grateful satisfactions, which crown that desire; and desire always eager, and never uneasy, always full, and never loved: the blessedness derived down to them, by their inseparable union to the fountain of all bliss; the light communicated to them from the original light; the happy change into an immutable nature, by seeing immutable God as he is, and being transformed into the likeness of him they see? ... And happy is that soul, which, refusing to be detained by low and viler objects, directs its flight to the noblest and most exalted, and, like the eagle, builds its nest in the top of the rocks, and keeps its eye steady upon the Sun of righteousness.

NOVEMBER 30

I will Rise

The Son of Man is going to be delivered into the hands of men, and they will kill him. And when he is killed, after three days he will rise.

MARK 9:31

The sacred oracles and the histories of all ages acquaint us that God brings about the greatest things not only by small and unlikely means but by ways and means directly opposite to the carnal reasonings of unthinking men; he chooses things that are not to bring to naught those things which are. How did Christianity spread and flourish? By one who was despised and rejected of men, a man of sorrows and acquainted with grief, and crucified on a cross. He was despised and rejected, not merely by the vulgar and illiterate, but the Rabbis and Masters of Israel, the Scribes and Pharisees, who by the Jewish churchmen were held too in so high a reputation for their outward sanctity, that it became a common proverb, "If only two went to heaven, the one would be a Scribe, and the other a Pharisee." Yet they were the ones who endeavored to silence the voice of all his miracles and doctrine with "Is this not the Carpenter's son?" Or worse, "He is mad, why do you listen to him? He has a devil and casts out devils by Beelzebub, the prince of devils." Their hatred not only followed him to, but after death, when in the grave, when they mocked his promise to rise again. But see: he burst the bars of death asunder and proved himself to be the Son of God with power by rising the third day from the dead.

DECEMBER 1

Victory over Satan

The God of peace will soon crush Satan under your feet. The grace of our Lord Jesus Christ be with you.

ROMANS 16:20

During Christ's temptation by Satan, Satan said, "All these things (a mighty all indeed – a mere imaginary bubble!) will I give you, if you fall down and worship me." This was indeed a desperate parting stroke. It is now high time for you, Satan, O you enemy of souls, to be commanded to depart! Filled with a holy resentment at such hellish treatment, and impatient of the very thought of alienating the least part of his heart and affections from his Father, or dividing them between his God and the world, Jesus said to him, "Get away you Satan, you grand adversary; for it is written, 'You shall worship the LORD your God, and him only shall you serve.' This is the great commandment of the law, the commandment my Father gave unto his Israel of old, and would thou have me, who came to fulfill the law and the prophets, thus shamefully to be a transgressor of it? Get away you – I will bear your insolence no longer. Your other temptations were hellish, like yourself, but this intolerably so. Get you therefore away, Satan; my heavenly Father is the Lord my God, and him only will I serve." And now the battle is over; the important combat is ended; Jesus has won the field. Satan is routed, and totally put to flight. Then, when the devil found that Jesus could withstand even the golden bait, the lust of the eye and pride of life, in the two last, as well as the lust of the flesh in the first temptation, despairing of the least success, and quite stunned with that all-powerful "Get you away, Satan," he left him. Praise God for Christ's resounding victory over Satan!

DECEMBER 2

Victory over Temptation

And lead us not into temptation, but deliver us from evil.
MATTHEW 6:13

The great and important duty that is incumbent on Christians is to guard against all appearance of evil, to watch against the first risings in the heart to evil, and to have a guard upon our actions that they may not be sinful. It is true the devil is tempting us continually. Our own evil hearts are ready to join with the tempter, to make us fall into sins, that he thereby may obtain a victory over us, and that we may be his subjects, his servants, his slaves. Then by-and-by he will pay us our wages, which will be death temporal, and death eternal. Our Lord Jesus Christ saw how his people would be tempted, and that the great enemy of their souls would lay hold of every opportunity to keep poor sinners from coming to the Lord Jesus Christ, hurrying them with temptation, to drive them to some great sins. Then if he cannot gain them over, he tempts them to fall into a smaller sin, and suit his temptations time after time. When he finds none of these things will do, he often transforms himself into an angel of light, and by that means makes the soul fall into sin, to the dishonor of God, and the wounding of itself. The Lord Jesus, seeing how liable his disciples and all others would be to be overcome by temptation, advises them when they pray, to beg that they might not be led into temptation. It is so dangerous to engage so subtle and powerful an enemy as Satan is, that we shall be overcome as often as we engage, unless the Lord be on our side. My brothers, if you were left to yourselves, you would be overcome by every temptation with which you were beset.

DECEMBER 3

A Complete Savior

And be found in him, not having a righteousness of my own that comes from the law, but that which comes through faith in Christ.

PHILIPPIANS 3:9

Satan is an enemy to God and goodness; he is a hater of all truth. Why else did he slander God in paradise? Why did he tell Eve, "You shall not surely die?" He is full of malice, envy and revenge. What else could induce him to tempt innocent men in paradise? He is remarkable for his subtlety, for not having power given him from above, he is obliged to wait for opportunities to betray us and catch us by guile. Therefore, he made use of the serpent to tempt our first parents. To lie in wait to deceive is another part of his character. Though this character is given of the devil, if we were to examine our own hearts, we should find many of the tempter's characters legible in us. You may value yourselves as fine rational creatures and noble beings. You were so, as you first came out of God's hands, but now you are fallen. There is nothing lovely or desirable in man; his heart is a sink of pollution, full of sin and uncleanness. Yet our modern, polite preachers tell us, that there is a fitness in men, and that God, seeing you a good creature, gives you his grace. But this, though it is a modern, polite and fashionable way of talking, is very unscriptural. Many pulpits ring of nothing more than doing no one any harm, living honestly, loving your neighbor as yourselves, and doing what you can, and then Christ is to make up the deficiency. This is making Christ to be half a Savior, and man the other part; but I say, Christ will be your whole righteousness, your whole wisdom, your whole sanctification, or else he will never be your whole redemption.

DECEMBER 4

Safety in Christ

Little children, you are from God and have overcome them, for he who is in you is greater than he who is in the world.

1 JOHN 4:4

Why does the devil tempt you? It is out of envy to you and to the Lord Jesus Christ that he endeavors to keep you from trusting in and resting with Jesus; and if he can only keep you from laying hold of Christ by faith, he knows he has you safe enough. And the more temptations you are under, according to their nature and greatness, you are more hurried in your minds, your thoughts and affections are more unsettled, and you are more apt to conclude that if you were to go to Christ at present he would not receive you. But this is the policy of the tempter, to make you have low and dishonorable thoughts of the blessed Jesus; and so by degrees he works upon your minds so that you are careless and indifferent about Christ. This, my brothers, is the design of the tempter. Nothing will please him more than to see you ruined and lost forever. He tempts you for that end, that you may lose your interest in Jesus Christ, and that you may dwell with him and apostate spirits to all eternity. He knows that Jesus Christ died for sinners, and yet he would try to keep souls from seeking to this city of refuge for shelter, and from going to Gilead for the true balm. Oh! Flee to and rest in the precious Savior Jesus Christ to whom all power is given in heaven and on earth, who is able to deliver you from the evil one and secure your eternal safety.

DECEMBER 5

Be Watchful

Be sober-minded; be watchful. Your adversary the devil prowls around like a roaring lion, seeking someone to devour.
1 PETER 5:8

When Satan finds he cannot allure you by flattery, he will try you by frowns and the terrors of this world. He will stir up people to point at you and cry, "Here comes another troop of his followers." He will stir them up to jeer, scoff, backbite and hate you; but if he still finds this will not do, then he throws doubts and discouragements in your mind, whether the way you are in is the true way or not. Or he will suggest, "What! Do you expect to be saved by Christ? He did not die for you, for you have been too great a sinner. You have lived in sin so long, and committed such sins against Christ such that he will not forgive." Thus he hurries poor sinners almost into despair. And very often, when the people of God are met to worship him, he sends his agents, the scoffers, to disturb them. But the Lord is on our side, and so prevents all the attempts of wicked and designing men to disturb and disquiet us. Lord Jesus, forgive them who are thus persecuting your truth! Jesus, show them that they are fighting against you, and that it is hard for them to kick against the pricks! These, my brothers, are some of the ways Satan takes, in his temptations, to bring you from Christ. Many more might be named, but these are sufficient, I hope, to keep you on your guard, against all that the enemy can do to hinder you from coming to Christ.

DECEMBER 6

Divine Assistance

In all circumstances take up the shield of faith, with which you can extinguish all the flaming darts of the evil one;

EPHESIANS 6:16

My dear friends, let me beseech you to go to Jesus Christ. Tell him how you are assaulted by the evil one who lies in wait for your souls. Tell him that you are not able to master him in your own strength. Beg his assistance, and you shall find him ready to assist you, and to be your Guide, your Comforter, your Savior, and your all. He will give you strength to resist the fiery darts of the devil. You can nowhere find one so proper to relieve you, as Jesus Christ. He knows what it is to be tempted; he was tempted by Satan in the wilderness. Jesus will give you the assistance of his Spirit to resist the evil one, and then he will fly from you. In Christ Jesus you shall have the strength you stand in need of, and the devil shall have no power. Therefore fear not, for in the name of the Lord we shall overcome all our spiritual Amalekites. Let the devil and his agents rage, let them breathe out threatening, yes, let them breathe out slaughters, yet we can rejoice in this, that Jesus Christ has them in his power, and they shall go no farther than he permits them. They may rage horribly, but they can go no farther, until they have got more power from on high. Praise be our Savior for his power and love!

DECEMBER 7

Amazing Love

His mouth is most sweet: yea, he is altogether lovely. This is my beloved, and this is my friend, O daughters of Jerusalem.
SONG OF SOLOMON 5:16

O you who have found Jesus Christ assisting and supporting you in all the temptations of this life, have you not found him to be a gracious Master? Is he not the chiefest of ten thousand, and altogether lovely? Now you see a form and comeliness in Christ, which you never saw before. O, how do you and I wish we had known Jesus sooner, and that we had more of his love. It is condescending love, it is amazing love, it is forgiving love, it is dying love, it is exalted and interceding love, and it is glorified love. Jesus Christ loved me before I loved him; he saw me polluted in blood, full of sores, a slave to sin, death and hell, and running to destruction, and then he passed by and said to my soul, "Live." He snatched me as a brand plucked from the fire. It was love that saved me; it was all of the free grace of God, and that alone. The little experience I have had of this love makes me amazed at the condescension, love and mercifulness of the blessed Jesus, that he should have mercy upon such a wretch as I. O, my friends, the kingdom of God is within me, and this fills me so full of love, that I would not want to be in my natural state again, not for millions of millions of worlds. I long to be with Jesus, to live with the Lord that bought me, to live forever with the Lamb that was slain, and to sing Hallelujahs unto him. Eternity itself will be too short to set forth the love of the Lord Jesus Christ. Indeed I cannot forbear speaking again, and again, and again, of the Lord Jesus.

DECEMBER 8

Rest for your Souls

Come to me, all who labor and are heavy laden, and I will give you rest.

MATTHEW 11:28

If there are any reading who are strangers to the love of the Lord Jesus Christ, do not despair, but come unto Christ. He will have mercy upon you, he will pardon all your sins, he will heal all your backslidings, and he will love you freely, and take you to be with himself. Come therefore, O my guilty brothers, unto Jesus, and you will find rest for your souls. You do not need to fear or despair, when God has had mercy upon such a wretch as I. He will save you also, if you will come unto him by faith. Why do ye delay? What! Do you say you are poor, and therefore ashamed to come? Christ does not mind your poverty. Come in all your rags, in all your pollution, and he will save you. Do not depend upon anything but the blood of Jesus Christ. Do not stand out an hour longer, but give your hearts to Christ. Give him the firstlings of the flock; come unto him now, lest he should cut you off before you are prepared, and your soul be sent to that pit from where there is no redemption. Do not waver, but give him that which he desires, your hearts. It is the heart the Lord Jesus Christ wants, and when you have an inward principle wrought in your hearts by this same Jesus, then you will feel the sweetness and pleasure of communion with God.

DECEMBER 9

Two Callings

The hand of the diligent will rule, while the slothful will be put to forced labor.

PROVERBS 12:24

Friends, I beseech you to let love, kindness, meekness, patience and long-suffering be found in you, as they were in the blessed Jesus Christ. I beseech you not to neglect the frequent coming together, to tell each other what great things the Lord Jesus Christ has done for your souls, and to build up, confirm and strengthen those who are weak in faith. However, I do not now encourage you to leave your lawful callings, and your business, in which God, by his providence, has placed you in this life. For you have two callings, the one a general calling, and the other a special one. It is your duty to consider your families, and if you neglect them out of any pretence whatsoever, such as going to church, or to societies, then you are out of the way of your duty, and offering that to God which he does not command you. But then, my friends, you are to take care that the things of this life do not hinder the preparing for that which is to come. Do not let the business of the world make you unmindful of your souls. In all your moral actions and in the business of life, take care to let all be done with a view to the glory of God, and the salvation of your souls.

DECEMBER 10

Warning against Worldliness

Set your minds on things that are above, not on things that are on earth.

COLOSSIANS 3:2

When Paul preached at Athens, he told the Athenians that as he passed by and beheld their devotions, he perceived they were in all things too superstitious. But if this apostle were to rise, and come to publish the glad tidings of salvation in any of our populous cities, he would see no reason why he should charge the inhabitants with this. Rather, as he passed by and observed the tenor of their life, he could say, "I perceive in all things you are too worldly-minded. You are too eagerly bent on pursuing your lawful business; so eagerly, as either wholly to neglect, or at least too heedlessly to attend on, the one thing that is needful. There cannot then be a greater charity shown to the world, than to sound an alarm in their ears, and to warn them of the inexpressible danger of continually grasping after the things of this life, without being equally, no, a thousand times more concerned for their well-being in a future state. And there is still the more occasion for such an alarm, because worldly-mindedness so easily and craftily besets the hearts of men. For out of pretence of serving God, in laboring for the meat which perishes, they are insensibly lulled into such a spiritual slumber, as to scarcely perceive their neglect to secure that which endures to everlasting life.

DECEMBER 11

Created for Holiness

Worship the Lord *in the splendor of holiness; tremble before him, all the earth!*

Psalm 96:9

For the perfecting this true religion in our hearts, the eternal Son of God came down and shed his precious blood. By this alone can we become the sons of God. If we were to judge by the common practice of the world, we might think we were sent into it for no other purpose than to care and toil for the uncertain riches of this life. But if we consult the Scriptures, they will inform us that we were born for nobler ends, to be born again from above, to be restored to divine likeness by Jesus Christ, our second Adam, and to thereby be made fit to inherit the kingdom of heaven. All creatures, even the busiest people, must fulfill the end for which they were created. Some think that religion only belongs to the clergy, but what a fatal mistake this is, seeing all persons are called by God to the same state of inward holiness. As we are all corrupt in our nature, so must we all be renewed and sanctified. And though it must be granted that the clergy lie under double obligations to be examples to believers, as being more immediately dedicated to the service of God, yet as we have been all baptized with one baptism into the death of Christ, we are all under the necessity of performing our baptismal covenant, and perfecting holiness in the fear of God. For the Scriptures point out to us only one way of admission into the kingdom of Christ, through the narrow gate of a sound conversion. He that does not enter into the sheepfold by this door, whether clergy or layman, will find, to his everlasting confusion, that there is no climbing up another way.

DECEMBER 12

Deceitfulness of Riches

Do not lay up for yourselves treasures on earth, where moth and rust destroy and where thieves break in and steal, but lay up for yourselves treasures in heaven, where neither moth nor rust destroys and where thieves do not break in and steal. For where your treasure is, there your heart will be also.

MATTHEW 6:19-21

One may imagine at first that there is something of the highest concern and utmost importance in our temporal affairs, since they divert so many from purifying their hearts by faith which is in Christ Jesus. A covetous miser, who neglects religion by being continually intent on seeking great things for himself, and those of his own household, flatters himself that he herein acts most wisely. And at the same time he will censor and condemn a young prodigal, who has no time to be devout, because he is so perpetually engaged in wasting his substance by riotous living, and following harlots. But it will be yet a little while, and all men will be convinced that they are as much without excuse who lose their souls by hunting after riches, as those who lose them by hunting after sensual pleasures. For though business may assume an air of importance when compared with other trifling amusements, yet when put in the balance with the loss of our precious and immortal souls, it is equally frivolous, according to that of our Savior. Christ says in Matthew 16:26, "For what will it profit a man if he gains the whole world and forfeits his soul? Or what shall a man give in return for his soul?"

DECEMBER 13

True Riches

I am a sojourner on the earth; hide not your commandments from me!

PSALM 119:19

If we were always to live in the world, then worldly wisdom would be our highest wisdom. But since we have no continuing city here, and were only sent into this world to have our natures changed and fit ourselves for that which is to come, then to neglect this important work for a little worldly gain is, with Esau, to sell our birthright for a mess of pottage. Alas! Even Christians who are commanded to "seek first the kingdom of God and his righteousness," and all other real necessary things shall be added unto them, are fearful that if they should do so, all other necessary things would be taken from them. They are strictly forbidden to be anxious for tomorrow, and yet they rest not night or day, but are continually heaping up riches for many years, though they know not who shall gather them. Is this acting like persons that are strangers and pilgrims on earth? Or rather, is it not directly deserting the service of Christ, and listing themselves under the banner of the world? The Almighty could say to each of them, as he did to the rich fool, "This night shall your soul be required of you." What would all those things profit them then? If eternal life could be purchased with money, or if men could carry their stocks beyond the grave to buy oil for their lamps, that is, grace for their hearts, when they should be called to meet the bridegroom, there might be some reason why God might bear with them. But since their money is to perish with them, would it not be much more prudent to spend the short time they have here allotted them, in buying oil while it may be had, and not, for fear of having a little less of that which will quickly be another man's, eternally lose the true riches?

DECEMBER 14

Living for Eternity

As we look not to the things that are seen but to the things that are unseen. For the things that are seen are transient, but the things that are unseen are eternal.

2 CORINTHIANS 4:18

Let me exhort all people, both high and low, rich and poor, to make the renewal of their fallen nature the one business of their lives, and to let no worldly profit or worldly pleasure divert then from the thoughts of it. Let the cry, "Behold, the bridegroom cometh," be always sounding in our ears, and let us live as creatures that are every moment liable to be hurried away by death to judgment. Let us remember that this life is a state of infinite importance, a point between two eternities, and that after these few days are ended, there will remain no more sacrifice for sin. Let us be often asking ourselves, how we shall wish we had lived when we leave this world? And then we shall always live in such a state, as we shall never fear to die in. Whether we live, we shall live unto the Lord; or whether we die, we shall die unto the Lord; so that, living or dying, we may be the Lord's. To this end, let us beseech God, the protector of all them that put their trust in him, without whom nothing is strong and nothing is holy, to increase and multiply on us his mercy, that with him as our ruler and guide, we may so pass through things temporal, that we finally lose not the things eternal; through Jesus Christ our Lord.

DECEMBER 15

True Christianity

Jesus answered him, "Truly, truly, I say to you, unless one is born again he cannot see the kingdom of God."

JOHN 3:3

The duties that belong to Christianity are generally known, and yet, how amazing it is that there is so little that is practiced! There is much of it in name and show, but little of it in the heart and conversation. Indeed, if going to church, and to the sacrament, or being called after the name of Christ, and being baptized in that name, will make us Christians, then perhaps all of us would have a claim thereto. But if it consists in matters of the heart, that there must be an inward principle wrought in us by faith; that there must be a change of the whole nature, a turning from sin unto God; a new birth of which we experience the pangs; and that you must feel yourselves weary and heavy laden with your sins before you will seek for deliverance from them; if these are all to be the case, then alas! How many there are who please themselves with an outside show, a name to live on while they are dead! And how few there are who have any share in this spiritual state, in this true and living name! How few are they who are weary and heavy laden with their sins, and seek to Christ for rest! They say in a formal customary manner, "We are sinners, and there is no health in us," but how few feel themselves to be sinners, and are so oppressed in their own spirits, that they have no quiet nor rest in them, because of the burden of their sins, and the weight that is fallen and lays on their minds! The only true rest that abides is found when Christ comes into your souls and pardons you, without any respect to your works, either past, present, or to come.

DECEMBER 16

From the Heart

This people honors me with their lips, but their heart is far from me;

MATTHEW 15:8

Those who think themselves good enough for heaven and are pleased that they are not as bad as others, are not weary or heavy laden. No, these are Pharisees who are not thus troubled; they laugh and jest at those who talk about feeling their sins, and think that there is no occasion to make so much ado about religion. They think that if they only mean well, and say their prayers, as they call them, it is sufficient. Yet although they may say a prayer, yes, thousands of prayers, all the while they are only offering up the sacrifice of fools. They may call God "Father" every day, when it is only mocking of God, and offering up false fire unto him. It would be just for him to deal with them as he did Nadab and Abihu, to destroy them and cut them off from the face of the earth. But he is waiting to be gracious, and willing to try a little longer, whether you will bring forth any thing more than the leaves of an outward profession, which is not all that the Lord requires. No, he wants the heart, and unless you honor him with that, he does not regard your mouths, when the other is far from him. You may repeat your prayers all your lives, and yet you may never pray over one. Therefore, while you flatter yourselves that you are good enough, and that you are in a state of salvation, you are only deceiving your own souls, and hastening on your own destruction. Oh, come unto Jesus Christ, not as being good enough, but as vile sinners, as poor, and blind, and naked, and miserable, and then Jesus will have compassion on your souls.

DECEMBER 17

Sensing our Sin

For I will declare mine iniquity; I will be sorry for my sin.
PSALM 38:18

My friends, there are those who are not weary and heavy laden with a sense of their sins, who can delight themselves in the entertainments of the age, and follow the sinful diversions of life. They know not what it is to weep for sin, or humble themselves under the mighty hand of God; they can laugh away their sorrows, sing away their cares, and drive away these melancholy thoughts. The talk of death and judgment is irksome to them, because it damps their mirth. They could not go to their assemblies in peace if they thought of their sins. If they are not thoughtful about their sins, they will never be weary and heavy laden of them. But at the Judgment Day, all will be over. They shall lose all their carnal mirth; all their pleasure and delight will be gone forever. They think now, that if they were to fast or to pray, and meditate and mourn, they should be righteous over much, and destroy themselves. Alas, my brothers, what misery must that life be, where there are no more pleasant days! How miserable will your life be when all your joys are over, when your pleasures are all past, and no more mirth or pastime! Do you think there is one merry heart in hell? One pleasing countenance? Or jesting, scoffing, swearing tongue? A sermon now is irksome, but then you would give thousands of worlds, if in your power, for one tender of mercy, for one offer of salvation by the blood of Jesus Christ, which now you so much despise. O, may you be awakened with a sense of your sin, and find rest in Jesus.

DECEMBER 18

Full Dependence

And I will give them one heart, and a new spirit I will put within them. I will remove the heart of stone from their flesh and give them a heart of flesh,

EZEKIEL 11:19

When you are obliged to cry out under the burden of your sins, and do not know what to do for relief, then you are weary of your sins. It does not consist in weariness all of a sudden; no, it is the continual burden of your soul. It is your grief and concern that you cannot live without offending God and sinning against him. And these sins are so many and so great that you fear they will not be forgiven. But what is meant by coming to Christ? My friends, it is not coming with your own works. No, you must come in full dependence upon the Lord Jesus Christ, looking on him as the Lord who died to save sinners. Go to him, tell him you are a lost, undone and miserable sinner, and that you deserve nothing but hell. When you thus go to the Lord Jesus Christ, in full dependence on him, you will find him to be an able and a willing Savior. He is pleased to see sinners coming to him with a sense of their own unworthiness, and when their case seems to be most dangerous, most distressed, then the Lord in his mercy steps in and gives you his grace. He puts his Spirit within you, takes away your heart of stone, and gives you a heart of flesh. Stand not out then against this Lord, but go unto him, not in your own strength, but in the strength of Jesus Christ.

DECEMBER 19

Soul Rest

Take my yoke upon you, and learn from me, for I am gentle and lowly in heart, and you will find rest for your souls.

MATTHEW 11:29

Christ gives an exhortation to all of you, high and low, and rich and poor, to come to him that you may have rest. And if Jesus Christ gives you rest, you may be sure that it will be rest indeed. It will be such a rest as your soul desires; it will be a rest which the world can neither give nor take away. O come all of you this night, and you shall find rest; Jesus has promised it. Here is a gracious invitation, and do not let a little rain hurry you away from the hearing of it. Consider what the devil and damned spirits would give to have the offer of mercy, and to accept of Christ, that they may be delivered from the torments they labor under, and must do so forever, or how pleasing would rain be to them to cool their parched tongues. But they are denied both, while you have mercy offered to you, free and rich mercy to come to Christ. Here is food for your souls, as the rain brings forth the fruits of the earth as food for your bodies. Here is mercy upon mercy. Let me beseech you to come to Christ, and he will give you rest for your souls. O my weary, burdened friends, go to Christ in this manner, and though you are weary, you will find rest from him before you come. Let not anything short of the Lord Jesus Christ be your rest, for wherever you seek you will be disappointed. But if you do seek him, there you will find a fullness of everything which your weary soul desires. Go to him this night; here is an invitation to all you who are weary souls.

DECEMBER 20

A Firm Foundation

He is like a man building a house, who dug deep and laid the foundation on the rock. And when a flood arose, the stream broke against that house and could not shake it, because it had been well built.

LUKE 6:48

Let me beseech you to take Jesus without anything of your own righteousness. For if you expect to mix anything of yourself with Christ, you build upon a sandy foundation. But if you take Christ for your rest, he will be that unto you. Let me beseech you to build upon this Rock of ages. Think of the gracious invitation, "Come unto me." It is Christ that calls you. And will you not go? If your souls were not immortal, and you in danger of losing them, I would not thus speak unto you, but the love of your souls constrains me to speak. I think this would constrain me to speak to you forever. Come then by faith, and lay hold of the Lord Jesus. Though he is in heaven, he now calls you. Come, all you drunkards, swearers, sabbath-breakers, adulterers and fornicators; come, all you scoffers, harlots, thieves and murderers, and Jesus Christ will save you. He will give you rest, if you are weary of your sins. O come lay and hold upon him. For your life receive him. Behold the Bridegroom cometh; may it be this night that your cry may be made. God grant that you may begin to live so that when the King shall come, you will have nothing to do but to commit your soul into the hands of a faithful Redeemer.

DECEMBER 21

Cure for Misery

Wretched man that I am! Who will deliver me from this body of death? Thanks be to God through Jesus Christ our Lord! So then, I myself serve the law of God with my mind, but with my flesh I serve the law of sin.

ROMANS 7:24-25

Until you are aware of your misery and lost condition, you are a servant to sin and to your lusts. You are under the bondage and command of Satan, doing his drudgery, under the curse of God, and liable to his judgment if you die impenitent. Look back into your lives, call to mind your sins, as many as you possibly can, the sins of your youth as well as of your riper years. See how you have departed from a gracious Father and wandered in the way of wickedness, in which you have lost for yourselves the favor of God, the comforts of his Spirit, and the peace of your own consciences. Then go and beg pardon of the Lord through the blood of the Lamb for the evil you have committed, and for the good you have omitted. Likewise, consider the heinousness of your sins; see what very aggravating circumstances your sins are attended with. See how you have abused the patience of God, which should have led you to repentance. And when you find your heart hard, beg of God to soften it, and cry mightily unto him. He will take away your stony heart, and give you a heart of flesh.

DECEMBER 22

Promise Manifested in the Flesh

I will put enmity between you and the woman, and between your offspring and her offspring; he shall bruise your head, and you shall bruise his heel.

GENESIS 3:15

On reading to you the words of Genesis 3:15, I may address you in the language of the holy angels to the shepherds that were watching their flocks by night: "Behold, I bring you good tidings of great joy." For this is the first promise that was made of the Savior to the apostate race of Adam. We generally look for Christ only in the New Testament; but Christianity, in one sense, is nearly as old as the creation. It is wonderful to observe how gradually God revealed his Son to mankind. He began with the promise in the text, and this the elect lived upon until the time of Abraham. To him, God made further discoveries of his eternal council concerning man's redemption. Afterwards, at sundry times, and in divers manners, God spoke to the fathers by the prophets, until at length the Lord Jesus Christ himself was manifest in flesh, and came and tabernacled among us. Although this first promise must certainly be dark to our first parents, in comparison of the great light which we now enjoy, yet, dark as it was, we may assure ourselves they built upon it their hopes of everlasting salvation, and by that faith were saved. Mercy cried out, "Spare these sinners," displaying God's amazing divine love.

DECEMBER 23

Confession

But the Lord God called to the man and said to him, "Where are you?"

GENESIS 3:9

In the Garden of Eden, we read that the Lord God called unto Adam (for otherwise Adam would never have called unto the Lord) and said, "Adam where are you? How is it that you come not to pay your devotions as usual?" Christians, remember that the Lord keeps an account of when you fail to come to worship. Whenever you are tempted to withhold your attendance, imagine that you hear the Lord God calling unto you, and saying, "O man, O woman, where are you?" It may be understood in another and better sense: "Adam, where are you? What condition is your poor soul in?" This is the first thing the Lord asks and convinces a sinner of, when he prevents and calls him effectually by his grace. He also calls him by his name, for unless God speaks to us in particular, and we know how poor, miserable, blind and naked we are, we shall never value the redemption wrought out for us by the death and obedience of the dear Lord Jesus. Adam answered the Lord, "I heard the sound of you in the garden, and I was afraid, because I was naked, and I hid myself." See what cowards sin makes us. If we knew no sin, we would know no fear. God answered, "Who told you that you were naked? Have you eaten of the tree of which I commanded you not to eat?" God knew very well that Adam was naked, and that he had eaten of the forbidden fruit. But God wanted to hear it from Adam's own mouth. Thus God knows all our necessities before we ask, but yet insists upon our asking for his grace, and confessing our sins. For, by such acts, we acknowledge our dependence upon God and thereby give glory to his great name.

DECEMBER 24

Grace to Withstand Sin

Let us then with confidence draw near to the throne of grace, that we may receive mercy and find grace to help in time of need.

HEBREWS 4:16

In Adam we contracted pride by the fall. In the garden Adam was unwilling to lay the blame for his sin upon himself. His answer to God, "The woman which you gave me, she gave me of the tree, and I did eat," is full of insolence towards God, enmity against his wife, and disingenuity with respect to himself. For he reflects upon God: "The woman which you gave me," as much as to say, "If you had not given me that woman, I would not have eaten the forbidden fruit." When men sin, they lay the fault upon their passions, then blame and reflect upon God for giving them those passions. Their language is, "The appetites that you gave us, they deceived us, and therefore we sinned against you." But, as God punished Adam for hearkening to the voice of his wife, so he will punish those who hearken to the dictates of their corrupt inclinations, for God compels no man to sin. Adam might have withstood the solicitations of his wife, if he would. And so, if we look up to God, we will find grace to help in the time of need. The devil and our own hearts tempt, but they cannot force us to consent, without the concurrence of our own will. Our condemnation is of ourselves, and it will evidently appear so at the great day, if we do not repent of our sin and pride.

DECEMBER 25

Sin Disunites

Against you, you only, have I sinned and done what is evil in your sight, so that you may be justified in your words and blameless in your judgment.

PSALM 51:4

Sin disunites the most united hearts; it is the bane of holy fellowship. Those who have been companions in sin here, if they die without repentance, will both hate and condemn one another hereafter. All condemned souls are accusers of their brothers. Thus it is, in some degree, on this side the grave. In the garden Adam said, "The woman whom you gave to be with me, she gave me of the tree, and I did eat." What a disingenuous speech was here! Adam makes use of no less than fifteen words to excuse himself, and only one or two (in the original) to confess his fault, if it may be called a confession at all. "The woman whom you gave to be with me, she gave me of the tree," here are fifteen words, followed by "and I did eat." With what reluctance do these last words come out? How soon are they uttered? Thus it is with an un-humbled, unregenerate heart. It will lay the fault upon the dearest friend in the world, nay, upon God himself, rather than take shame to itself. We are all subject to the pride by the fall, until our hearts are broken and made contrite by the Spirit of Christ. May we be like David who was willing in Psalm 51:4 to confess his faults, and was truly sorry for his sins.

DECEMBER 26

Final Victory

When the perishable puts on the imperishable, and the mortal puts on immortality, then shall come to pass the saying that is written: "Death is swallowed up in victory."

1 CORINTHIANS 15:54

In every believer there are two seeds: the seed of the woman, and the seed of the serpent, the flesh lusting against the spirit, and the spirit against the flesh. It is with the believer, when quickened with grace in his heart, as it was with Rebekah, when she had conceived Esau and Jacob in her womb. She felt a struggling, and began to be uneasy. "If it be so," said she, "Why am I thus?" Thus grace and nature struggle (if I may so speak) in the womb of a believer's heart; but as it was there, "The elder shall serve the younger," so it is here. Grace in the end shall get the better of nature; the seed of the woman shall crush the serpent's head. Many of you that have believed in Christ perhaps may find some particular corruption yet so strong that you are sometimes ready to cry out with David, "I shall fall one day by the hand of Saul." But fear not, the promise in the text insures the perseverance and victory of believers over sin, Satan, death, and hell. What if indwelling corruption does yet remain, and the seed of the serpent bruise your heel, in vexing and disturbing your righteous souls? Fear not; though faint, yet pursue. You shall yet bruise the serpent's head. Christ has died for you. Yet a little while, and he will send death to destroy the very being of sin in you.

DECEMBER 27

Union by Faith

Therefore, holy brothers, you who share in a heavenly calling, consider Jesus, the apostle and high priest of our confession,
HEBREWS 3:1

O what a holy familiarity there is between God and the holy souls that are united to him by faith in Jesus Christ! Abraham was reconciled to God by the death and obedience of Christ, which he rejoiced in, and saw by faith afar off. He did not, like guilty Adam, seek the trees of the garden to hide himself from, but took pleasure in conversing with God, and talked with him as a man talks with his friend. O that Christ-less sinners knew what it is to have fellowship with the Father and the Son! They would envy the happiness of saints, and count it all joy to be termed enthusiasts and fools for Christ's sake. Well might the apostle, speaking of Abraham, say that "against hope he believed in hope, and being strong in faith, gave glory to God," for, had he not been blessed with faith which no man ever before had, he might have refused to comply with the severe command of God to offer his son Isaac. As before by faith he considered not the deadness of Sarah's womb, when she was past age, but believed on him who said, "Sarah your wife shall bear you a son indeed," so now, being convinced that the same God spoke to and commanded him to offer up that son, and knowing that God was able to raise him from the dead, without delay he obeyed the heavenly call.

DECEMBER 28

Choose this Day

Choose this day whom you will serve … But as for me and my house, we will serve the LORD.

JOSHUA 24:15

These words contain the holy resolution of pious Joshua, who in the preceding verse gave a most moving, affectionate discourse, recounting to the Israelites what great things God had done for them. He reminded them, in the most pressing terms, that since God had been so exceeding gracious unto them, they could do no less than, out of gratitude for such uncommon favors and mercies, dedicate both themselves and their families to his service. By the same engaging motive does the prophet Samuel afterwards enforce their obedience to the commandments of God in 1 Samuel 12:24: "Only fear the Lord and serve him faithfully with all your heart. For consider what great things he has done for you." But then, that they might not excuse themselves (as too many might be apt to do) by his giving them a bad example, or think he was laying heavy burdens upon them, he tells them in the text that whatever regard they might pay to the doctrine he had been preaching, yet he (as all ministers ought to do) was resolved to live up to and practice it himself. "As for me and my house, we will serve the Lord." A resolution like this is no less becoming and no less necessary for every true son of Joshua that is entrusted with the care and government of a family in our day. If it were ever seasonable for ministers to preach about this matter, and for people to put family-religion into practice, it was never more so than in the present age; since it is greatly to be feared, that out of those many households that call themselves Christians, there are but few that serve God in their respective families as they ought.

DECEMBER 29

Thanksgiving

Oh give thanks to the L*ORD; call upon his name; make known his deeds among the peoples!*

1 CHRONICLES 16:8

Meet and right it is to sing
Glory to our God and King;
Meet in ev'ry Time and Place,
To rehearse his solemn Praise.

Join ye Saints, the Song around,
Angels help the cheerful Sound;
Publish thro' the World abroad,
Glory to th' eternal God.

Praises here to you we give,
Gracious you our Thanks receive
Holy Father, sov'reign Lord.
Ev'ry where be you ador'd.

Tho' th' injurious World exclaim,
Sing we still in Jesus' Name:
Savior you we ever bless,
You our Lord and God confess.

DECEMBER 30

A Great Cloud

Therefore, since we are surrounded by so great a cloud of witnesses …

HEBREWS 12:1A

Various are the pleas and arguments which men of corrupt minds frequently urge against yielding obedience to the just and holy commands of God. But, perhaps, one of the most common objections that they make is this that our Lord's commands are not practicable because they are contrary to flesh and blood. Consequently, they believe that he is a hard taskmaster, reaping where he has not sown and gathering where he has not strewed. These we find were the sentiments of that wicked and slothful servant mentioned in Matthew 25, and are undoubtedly the same with many which are maintained in the present wicked and adulterous generation. The Holy Spirit foreseeing this has taken care to inspire holy men to record the examples of many holy men and women, who, even under the Old Testament dispensation, were enabled cheerfully to take Christ's yoke upon them, and counted his service perfect freedom. The large catalogue of saints, confessors, and martyrs, drawn up in Hebrews 11 abundantly evidences this truth. What a great cloud of witnesses have we there presented to our view! All were eminent for their faith but some shine with a greater degree of luster than others. The proto-martyr Abel leads the van. Next to him we find Enoch mentioned, not only because he was next in order of time, but also on account of his exalted piety. He is spoken of in the words of the text in a very extraordinary manner. We have here a short but very full and glorious account, both of his behavior in this world and the triumphant manner of his entry into the next. The former is contained in these words, "And Enoch walked with God." … If so much as this can be truly said of you and me after our decease, we shall not have any reason to complain that we have lived in vain.

DECEMBER 31

Covenant of Grace

He remembers his covenant forever.

PSALM 105:8

Faith and obedience are conditions, if we only mean that they, in order, go before our salvation; but I deny that these are proposed by God to Adam or that God treats with him in this promise as he did before the fall under the covenant of works. For how could that be, when Adam and Eve were now prisoners at the bar, without strength to perform any conditions at all? The truth is this: God, as a reward of Christ's sufferings, promised to give the elect faith and repentance in order to bring them to eternal life: and both these and every thing else necessary for their everlasting happiness are infallibly secured to them in this promise, as Thomas Boston, that excellent Scottish divine, clearly shows in his *A View of the Covenant of Grace*. This is by no means an unnecessary distinction; it is a matter of great importance: for want of knowing this, people have been so long misled. They have been taught that they must do so and so, as though they were under a covenant of works, and then for doing such works that they should be saved. Whereas, on the contrary, people should he taught that the Lord Jesus was the second Adam, with whom the Father entered into a covenant for fallen man; that they can now do nothing of or for themselves, and should therefore come to God beseeching him to give them faith by which they shall be enabled to lay hold of Christ's righteousness; and that faith they will then show forth by their works out of love and gratitude to the ever blessed Jesus, their most glorious Redeemer, for what he has done for their souls. This is a consistent scriptural scheme: without holding this, we must run into one of those two extremes: Antinomianism on the one hand or Arminianism on the other. From both may the good Lord deliver us!

Scripture Index

1 Corinthians

2 Corinthians

Galatians

Ephesians

Philippians

Christian Focus Publications

Our mission statement –

STAYING FAITHFUL

In dependence upon God we seek to impact the world through literature faithful to His infallible Word, the Bible. Our aim is to ensure that the Lord Jesus Christ is presented as the only hope to obtain forgiveness of sin, live a useful life and look forward to heaven with Him.

Our books are published in four imprints:

CHRISTIAN FOCUS

Popular works including biographies, commentaries, basic doctrine and Christian living.

CHRISTIAN HERITAGE

Books representing some of the best material from the rich heritage of the church.

MENTOR

Books written at a level suitable for Bible College and seminary students, pastors, and other serious readers. The imprint includes commentaries, doctrinal studies, examination of current issues and church history.

CF4•K

Children's books for quality Bible teaching and for all age groups: Sunday school curriculum, puzzle and activity books; personal and family devotional titles, biographies and inspirational stories – because you are never too young to know Jesus!

Christian Focus Publications Ltd,
Geanies House, Fearn, Ross-shire,
IV20 1TW, Scotland, United Kingdom.
www.christianfocus.com